TO BE
DISPOSED
BY
AUTHORITY

STUDIES IN IRISH HISTORY

edited by
T. W. MOODY
Professor of Modern History
University of Dublin

R. DUDLEY EDWARDS
Professor of Modern Irish History
National University of Ireland

J. C. BECKETT
Reader in Modern History
Queen's University, Belfast

VOLUME VI

THE FREEDOM OF THE PRESS
IN IRELAND
1784–1841

THE FREEDOM OF
THE PRESS IN IRELAND
1784–1841

by

BRIAN INGLIS

FABER AND FABER LTD
24 Russell Square
London

First published in mcmliv
by Faber and Faber Limited
24 Russell Square London W.C.1
Printed in Great Britain by
Latimer Trend & Co Ltd Plymouth

To

R. M. SMYLLIE

Acknowledgements

This book is based on a thesis accepted for the degree of Ph.D. of the University of Dublin in 1950, after a course of postgraduate research made possible through an educational grant under the forces post-war scheme.

I am particularly grateful for the help I have received from Professor T. W. Moody, my supervisor for two years in Trinity College, Dublin, and from Professor R. Dudley Edwards of University College, Dublin, both of whom read the manuscript and proofs. My thanks are due also to Dr R. B. McDowell of Trinity College, Professor T. D. Williams of University College, and Professor John Hall Stewart of Western Reserve University, Ohio, for suggestions and advice; and to the staffs of the libraries in which I worked, particularly of the National Library of Ireland.

In a work of this nature, assistance in the initial exploratory stage is of the greatest value. I received it from the late Francis O'Kelley, whose knowledge of the Irish press in the 18th century was encyclopaedic. My hope was that this book would be complementary to a work by him on the bibliography and biography of the press. Perhaps such a book may still be compiled from the material which he collected and from which he helped others so ungrudgingly.

In conclusion, I am indebted to the Board of Trinity College, Dublin, for a most generous grant in aid of publication.

Contents

CONTENTS

Table of Abbreviations

B.M., Add. MSS   British Museum: additional manuscripts
Commons Jn.   Journals of the house of commons
E.H.R.   English Historical Review
H.M.C.   Historical Manuscripts Commission
I.H.S.   Irish Historical Studies
Ir. parl. reg.   Irish parliamentary register
I.S.P.O.   Irish state paper office, Dublin Castle
Lords Jn.   Journals of the house of lords
N.L.I.   National Library of Ireland
Off. papers   Official papers, 2nd series (in I.S.P.O.)
Parl. deb.   Parliamentary debates
P.R.O., H.O.   Public record office, London (Home Office papers)
P.R.O.I.   Public record office, Ireland (Four Courts, Dublin)
Reb. papers   Rebellion papers (in I.S.P.O.)

NEWSPAPERS

(*a*) General abbreviations

D.	Dublin
E.	Evening
I.	Irish
J.	Journal
M.	Morning
N.	Northern
(*P*)	Pamphlet

(*b*) Individual newspapers

F.D.J.	Faulkner's Dublin Journal
Hib. J.	Hibernian Journal
Hib. Tele.	Hibernian Telegraph
S.N.L.	Saunders' News-Letter
Vol. J.	Volunteer's Journal

Introduction

The phrase 'the freedom of the press' was often used in Ireland, during the later part of the eighteenth century. It did not imply that the press had secured, or ought to secure, any formal legislative guarantees; it merely emphasized the contrast with the relative lack of freedom of the press in other countries—in two essentials. Publication could be made by anybody without previous licence, or submission of the MS for censorship; the publisher might later be brought up on a charge of libel, or sedition, or blasphemy, but he was not compelled to obtain permission to publish. And if he was charged, he could only be tried and convicted in the ordinary courts, before a jury; there were no special tribunals to deal with press cases.

Theoretically, therefore, the freedom of the press in Ireland was based upon trial by jury. Publishers knew that they must avoid anything that in the opinion of the ordinary juryman would constitute a libel. Until Fox's Libel Act was re-enacted for Ireland in 1794, judges claimed the right to determine whether or not a publication was libellous, leaving to the jury only the decision on the fact of publication; but for some years previously, juries were disputing this right with the bench. If the judge's decision appeared to them to be unfair, they could—and on occasion, did—find the defendant not guilty of publication, in order to ensure his acquittal.

This safeguard of trial by jury ought to have ensured that the press would be free to reflect public opinion—the opinion, at least, of that section of the population from which juries were drawn. Different juries might vary in their viewpoint, and at different times, the temperature of public opinion altered, so that a phrase which was innocent one year might be considered seditious the next. Still, the system should have allowed tolerance of a wide range of views in journals, periodicals and pamphlets, except in times of civil disturbance. It was this freedom— not any absolute right of publication—that was inherent in the popular conception of the freedom of the press.

With this in mind, my purpose has been to trace the course of the relations of press and state in Ireland from 1784, when statutory limitations were first enacted to curb the activities of the press, to the period of whig administration of 1835–41, which gave Ireland a period of unusual tranquillity, reflected in the newspapers, before the threat of rebellion once more brought the press and the administration into conflict. In the intervening years, various expedients were used to deprive the press of the protection which the jury system theoretically gave them. Juries were packed, or intimidated, or circumvented by legal tricks. The executive and the legislature joined with the judiciary in employing devices to harass newspaper owners, or silencing them by force or with favours. At times—in the rebellion years, and during Robert Peel's chief-secretary-ship—the Irish newspapers virtually ceased to criticize the government. But their weakness and their lack of influence, during these periods, was to prove one of the strongest arguments in favour of the restoration of their independence. Gradually it came to be recognized that newspapers could safely and profitably be left to form a 'fourth estate', designed not to make or to administer but to criticize the law. The actual term, fourth estate, did not become common currency until the 1820s, but the idea had been put forward—and quoted in the Dublin newspapers—in 1784, by the British advocate Erskine: 'other liberties are held under government, but the liberty of opinion keeps governments themselves in subjection to their duties'. A free press was a constitutional safety valve, without which the transition to a democratic society could not have been accomplished.

I have tried, therefore, to show how the idea of the freedom of the press developed in Ireland, and the way in which the restrictions imposed upon the newspapers delayed their growth into a fourth estate. Earlier writers on the press in Ireland, admittedly, have contended that the press Ireland required at the time was not of a fourth-estate character. Their argument has been that when a country is engaged upon a struggle for independence, the test of a newspaper is its devotion to the national cause. This was a point of view that Daniel O'Connell held—that independent newspapers should set aside their various opinions, and range themselves under his leadership. But in this work, it is with the press in its capacity as a potential fourth estate, rather than with its value as an instrument of nationalism, that I have been mainly concerned—though the two strands are often intertwined.

Just as the temptation to make opposition journalists into great Irish patriots proved irresistible to some earlier writers, so in my own case the temptation has been to accept at their face value the utterances and actions of newspaper editors who claimed to be interested in the preservation of the freedom of the press. Perhaps it is as well to stress that,

16

admirable men though many of these editors were, the concept of a free press is not based upon the honesty and integrity of editors, any more than the concept of equality before the law is based upon the honesty and integrity of barristers. The case of barristers and editors is not an exact parallel, but it is useful to keep in mind as a corrective against too romantic a view of the journalists who suffered in the cause of press freedom. Conversely, the temptation has been to condemn those who opposed or helped to undermine the freedom of the press. It is difficult to think of men like Francis Higgins and John Giffard except as Dickensian villains. But the instructive case of William Paulet Carey is enough to warn against such verdicts. Journalism has produced many an honest Enobarbus, to be corrupted by the fortunes of the Antonys to whom they attached themselves.

One other qualification must be made. The importance of the press at any time obviously cannot be judged on the newspapers' estimates. Using newspapers as sources, it is easy to credit them with more power than they possessed. In the period I have covered it is safe to say that the press reflected, rather than influenced, trends; but in a work about the press the tendency is to attribute to newspapers, individually or collectively, a greater importance than they deserve. The evidence which is available is unfortunately not sufficient to justify an estimate of the influence of the press at any time in this period; all that can be said with certainty is that the newspapers themselves are not a reliable guide.

Chapter I. 1784-8

1. THE IRISH PRESS IN 1784

Resolved, *nem. con.*, that the said paper is a daring, false, scandalous and seditious libel on the proceedings of this house, tending to promote discontents among his majesty's subjects, to create groundless jealousies between the kingdom and Great Britain, to alienate the affections of the people from his majesty's government, and to excite an opposition to the laws of the land.

The Irish house of commons followed this resolution, made on 5 April 1784,[1] with an order that the printers and publishers of the paper, the *Volunteer's Journal, or Irish Herald*, should be taken into custody. On the 6th, a similar order was made for the arrest of the printer of the *Freeman's Journal*. Two days later, the chancellor of the exchequer, John Foster, brought in a bill to prevent abuses in the press, precipitating the first serious clash between press and government in Ireland.

Before 1780, although individual newspapers had occasionally provoked the government's wrath, it had rarely shown much concern about the press as a whole. Newspapers for the most part had been small commercial sheets, published primarily to circulate advertisements. News was included almost as an afterthought, to fill up space. Often a single individual would be owner, printer, publisher, editor and manager combined, running the paper with the help of journeymen printers. Even the well-established newspapers had no staffs, in the modern sense, of either reporters, or sub-editors. Circulations were small; owners were satisfied if they reached four figures and, as advertisers were not prepared to pay high rates to reach so limited a circle of readers, profits were meagre. This discouraged owners from employing writers of their own, so that the papers remained featureless, unless they could command a flow of free contributions, such as letters, from outside.

The bulk of the news was copied direct from the English news-

[1] *Ir. parl. reg.*, iii. 144.

papers, to save expense; the selection, too, could be left to the printers, who took as much as they needed to fill the paper, with very little regard to the content. Home news was neglected. Sketchy reports of debates in parliament or in the Dublin city commons were supplemented by a few paragraphs about murders, assaults and robberies, and the arrests, sentences and executions that followed them, each Dublin paper copying from the columns of its rivals any occurrences it had not itself received. The combined resources of the whole Dublin press rarely provided enough home news—apart from reports of debates—to fill a column; whereas news taken from the London papers might occupy half of its four pages.

Irish newspapers at this period were as alike as a row of Georgian houses, each differing slightly in outward appearance, but barely distinguishable to the casual eye. In this they followed the English example, except that the London newspapers, having no source from which to copy news as the Dublin newspapers did from them, were compelled to take a more active interest in events around them. Controversy, the London owner had found, helped to fill a newspaper, and after John Wilkes had shown the way with his *North Briton* there had been many conflicts in London between press and administration, frequently ending in the courts with prosecutions for libel or sedition. The Irish newspapers did not then catch the infection. Their news columns could be filled free without recourse to controversial matter, and until a domestic problem appeared that could not be ignored, most proprietors were well satisfied to take their news from London sources.

Before the time of the Volunteer movement only one newspaper had achieved a reputation in controversy. The *Freeman's Journal*, for which Lucas and Grattan had written, had been the only newspaper 'that upheld liberal principles, that raised a public spirit where there had been none, and kept up a public feeling when it was sinking, and to which, in a great degree, Ireland was indebted for her liberties'; but after the death of Lucas in 1771 the impetus he had given to the paper slackened. So little cause for worry did the *Freeman* or its contemporaries give to the government during the next few years that in 1780 a pamphleteer could remark that no newspaper had been prosecuted within living memory.[1] The freedom of the press was not threatened because so little was printed that could be termed subversive.

The growth of the Volunteer movement brought about the change. New papers were started; old papers began tentatively to include

---

[1] Anon., *Thoughts on newspapers* (P) 1780, p. 5.; *Grattan memoirs*, i. 92.

polemical material—resolutions passed by the Volunteers, letters demanding independence or the repeal of Poynings' Act, and editorial comment. The government grew uneasy, but still they could not bring themselves to act. In 1780 the *Freeman* and other Dublin newspapers published certain Volunteer resolutions which the Irish houses of parliament thought libellous; the lord lieutenant was urged to prosecute,[1] but refused on the ground that to do so might aggravate rather than allay the discontent. He must have realized that to proceed against the newspapers for publishing the resolutions would be tantamount to prosecuting the Volunteers themselves; and that, the government dared not do.

By the year 1782, therefore, when the Irish parliament won its measure of legislative independence, the old style of advertising sheet had largely disappeared, giving place to livelier and more controversial newspapers. Any prospect there might have been that the press would slip back into its former ways after the revolution was dispelled by the dispute which arose in the patriot ranks between Grattan and Flood over the Renunciation Act, which set the patriot newspapers at each other's throats. When this dispute was settled, the newspapers found themselves joining forces again to oppose a government hardly less inimical to the patriot cause than that which had provoked their opposition in the '70s. Throughout the period 1780–4, the Irish press remained full of vitality.

During 1784 ten newspapers were being published, most of them thrice weekly, in Dublin alone. Only two retained some of the characteristics of the earlier period, rarely entering into the controversies that raged around them. *Faulkner's Dublin Journal*, the patriarch of Irish newspapers, had been founded by George Faulkner, Swift's publisher, in 1725. The historian, R. R. Madden, who worked painstakingly and impatiently through the files of Irish eighteenth-century newspapers, thought it 'with few exceptions the dullest, most spiritless, least political, polemical, literary, instructive, or entertaining of the Dublin newspapers'. He was hardly less critical of *Saunders' News-Letter*—'it could not have been more destitute of Irish news if it had been published in Iceland'. Advertisements sometimes took up as many as three out of the four pages. The proprietors ingenuously justified the existence of so much material copied from the English papers by claiming that they were securing the services of the best London journalists without cost. Both newspapers professed political neutrality, which in practice usually meant a negative support of the government of the day.

[1] *Lords jn. Ire.*, v. 218.

The best known of the opposition papers was still the *Freeman's Journal*, but its influence by 1784 had waned. Its chief rival the *Dublin Evening Post*, which had been founded in 1778, had usurped its place. The *Post* had from the first a vigorously patriotic tone, opening the year 1780 with a crow of delight over the possibility 'that badge of slavery, called Poynings' Act' might be repealed. A year later it was claiming the largest circulation of any paper in the country—4,000. It took Flood's part against Grattan, while the *Hibernian Journal*, also a patriot newspaper, followed Grattan, which brought the two into conflict. By 1784, however, this feud was dying. On the flanks were the violently anti-government *Volunteer's Journal*, and the government-owned *Volunteer Evening Post*. The *Volunteer's Journal* was set up in October 1783, quickly establishing itself as uncompromisingly radical. It even showed some interest in Catholic claims, for which the patriot press had until then shown little sympathy:

> When the men of Ireland forget their destructive religious prejudices, and embrace each other with the warmth of genuine religious philanthropy, then, and not till then, will they eradicate the baneful English influence, and destroy the aristocratic tyrants of the land

was written boldly across the front page of each issue. It discussed whether or not the connection with England should be maintained in a manner that left no doubt where its sympathies lay, and by April 1784 had worked itself up to the pitch of scurrility that moved the government to its retaliatory legislation. The *Volunteer Evening Post* was founded a month after the *Volunteer's Journal*, presumably as a counterweight. It protested impartiality, spoke of the value of a free press, and in December offered a gold medal for the best essay on the Volunteers. Nobody was deceived; the appearance of numerous government proclamations in its columns, and articles condemning parliamentary reform, revealed its real feelings.

A number of other newspapers of less importance sprang up in Dublin during this surge of journalistic activity in the early 1780s. The provincial press, too, showed signs of growth, though its real expansion was not to come until a few years later. In Belfast the *News-Letter*, one of the longest established newspapers, had supported the Volunteer movement; but after 1782 it began to drift into a more conservative course, and in 1783 the *Mercury* was set up in opposition. Newspapers were published in Cork and a few other provincial centres, notably Kilkenny, where *Finn's Leinster Journal* began to make a reputation for itself with fiery opposition to the government.

By 1784 the newspapers independent of government influence were either antagonistic to the government, or neutral. If the government wanted support, it had to be purchased. The executive and their supporters in parliament formed a powerful oligarchy, representing nobody but themselves; and the overwhelming majority of citizens, even of the limited well-to-do class who could afford to buy newspapers, were soon dissatisfied with the results of '82. The newspapers did not immediately reflect this dissatisfaction, partly because their attention had been distracted from the government by the quarrel between Flood and Grattan. By the winter of 1783–4 they were beginning to become aware of where their real enemies stood. The government must have watched with alarm the growing vigour of the opposition press; but months slipped by while they hesitated, uncertain whether to act, until the issue of the *Volunteer's Journal* for 5 April 1784 finally irritated them beyond endurance.

It was scurrilous by any standards. Extracts read in the house of commons included a demand for complete severance from England. 'The Rutland administration', it said, 'has in one month made more progress in infamy, than any preceding one could arrive at in two years.' The house of commons was referred to as a 'den of thieves', and 'a Gomorrah of iniquity'; some of its members were mentioned disparagingly by name, reference being made to a place obtained for 'the Honourable (! ! !) James Luttrell'. Abuse of this nature had been appearing for some weeks in the *Volunteer's Journal*; months before, it had denounced the 'prostitute accursed house of commons, whose conduct could not be sufficiently stigmatized', and had praised the Americans for their determination to fight for their freedom. But in this number a new note of menace had found its way into the paper—the threat of personal violence. An 'advertisement' announced:

> In a few days will be published
> in the WEAVER'S SQUARE
> The whole art and mystery of TARRING
> and FEATHERING a TRAITOR
> Dedicated to the rt. hon. John FOSTER.

Further editions were promised, dedicated to Luttrell, and to the attorney general John Scott, who had just been elevated to the bench. A cartoon on the front page showed a gibbet erected for traitors; underneath was the announcement that the starving manufacturers (Foster had just refused to impose protective tariffs on English cloth) had gathered round 'the den of thieves in College Green'—the house of commons—and 'from a numerous band of notorious malefactors dragged the arch-traitor, Jacky Finance, whom amid the execration of thousands they led to a gallows', from which the cartoon portrayed him hanging.

The government's declaration of war on the press—the order for the arrest of printers and the Press Bill—was not planned; it was the instinctive reaction of a group of men threatened with physical violence, and frightened by the threat, as well they might be. But the absence of a preconceived plan mattered little; the important point was that such action had been taken. Once the first move had been made, once the precedent had been established that the government could legislate against the press as a whole, there was nothing except the government's good sense and perspicacity—and in neither, as events were to show, was it well endowed—to prevent the campaign from continuing until newspapers of all shades of opinion had been brought to the point of unconditional surrender to the government's demands. Foster could say, and probably believe, that it was excesses to which he objected: not the power of the press, but the abuse of that power. But the decision on what constituted abuse was left to the administration; and it proved a stern judge in its own cause. Before the battle was called off, in 1785, the opposition press was to be reduced almost to impotence.

The events of the years 1784–5 are significant not only because this was the first general conflict between the press and government, but because the period happens to contain in microcosm an indication of the course of future clashes between them. The expedients that were later to be used by governments have received their first trial. They were later adapted and improved, but most of the methods by which the press might be brought to submission were given their initial tests in the months that followed the prosecution of the *Volunteer's Journal*.

2. CONFLICT, 1784–5

In analysing the methods used by the government in their dealings with the press, it is convenient to make a theoretical distinction between action by the executive, by the legislature, and by the judiciary, provided it is remembered that the distinction did not exist in practice. The various elements of the ruling oligarchy in Ireland had a remarkable unconscious homogeneity, whatever conscious views individuals might hold on the freedom of the press. When that freedom threatened their interest, the ministers, their supporters in parliament, and judges acted in unison. The opposition in parliament, although it contained many able men, was too small to influence decisions. Juries were the only doubtful elements. They would require careful 'packing' if the government was to be certain of their verdict. The government, however, quickly found ways to avoid trial by jury in press cases, thereby enabling the courts to function as part of the administrative machine. It is seldom easy to be certain who was responsible for any particular act of aggression against the newspapers. When the attorney general launched a prosecution it might be on his own initiative, or on orders from Dublin Castle—the term 'the Castle' then being used as a convenient synonym for the executive. But with this qualification, an attempt can be made to disentangle the different parts played by executive, legislature and judiciary in the Irish government's first contest with the press.

(i) *Newspapers and the executive*

The Castle could take action against the press either by repression or by purchase. Opposition newspaper owners could be prosecuted; or, they could be offered financial inducements to alter their allegiance. The executive in this period tried both methods.

*   *   *

Where the policy of repression was used the government had a choice of weapons. It could employ either the courts, or the Irish house of commons. The commons could act on their own initiative, without prompting from the Castle; but in the case of the proceedings against the *Volunteer's Journal*, it was clearly by the wishes of ministers—or a minister—that they took action. Members listened, not without some quiet amusement, to the extracts from the *Volunteer's Journal* read out on April 5 by Foster's wish; and, having heard them, ordered P. Donnelly, the printer and William Bingley, described as the publisher, into custody of the sergeant-at-arms. Later in the day, he returned saying that he had been unable to find them. The house passed a resolution asking the lord lieutenant to offer a reward for the apprehension of the writers, printers and publishers of the newspaper, and the attorney general was ordered to prepare to prosecute. The lord lieutenant gave his consent.[1]

On Foster's further complaints the following day, the printer and publishers of the *Evening Chronicle* and the *Freeman* were added to the sergeant-at-arms' list. Foster further claimed to have ascertained that a Matthew Carey was 'solely responsible' for the libels in the *Volunteer's*

---

[1] 8 Apr. 1784 (H.M.C., *Rutland*, iii. 864).

Journal; his name, too, went down, showing that Foster had already been faced with the uncertainty that was often to prove useful to the newspapers in the courts—the allocation of responsibility for libels. The commons had no clear idea of the distinction between printer, proprietor, publisher and editor (or 'conductor', a term in general use at the time). These jobs were not separate in the public mind, nor, indeed, in the newspaper offices themselves. The confusion helped newspapers to circumvent prosecutions; and it was to be deliberately encouraged even after the division of labour had begun to sort journalists into easily recognizable categories. This had not happened by 1784, when the terms were only used loosely.

Again, the sergeant-at-arms had to report failure. He had gone to a house in Abbey Street, where he had word that Carey was to be found, and had seen him there; but Carey had made his escape by leaping from a two-pair of stairs window. The lord lieutenant was petitioned to sanction a reward for his arrest. On April 13, Carey was taken in the offices of the *Volunteer's Journal*, which had continued publication as if nothing had happened, repeating and embroidering some of the libels. Brought before a magistrate, he tendered bail; but at that moment an order came to take the prisoner out of the court's jurisdiction and hand him over to the sergeant-at-arms—an act which the lord lieutenant, Rutland, in a despatch to London, admitted was 'contrived' in order to prevent him from obtaining his release on bail, and which led the *Dublin Evening Post* to mourn the lost liberty of the subject.[1]

The decision to bring him before the commons, instead of letting the law take its course, was due less to any sensitivity of members for their rights, than to the Castle's determination not to let him escape, as there was some small risk that he might, if the prosecution broke down on a technicality. The Castle may not yet have been fully aware of the strength of its hold on the courts, whereas a majority in the commons could be relied upon to do the Castle's bidding. Carey came before the house on the 19th. The Speaker warned him that he need not answer any questions which might incriminate him; the attorney general went further, and told him that if he had any sense he would answer no questions at all, as anything he said could be used in court as evidence against him. Carey denied the commons' right to deal with a case that was pending in the courts. Foster himself was afraid that if the commons dealt with Carey, the courts might later acquit him on the grounds that a man should not be punished twice for the same offence; but he must have

---

[1] *D.E. Post*, 17 Apr. 1784.

felt this to be the lesser risk. The opposition minority were uneasy. Even if the libels were proven Carey's treatment, they thought, had been scandalous. 'Three ranks of soldiers' had been sent to make his arrest, and after the prisoner had been forcibly removed from the power of the magistrate, he had been put in close confinement and denied the use of pen, ink and paper. Some speakers argued that Carey would have a good case against the house for wrongful arrest and imprisonment— advice which William Bingley, the supposed publisher of the *Volunteer's Journal*, who was by this time also in custody, was later to remember, to his cost.

Carey defended himself vigorously. He charged the sergeant-at-arms with unnecessarily harsh treatment; to judge by the evidence put before a committee set up to investigate the charge, he had grounds for complaint, but the sergeant was vindicated. Carey then obtained a writ of *habeas corpus*: but the magistrate before whom he was brought had to admit that the commons' jurisdiction overrode that of the courts.[1] The commons' answer was to keep Carey in custody, while the administration made arrangements to press the prosecution against him before the court of king's bench. Before these had been completed parliament was prorogued. Carey was automatically released; and he managed to escape, disguised as a woman, to America.[2]

Carey's influence on the future of the press in Ireland was substantial. By the violence of his onslaught on the government he had, within the space of six months, changed their attitude to the press from tolerance to detestation. A biographer has suggested that lameness as a child may have made Carey first shy, then aggressive, in adolescence; and as Carey himself was later to admit, the squibs and cartoons in the *Volunteer's Journal* are irresponsibly, rather than calculatedly, seditious. In America he settled down to become one of the most respected publishers in the country. Had the Irish government realized the manner of youth they were dealing with, and treated the case less seriously, they could have disposed of him without recourse to a general intimidation of the press. As it was, the *Evening Post* immediately sensed the danger, foreseeing that 'a strong precedent will be established which at a future day, perhaps not very distant, will prove a most formidable engine against our liberties'.[3] The *Post*'s proprietor, John Magee, was to have many

---

[1] *Vol. Journal*, 21 Apr. 1784.
[2] *Town and Country Magazine*, July 1784; *Dict. Amer. Biog.*: Gilbert, *History of Dublin*, iii. 320. For reminiscences of Carey's youth see also his autobiography and Bradsher's biography.
[3] *D. E. Post*, 29 Apr. 1784.

months in jail during which he could congratulate himself on the accuracy of his prediction.

There was no real need for the Castle to pursue its campaign against
the press any further. The *Volunteer's Journal* was the only newspaper in
which violent language had been unrestrained: other opposition newspapers had been critical, but none to the same pitch of scurrility. The
libels in the *Freeman's Journal* and the *Evening Chronicle*, it was stated
in their defence when their case came up before the house of commons,
had been copied innocently by journeymen printers from the *Volunteer's Journal*; and the commons accepted this excuse. The administration could have made a reasonable case for firm measures against newspapers which published incitements to violence: the harsh treatment
of the *Volunteer's Journal* staff could have been justified as the only way
to deal with a mad dog. But appetite was whetted by the action. Why
stop at the *Volunteer's Journal*—so the argument probably ran—when
half a dozen Dublin newspapers were in opposition? Those newspapers
had ridiculed the press bill: might they not be tempted to fall into the
ways of the *Volunteer's Journal*, if they were not taught a lesson? Would
not another prosecution—or, better, prosecutions—help to make them
more docile?

On June 26, the administration struck again, initiating proceedings
in the court of king's bench against three Dublin newspapers. The *Volunteer's Journal* had published a letter on the 21st alleging the growth of
military despotism in Ireland. The owners must have got wind of the
impending prosecution; on the 25th they protested that the article
should 'NEVER, NEVER have been inserted'; the MS had not been passed
for publication. As it had occupied two and a half columns on the front
page, the excuse was thin. It was, nevertheless, a peculiar choice for
prosecution, since the tone of the letter was not particularly offensive,
and the author, Handy Pemberton, was known to be eccentric.

The other two charges were still more odd. The *General Evening Post*
was accused, vaguely, of libelling the house of commons. It protested
ignorance of the nature of its offence, and the prosecution failed to offer
any enlightenment. The libel complained of in the *Hibernian Journal* consisted in the succession of two paragraphs in the domestic intelligence
column. They ran:

> Tarring a tailor is a small beginning, and the greatest revolutions have
> often proceeded from small causes, or inconsiderable acts—we hear that
> two Right Honourables are in contemplation.
> We are credibly informed that Mr. Foster and Mr. Beresford are not
> yet embarked for Holyhead, and in the present state of affairs, it is uncer-

tain whether they will take their flight together, or separate, from Waterford or Donaghadee.

The *Hibernian Journal* naturally maintained that no connection was intended between the two paragraphs. The attorney general realized, too late, that it would be difficult to prove them liars; and all that the abortive prosecution achieved was to give the jest publicity far more extensive than it would have had from the few hundred readers of the *Journal*.

Simultaneous action against three newspapers on such ill-chosen ground was a warning that the Castle had made up their mind to harass the opposition press, on any excuse. Another was offered a few weeks later. In August a butcher, convicted of assisting at the tar-and-feathering of a colleague who had failed to observe trade conventions, was whipped through the streets at the cart's tail, a sentence which brought out a mob so threatening that the military at one point opened fire, killing a bystander. The lord lieutenant sent an account of the event to England, alleging that the soldiers were fired upon first.[1] The *Volunteer's Journal* maintained that the volley had been provoked by no more than a stone hurled by a drunk; but that this, which had served the magistrate in charge as an excuse to give the order, 'Level well, and fire low, my boys.'

On the strength of this report the *Volunteer's Journal* was charged with seditious libel. Again, the Castle's plans miscarried; John Rorke, a respectable citizen of Ballsbridge, came forward to avow that he had heard and reported the words spoken by the magistrate, Alderman James. It was Rorke, therefore, and not the owner of the *Volunteer's Journal*, who stood his trial the following January. The result was nevertheless a warning to the press. Rorke's counsel wished to bring evidence that the words attributed to Alderman James had in fact been spoken. This defence was declared inadmissible by the bench, who held that the truth 'would not weigh a feather in the question'—a decision which relieved the prosecution of the onus of trying to prove that the words had not been spoken. The bench held that what mattered was whether publication of the words might lead to a breach of the peace, which they were more likely to do if the report was true. Rorke was found guilty, fined and imprisoned.[2]

As soon as they found that the *Volunteer's Journal* had again wriggled out of their grip, the administration took fresh proceedings against the

[1] P.R.O., H.O., 100/74.
[2] *Vol. Journal*, 26 Jan. 1785.

paper, for a letter which had appeared in its columns on August 25. The letter's general tone had been innocuous, but it had concluded with the injunction 'pull those tyrants from the seat of power'. This time, the law officers of the crown were careful to make sure they had the right man. Matthew Carey's successor as the registered proprietor and printer, James Dowling, was first paraded before the stamp commissioners for identification before he was placed in close confinement.[1] He was denied visitors—an unusual proceeding, for which the reason was soon discovered. As proprietor, it was Dowling's business to lodge all newsprint with the commissioners to receive the government stamp. The commissioners now refused the stamps on the grounds that they had no authorization from Dowling. After some argument they were persuaded to hand over the stamped paper that they had in stock, but they announced their determination to stamp no more. The *Volunteer's Journal* published their refusal, holding it up as illegal because it was equivalent to condemnation before trial: and the commissioners reluctantly gave way.

Less than a month later, the administration made a more direct assault on the *Volunteer's Journal*. The Dublin Sheriffs appeared with a squad of men and searched the office, breaking in doors, opening cases and ransacking cupboards, before retiring empty-handed. They refused to give any reason for the raid. According to the *Freeman*, the search had been for Thomas Carey, who had taken on the paper and had escaped by the same route as his brother, a ladder being placed permanently outside the window, against such contingencies.[2] The raid put beyond doubt the design of the government to break the *Volunteer's Journal*. In its first number of the new year, the paper spread over its front page the boast that in the previous nine months it had received:

2 informations *ex-officio*;
3 rules to show cause;
2 indictments for misdemeanours;
4 indictments for high treason.

Had there been real grounds for all these charges the government would presumably have been satisfied to leave the owners to the normal course of the law. The imprisonment without trial of two proprietors and members of the staff, the attempt to withhold stamps, and the raid by the sheriffs, all suggest that the Castle was aware that the case for the prosecution could not be expected to convince a jury.

The only excuse the administration could put forward was the un-

[1] Ibid., 30 Aug. 1784.
[2] *Freeman*, 13 Nov. 1784.

doubted difficulty of pinning libel on the right man in the courts. Dowling, for example, had been made the nominal proprietor of the *Volunteer's Journal*, in order to shield the real owners, the Careys. He was kept in jail for four months, under the threat of execution for high treason, until he signed an affidavit that the Careys, first Matthew and then his brother Thomas, were the true owners.[1] The Careys' father Christopher, a wealthy baker, was annoyed that Dowling, who had only been the nominal owner and who had won his release from jail by disowning Matthew and Thomas, should resume proprietorship of the paper. In the middle of January 1785 Christopher Carey took possession of the newspaper office, an action for which he was able to obtain sanction from the courts.[2] The next number of the paper, however, could not be called the *Volunteer's Journal, or Irish Herald* as before, because that title was still nominally Dowling's property. Instead, it appeared as the *Volunteer Journal, or Irish Advertiser*. The issue was unnumbered, and the motto changed from 'Liberty and my Native Land' to—appropriately—'Now or Never'; otherwise, except for the change of printer from 'Dowling' to 'Doyle', it could have passed unnoticed for its predecessor, and probably did. But, within a week Dowling had persuaded one Nicholson to put up the money to revive the *Volunteer's Journal, or Irish Herald*. For some time the two papers ran alongside, arguing vigorously, one with CAREY, the other with NICHOLSON, printed boldly at the top of the front page. Dowling alleged that Christopher Carey had connived with the government in an effort to stamp out the old *Volunteer's Journal*. If the charge was true, it would be an indication that the government had already learned the lesson that there were more effective ways of dealing with the press than straightforward repression. The Careys certainly came to terms with the government. Later in the year, Thomas was brought up on two charges before the king's bench: the first, that he had published the letter for which Dowling had been jailed, in the *Volunteer's Journal* of 25 August 1784: the second, that it had been printed again—in a fit of bravado, on the news of Dowling's arrest—a few days later. The first witness put up by the prosecution deposed that Thomas Carey had been away in Kilkenny on both occasions. The judges promptly instructed the jury to find the prisoner not guilty.[3] The circumstances of his acquittal were suspicious. There is no proof that the Careys and government came to terms before April 29, when Nicholson's and Carey's newspapers merged as the result of an agree-

[1] *Carey's Vol. Journal*, 21 Jan. 1785.
[2] Ibid.
[3] *Vol. Journal*, 1 June 1785.

ment. But although the *Volunteer's Journal* survived for some months, it did not recover its former vigour.

The dispute between the two *Volunteer's Journals* distracted them from their task of flaying the oligarchy; and from most of the other opposition papers, although they could be caustic enough, the government had less to fear. The *Dublin Evening Post*, however, had provoked Castle wrath with its steady advocacy of a reformed parliament, and its exposure of corruption and incompetence; and on January 28 an advertisement appeared in other Dublin newspapers from its proprietor, John Magee, giving his change of address to the New Jail, to which he had been committed.

The previous November, Magee had printed some resolutions passed at a meeting in Roscommon, calling, among other things, for the impeachment of the attorney general, John Fitzgibbon. An 'information' had been laid against the *Post* at the time, possibly without any intention of prosecuting, but just to hold a threat over the paper's head. Magee paid no attention: on January 25 his '*Post*-Script', which did general duty as a column of home news, gossip and comment, began: 'Never did an Irish administration cut so deplorable a figure as the present.' Two days later he was 'attached'—brought up on a special warrant—before the king's bench, and committed to jail. He was charged not with the original offence, but with contempt of court for a criticism in the *Post* of the procedure by which he had been committed. Scott, now Baron Earlsfort, sentenced him to a month's imprisonment, and a fine of £5, together with securities to keep the peace.[1]

It was not a heavy sentence: but that the proprietor of the most popular and most widely read newspaper in the country could be ignominiously jailed along with the common felons of Dublin, must have had more effect than all the threats and prosecutions against the *Volunteer's Journal* together. It was unnecessary for the government to pursue the prosecutions still pending from the previous summer. The newspaper proprietors had by this time been compelled to realize that they could be heavily penalized even by unsuccessful and frivolous prosecutions which never reached the courts.[2] As the newspapers complained, the law officers of the crown had a direct interest in promoting prosecutions, for which they were well paid. A defence had to be prepared in case the trial came on, as it might, at short notice. The courts demanded that the newspapers pay for copies of informations which had been laid against

---

[1] *Freeman*, 8 Feb. 1785.
[2] *Vol. Journal*, 28 June 1784.

them, which, at the regulation five words to a line, seven lines to a page, operated as a fine on its own account.

But the real danger from the executive's assaults lay in their change of purpose. Once the precedent had been firmly established that the newspapers could be prosecuted at the Castle's whim, the administration began to use the courts as a weapon to frighten the press into subjection. The actual sum of repression was quite small. Few prosecutions were pursued to a conclusion; it was the threat implied in them that really mattered. The houses of parliament, the Castle and the courts presented a formidable trio of adversaries, with unlimited powers of vengeance on anybody who irritated them. An editor, hesitating whether to insert some criticism of the government, might well fear that the ministry had made up their minds at the next excuse to strike at him and his newspaper.

The administration at first intended no more than to weed out scurrility and incitement to violence from the press, distinguishing between liberty and licence. Even after the initial prosecutions of the *Volunteer's Journal*, the lord lieutenant in a letter to England commented that although the press was still violent, fresh prosecutions might give the printers too great a sense of their own importance.[1] A week later he repeated this opinion. Violence in the press, he considered, worked no material ill-consequence. With this dispatch he enclosed—presumably with approval—a sensible and far-sighted petition from the Dublin city commons drawing attention to the threat to the freedom of the press which lay in the unrestrained power of the executive. But as soon as the government became involved in a conflict with the newspapers, tolerance vanished. In June, the lord lieutenant was complaining about their insolence[2] and although in November he could still write that he wished them to have the same 'free range of discussion and animadversion which is the right of the British press', he regretted that they were still licentious, and the attorney general had, in consequence, been compelled to proceed against some of them.[3] No doubt Rutland was sincere; but because he felt himself threatened, he could not see that the newspapers—except the *Volunteer's Journal*—were no more licentious than they had been at any time in the past five years. They were critical and occasionally annoying, but as he had said himself, that worked no material ill. The reaction to the *Volunteer's Journal* had produced a

---

[1] Rutland to Sydney, 21 Apr. 1784 (P.R.O., H.O., 100/12).
[2] H.M.C., *Rutland*, iii. 109.
[3] 25 Nov. 1784 (P.R.O., H.O., 100/13).

change in this attitude that was to have serious consequences in the future.

*   *   *

Before the Castle had committed itself to a policy of repression, it had already exerted influence upon newspaper owners and journalists by payments for services. When the strength of the Volunteer movement in 1781 began seriously to alarm the government, the chief secretary wrote to the British prime minister, Lord North, urging him to transmit some of the secret service money for this purpose. 'We have hitherto, by the force of good words, and with some degree of private expense, preserved an ascendancy over the press,' he wrote, 'but we are without the means of continuing it.' North's reply was unfavourable; and in a few days, the chief secretary was urging him to reconsider his decision. 'We much regret that your lordship had not found any means to assist us in the article of secret service. The press is the principal operative power in the government of this kingdom, and we are utterly without means to influence that power.'[1] The Irish administration was apparently unable to obtain funds with which to set up a newspaper of their own until 1782, when the *New Evening Post* was first published. Correctly expecting an outcry if their paper's affiliations were known, its editors claimed that in politics it would be 'impartial', a word already notorious as a convenient euphemism for support of the *status quo*. The opposition press at once denounced it as a ministerial wolf in sheep's clothing—except for the *Hibernian Journal*, then at variance with the rest of the opposition owing to its support of Grattan, which unguardedly asked what was wrong with the government having a paper of its own? The *New Evening Post* soon vanished from the streets; possibly in the fashion related by the English author of a history of the press:[2]

> The government, recognising the power of the press, and finding that it was all exerted against itself in Ireland, used every means to encourage the establishment of an organ in Dublin—but in vain. No printer would run the risk to his windows, if not to his life, of printing a newspaper on the government side, so in 1780 a press and types and a staff of English editors, printers and compositors were sent out, and a paper started with the title of the *Volunteer Evening Post*, professing to advocate the popular side. At last it was found wavering—the secret oozed out, and the Irish mob was up. The editor fled for his life and got away, but the printer—less fortunate—fell into the hands of the populace and was carried to the Tenter Fields and

[1] *Beresford correspondence*, i. 170–1.
[2] Andrews, *History of British journalism*, i. 294.

tarred and feathered. The paper broke down and the press, types and materials were advertised for sale; but no one would have anything to do with the obnoxious saxon things, and after three years printer, plant and all were fetched back to England.

Although almost every verifiable reference this Alexander Andrews made to Irish newspapers in his history is inaccurate, and this story has many of the ingredients of legend, it may have had a basis in fact. But the newspaper can not have been the *Volunteer Evening Post*, whose first issue did not appear until the autumn of 1783 and which outlived the tar-and-feather period. The exact nature of the *Volunteer Evening Post's* connection with the administration remains uncertain, but it was certainly under governmental control—not independently owned and supporting the government from choice. Its circulation was negligible. Advertisers—not infallible judges of a newspaper's popularity, but by their likes and dislikes affording a rough guide—ignored the *Volunteer Evening Post*, which was forced to rely almost exclusively for revenue on government proclamations, published in great quantities. One issue had less than a column of commercial advertisements, to six columns of government advertisements and proclamations. Unwilling, therefore, though they must have been to admit that their own newspaper served little purpose, the Castle must have begun to wonder whether it would not be more effective to win over one of the popular opposition papers to their support.

In 1782 signs of a change of heart began to appear in the *Freeman's Journal*, for long the most influential opposition paper. Government proclamations were found in its advertisement columns. This, though not invariably proof that a newspaper was supporting the administration, was unusual in one that had been unwavering in opposition. Possibly the administration were endeavouring to buy their way into the *Freeman's* favour; if so, they were temporarily disappointed, for in October it suddenly lashed out at the 'Castle scribes' for garbling a speech by Charles James Fox, referred to the 'curse of the administration', and backed Flood in his quarrel with Grattan.[1] The proclamations abruptly ceased.

The *Freeman*, however, had lost its position as the leading opposition newspaper. The reason can be guessed from a despatch written by the lord lieutenant in March 1783. Loyal addresses had been sent to the government from various bodies in the state, and the opposition had endeavoured to insinuate that these had been solicited by the administra-

[1] *Freeman*, 22 Oct. 1782.

tion. 'Higgins has had a variety of letters,' the lord lieutenant wrote,[1] 'some directly and some obliquely charging the government with these dealings, all of which he has refused to insert, specifying the subjects to the public and the reasons why he did not admit them.' Francis Higgins, the notorious 'Sham Squire',[2] had a few years previously secured an editorial post on the *Freeman* and, unknown to the proprietors, was in Castle pay. With characteristic ingenuity he contrived that this 'specifying the subjects to the public' should be done in such a way that the lord lieutenant, who knew what the paragraph referred to, imagined that the public would understand its significance. To the casual reader, however, it must have been meaningless.

In other words, Higgins was keeping up a pretence of patriotism for the benefit of the proprietors at the same time as he was ingratiating himself with the administration. Although he performed the difficult feat skilfully, he must have lost the *Freeman* many puzzled subscribers in the process.

For a time, the *Freeman* continued its equivocal way. Foster's Press Bill was opposed, but the most prominent criticism, a letter signed 'Junius', is sufficiently diffuse in its sentiments to suggest that it was put in only as a sop to the opposition; and in its attitude to the tar-and-feathering of sellers of imported goods, then in full swing, there was little to distinguish the *Freeman* from the Castle's *Volunteer Evening Post*. On 2 June 1784, however, a letter from the proprietors—given the lead on the front page—made a new profession of 'impartiality'. This unmistakable sign of government sympathies was reinforced by the reappearance of Castle proclamations among the advertisements, bringing the advertisements up from the two columns to which they had dwindled —evidence of the declining influence of the paper—to over four and a half. The *Freeman* had become, and was to remain for many years, a government newspaper.

It is unlikely that the administration had planned this *coup*. Probably Higgins had seen in government support the means to further his ambitions, and had persuaded the Castle that he could do a great service for them by altering the *Freeman's* allegiance. Nor is it likely that they suggested the policy of trying to satisfy their supporters and patriots alike, by maintaining the *Freeman* as ostensibly an opposition journal: Higgins was serving two masters, and probably he was trying to satisfy both until such time as he could persuade them to come to terms. The dwindling circulation and profits of the paper, reflected in the falling-off

[1] 23 Mar. 1783 (H.M.C., *Fortescue*, i. 203).
[2] See p. 54

of advertisements, must have reinforced his arguments with the owner, and may have clinched them. Whoever was responsible for the plan, when the newspapers began to give trouble again a few years later the administration were quick to remember it and put it into operation again.

To have won over the *Freeman* must have seemed to the government a decidedly satisfactory achievement. But, in the event, it brought them little benefit. Government papers were not popular, and as soon as their sympathies became known, circulation fell. The *Volunteer Evening Post* never attracted advertisements, and the *Freeman*, to judge by appearances, lost ground as soon as it began to waver in its allegiance. All that the administration were in fact achieving was a transference of readers to other newspapers. This was to prove expensive. The Castle had found two ways of subsidizing their newspapers: one directly, with secret service money: the other indirectly, through payments for the publishing of proclamations. The amounts disbursed from the secret service fund were never made public: but the figures of payments to newspaper owners for proclamations and government advertisements were later laid before the Irish commons.[1] They showed that before 1780 proclamations and government advertisements had been confined almost entirely to the *Dublin Gazette*, the official Castle publication, not in the strict sense a newspaper. Subsequently, the *Freeman* and the *Volunteer Evening Post* had received large sums from the re-publication of these advertisements from the *Gazette*. The amount paid to the *Volunteer Evening Post* each year ran into four figures. In 1774 the expenditure incurred by the government for inserting proclamations in the newspapers had been £276: in 1785 it was over £4,000.[2] The Castle claimed that the necessity for the proclamations—warnings about disturbed areas, rewards offered for the arrest of felons, etc.—had become greater. Opposition members asked why, in that case, most of the proclamations should go to Castle newspapers which were not read? The sums that had been received by individual newspapers for publishing proclamations in 1786, it was disclosed, were divided between the two Castle newspapers: the *Freeman* took £650 and the *Volunteer Evening Post*, £1,350, the rest going to the official *Gazette*.[3] For those days, these were big incomes; enough to maintain a newspaper without the help of private advertisers, and more than enough to tie a proprietor effectually to the government, in the knowledge that independence would precipitate the loss of his livelihood.

[1] *Commons jn. Ire.*, xii. Appx. lxii.
[2] *Ir. parl. reg.*, vi. 106.
[3] Ibid., vii. 83.

Although the accounts for this period have not survived, secret service money was being used to buy patriot writers over to the Castle's service. Higgins had a pension[1]: and as early as 1780 the lord lieutenant had boasted that he had seduced Frederick Jebb away from the patriots with a promise of £300 a year.[2] Jebb had won a reputation as the Irish Junius by some fiery articles over the signature of *Guatimozin* which appeared in the *Freeman*: he was to be equally fiery, though less effective on the government's behalf, and his 'conversion' was considered as a considerable acquisition.[3] Probably there were other journalists also in the Castle's pay.

(ii) *Newspapers and the legislature*

The two houses of parliament were closely tied to the administration by patronage and interest. They could co-operate in the subjugation of the press in two ways: by the enforcement of their privileges, and by the enactment of restrictive laws. In the period 1784–5, both methods were adopted.

*   *   *

Until the 1770s the English houses of parliament had looked upon publication of reports of their debates as a breach of privilege. Although action against the publisher was usually only taken when the matter printed gave either house cause for annoyance, publication alone was sufficient to constitute a breach of privilege, no matter how accurate or inoffensive the report might be. In 1771, an attempt was made to contest this point by Alderman John Wilkes and the lord mayor of London who, sitting in their judicial capacity, sentenced a parliamentary messenger, despatched to arrest a printer, for assault. The commons retaliated by sending the lord mayor to the Tower: but the reaction of the London mob was so menacing that, although neither house formally relinquished its claims, newspapers were tacitly permitted to report debates without fear of retaliation—except when either house felt itself the victim of calumny.[4]

The Irish houses of parliament had less clear-cut views on the subject. Before 1782, they had occasionally taken action against the press. When

[1] Higgins to E. Cooke, 18 May 1801 (Reb. Papers 620/18/14).
[2] Madden, *Irish periodical literature*, ii. 430.
[3] *General Evening Post*, 8 May 1781.
[4] C. Grant Robertson, *Select statutes*, p. 337.

the house of commons had resolved in 1749 that some publications of Charles Lucas's reflected on their dignity, they ordered him and his publisher to be sent to the Newgate;[1] but they were content to leave his prosecution to the state, as they were again in 1780 when both houses denounced the *Hibernian* and the *Freeman's Journals* for publishing certain inflammatory Volunteer resolutions.[2] Only on rare occasions had they acted for themselves. When the earl of Clanricarde complained that he had been maligned under the feeble disguise of 'E . . . . C . . . .' in the *Dublin Evening Post* in 1781, the printer was committed to prison until, a fortnight later, a penitent apology secured his release.[3]

The subject was discussed at some length in the house of lords on 11 December 1783 when, on Lord Mountmorres complaining that he had been misrepresented in the *Volunteer's Journal*, the house ordered the printer to appear before them. As the printer was able to show that this misrepresentation complained of had been copied from a government newspaper—the *Volunteer Evening Post*—the lords let the matter drop. The debate, however, showed how little formed members' ideas were on their rights. Lord Mornington claimed that printers had acquired from immemorial usage the right to publish parliamentary debates, and that the charge of misrepresentation would have to be proved; but Lord Carhampton thought it was a breach of privilege for anyone to presume, without leave of the house, to publish its debates at all (Carhampton was the father of Luttrell, who had been Wilkes's opponent in the Middlesex election, and had been liberally bespattered with abuse by the popular press in London). The house inclined to take a middle view. The printer was told that, although no action would be taken against him, he had been guilty of a breach of privilege in publishing the debate without permission.

The lords, in effect, were saying that a newspaper could continue to publish reports of parliamentary debates, but that they reserved the right to punish it if the report gave offence, without argument about the rights and wrongs of the case—simply on proof of publication. This was the position when the conflict between administration and press began in April 1784. Parliamentary privilege proved one of the most useful weapons against the press that the administration possessed. The houses of parliament, the newspapers soon discovered, were above the law. They could remove a prisoner from the magistrate, sentence and punish him—and then hand him back to the magistrates to be dealt with as if

[1] *Commons jn. Ire.*, v. 14.
[2] Ibid., x. 194.
[3] *Lords jn. Ire.*, v. 241, 253.

nothing had happened, in spite of the common law precept that no man should suffer twice for the same offence. Matthew Carey found this, to his cost: but the house of commons in his case were less concerned to uphold their privileges than to make certain that he did not escape punishment. They were satisfied to hand him over to the courts—or would have been, had not parliament been prorogued. It was reserved for Carey's colleague William Bingley to give the commons the opportunity to show their strength.

Bingley was named by Foster on April 5 as the publisher of the *Volunteer's Journal*. Arrested a few days later, he was taken before a judge of the king's bench. The judge, who heard the case in his own home, admitted him to bail; but before Bingley could leave, the deputy sergeant-at-arms of the house of commons arrived to arrest him. The sergeant was reprimanded by the judge, who gave Bingley a safe-conduct out of his parlour. He was promptly rearrested[1] in the hall and, like Carey, put into close confinement—so close that when he was brought before the commons on April 19 he claimed that he would have been able to prove to their satisfaction that he had nothing to do with the direction of the paper, but that he had not been allowed to see anyone in order to arrange to obtain witnesses. He reminded the house that he had already entered into a recognizance of no less than £2,000 to appear for trial before the king's bench. The following day he was able to produce some respectable citizens to vouch for his story that he was only a clerk in the *Volunteer* office, and he was discharged. On May 1 he was informed by the king's bench that his attendance would not be required before them unless he received notification, which was as much as to say that he would not be prosecuted if he gave no more trouble. 'Merciful proceedings', was the *Dublin Evening Post's* sarcastic comment.

There the affair would have rested, if Bingley had not been born to trouble. Whether he guessed it or not, his arrest had been made on the strength of his past. The earl of Mornington referred to him as 'Bingley of famous memory',[2] and in a dispatch from the Castle the chief secretary, Orde, wrote that 'the *Volunteer's Journal* is the property of Matthew Carey and of William Bingley, late a printer in London, who was prosecuted there for offences of a similar nature, and is supposed to be instrumental in all this mischief'.[3] Bingley had been the friend and disciple of Wilkes, from whom he had taken on the publication of the *North*

[1] *Reformist*, 21 Feb. 1785; *D. E. Post*, 17 Apr. 1784.
[2] H.M.C., *Fortescue*, i. 230.
[3] 7 Apr. 1784 (P.R.O., H.O., 100/12).

Briton after the prosecution for No. 45 had compelled Wilkes to withdraw from the paper. Most of Bingley's work had to be done from jail, as an English court ruled that No. 50 was libellous. It was ten weeks before he had been admitted to bail; and then, because he had refused to answer questions until brought to trial, he had been imprisoned for a further eighteen months without trial before being released on a *nolle prosequi*—a procedure that had not escaped the attention of Junius.[1]

On his own account, Bingley had come to Ireland to forget the past. He had taken up farming in Donegal; but financial straits had compelled him to return to his old profession in Dublin. What influence he had in the *Volunteer's Journal* it is impossible to say, but he managed to satisfy Foster and the commons that he had none. This only increased his sense of grievance, which continued to rankle. A year later he adopted a suggestion that had been made by a sympathizer in the commons, and brought an action against the sergeant-at-arms for wrongful imprisonment.

In spite of his past experiences, Bingley must have felt that he had a good case. His arrest had been of dubious legality, and his confinement harsh; he ought not to have been taken up at all, as some days before he had been arrested Foster had named Carey as solely responsible for the libels. The commons had admitted this by letting Bingley go free. So confident was he of compensation that he refused a collection made for him by some members of the house, who thought he had been unjustly treated, in case the courts should dismiss his action on that account.[2]

The commons were informed of the action pending against the sergeant-at-arms on 16 February 1785. They promptly ordered that Bingley should appear before them the following day—'in custody', the choleric Sir Henry Cavendish suggested, but other members thought this was hard on someone whose only fault was seeking redress of a grievance in the courts. Foster replied that the house was the judge of its own privileges, and the attorney general denied that the courts were competent to judge the house. In that case, a member of the opposition inquired, should not the court which issued the writ be attached and brought before the bar of the house? The solicitor general hurriedly disclaimed any such intention.

Bingley told the commons that he had no intention of bringing an

[1] *Reformist*, 21 Feb. 1785: *A treatise on the origin of attachments and informations* (P), 1785.
[2] *Reformist*, 21 Feb. 1785.

action against them—only against the sergeant-at-arms, for abusing his authority. The brusque reply was that they were not interested in the merits of his case. All they wished to ask him was, did he intend to proceed with this action in the courts? Bingley refused to commit himself: his solicitor, who had been showing signs of increasing agitation, seized the excuse to abandon his client, who was again committed to custody in Newgate jail. Three weeks later he petitioned the house, promising to answer their questions. They ruled that he had not shown proper submission, and ignored his request. On May 26 he was given permission to appear as a witness in the trial of Thomas Carey, but it was not until August 2 that another petition, which amounted to unconditional surrender, was adjudged sufficiently penitent for the commons, a week later, to order his discharge—waiving the usual fees.

Both houses, in brief, arrogated to themselves the right to deal with individuals exactly as they pleased. In times when they had nothing to fear from the press, they could be tolerant: when frightened they were tyrannical; and from their decisions the newspaper owner had no appeal.

* * *

Two types of legislation could be employed by parliament in its dealings with the press: direct—whereby regulations were made about the printing and publication of newspapers; and indirect—whereby laws would be passed ostensibly to obtain revenue, but having as a secondary effect the diminution of newspapers' profits.

The bill 'to secure the liberty of the press' which Foster brought before the commons in April 1784 was an example of direct legislation. It bore all the signs of hurried composition. The earl of Mornington, who was in close touch with the Castle, complained in his correspondence that neither he nor the chief secretary, Orde, had seen the bill before it was introduced. He approved certain clauses, but felt that there were others that had been included without sufficient thought, and he had made up his mind to have the bill altered or, failing that, to oppose it in the lords. As it was, he feared that the Castle would be blamed for the bill by the public, who could not know that it had not even been told.[1]

His annoyance was shared by the influential John Beresford who wrote that although he reprobated violence, he doubted the prudence of an attempt to restrain the press at that time. Beresford unjustly

[1] 10 Apr. 1784 (H.M.C. *Fortescue*, i. 228).

blamed Orde for involving government supporters without prior consultation.[1] The prevailing uncertainty makes it probable that it was Foster, against whom the worst scurrilities were aimed, who prepared the bill; certainly he introduced it.

The first clause required printers, publishers and proprietors in a newspaper to give their names and addresses to the stamp commissioners. The object was to make certain of catching somebody in the event of a successful prosecution for libel—even if it was not the man responsible. This was not unreasonable, nor could much objection be taken to the clause which made it illegal for newspapers to accept payment for the publication of libels, or to extort payment not to publish them. The section of the bill which aroused most opposition was that requiring each proprietor to lodge the sum of £500 as security. This in effect meant that proprietors were held to special bail, though that had been only intended for very grave offences. Small newspapers, it was pointed out, would not find it easy to raise the money. One other clause, providing for the arrest of newsvendors of publications containing libels, came in for criticism; a blind hawker, it was said, might suddenly find himself in jail. Grattan summed up the prevailing opinion in committee. Part of the bill he thought necessary, as 'one paper teems with exhortations and incitements to assassination'; but a clause requiring the printer to make known his name was all that was needed. It was agreed to strike out the controversial clauses—a decision that satisfied Mornington, who supported the bill in the house of lords, writing to Grenville in England that the bill in its amended form met his objections, and was, he believed, inspired by them'.[2] The special bail requirement was omitted, and the clause affecting newsvendors modified; they were not to be arrested provided that they disclosed where they had obtained the offending newspaper.

The amended bill received the king's assent, becoming law on June 1. In its final form it contained little direct threat to the freedom of the press. The threat lay rather in the act's implications. Almost certainly it would have been less moderate if its sponsors had been less precipitate. The attitude of Orde, Mornington and Beresford, and presumably of many colleagues, would not have been as liberal had they not resented the introduction of legislation about which they had not been consulted.

Otherwise, the bill was chiefly remarkable for the resistance it provoked in the Dublin newspapers during its passage. With the single ex-

[1] *Beresford correspondence*, ii. 256.
[2] H.M.C., *Fortescue*, i. 230.

ception of the government *Volunteer Evening Post*, they were unanimous in their execration of the bill 'for "securing"—*alias* annihilating, the liberty of the press'—in its original form. The lord lieutenant's later assertion in a dispatch to London, that most printers favoured the bill,[1] may have been true of the act in its final version; it certainly was not true of the draft originally presented. The *General Evening Post* called it 'the most flagrant direct attack ever attempted upon the liberties of Ireland'. The *Dublin Evening Post* warned the commons that juries would not suffer the freedom of the press to be assailed by 'the prostitute and corrupt minions of a tyrannic power'. The *Volunteer's Journal* had another cartoon of a gibbet with 'Jacky Finance' Foster lying below, the inference being that his corpse was so execrated that no one would take it away for burial. Even *Faulkner's Journal*, which Foster had referred to in the commons as 'generally chaste enough', and which rarely ventured any comment whatsoever, said that on similar principles they could expect a bill for the perfect security of the liberty of subjects by sending them in chains to Newgate prison.

All this, admittedly, was before the bill had been amended. In any case the opposition was not so impressive as it sounds: the criticisms were less spontaneous than they appeared. The newspapers took each other's news and comments as a matter of course. On April 10, for example, the *Freeman* included two paragraphs, one calling upon the seconder of the bill to withdraw his support, the other commenting generally on press liberty. Later that same day, the *Dublin Evening Post*, included both these paragraphs, adding one of its own praising Dublin University for their support of the cause of press freedom. The *General Evening Post* did the same. Next morning, the three paragraphs were reproduced word for word in the *Volunteer's Journal*; and two of them by the *Hibernian Journal*, which omitted the praise for Dublin University. On the 13th, *Faulkner's Dublin Journal* joined in, with slight alterations in the wording; and the following day all three paragraphs appeared in *Finn's Leinster Journal*.

It would be unwise, therefore, to put too high a value on the unanimity with which the newspapers rallied to defend the freedom of the press, or to single out individual newspapers for special mention. A solemn protest against the act may have been inserted by some apprentice journeyman, who could barely read, trying to fill the paper's columns. Although over a period of weeks a newspaper's opinions can be detected, they can rarely be judged by isolated paragraphs. The *Volunteer's Jour-*

[1] Ibid., *Rutland*, iii. 94.

nal, the most opinionated of the Dublin press, was at the same time the most inveterate robber of other papers' material.

The reaction against the bill as originally drafted, was nevertheless strong, in the commons as well as in the press. Foster had rushed it before the house and the accusation was made that he had brought it in after many members had returned home, under the impression that no more important bills were to be brought up that session—not that this would have affected the outcome. An influential element in the house were in favour of still more drastic measures to curb the press—the law officers of the crown, in whose hands lay the freedom of the press, among them. The prime sergeant expressed his 'thorough detestation' of newspapers; Sir Henry Cavendish, the diehard tory of his day, and Luttrell, would all have liked to see the bill go through as originally drafted; and a member of the Beresford family wanted corporal punishment revived for refractory journalists.[1] The newspapers had some reason to feel that the act, for all its final moderation, might prove a dangerous precedent.

Yet the Press Act was not so dangerous to the future of the independent newspapers as legislation initiated the following March, when the chancellor of the exchequer dealt what the *Dublin Morning Post* referred to as 'the finishing blow to the liberty of the press'—the imposition of a higher rate of duty on newspapers' stamps, and an increase in the advertisement tax.

A stamp duty of one halfpenny a copy, and an advertisement duty of twopence upon each advertisement printed, had been imposed a few years before. Now, the stamp duty was to be raised to one penny and the advertisement tax to one shilling. The opposition newspapers contended that such an impost could only be made not with a view to raising revenue but to cripple the independent press. The advertisement tax, for example, was clearly discriminatory against the opposition papers because proclamations and government advertisements, upon which the Castle papers relied, were exempted.

The new duties came into force on March 25, after which date, as the newspapers had warned their subscribers, prices were raised from 1½d to 2d, and the advertisement duty passed on by higher rates to advertisers. As the papers had feared, advertising fell off sharply. The number of advertisements in the *Belfast Mercury* fell by one third, and the *General Evening Post* lost four columns—a full sheet—of advertising matter. The greatest sufferer was the *Volunteer's Journal*, which was reduced for a time to a single sheet—two pages—and was much reduced

[1] *Vol. Journal*, 14 Apr. 1784.

in size when it returned to its original four page layout. The Castle papers protested that they were suffering for the sins of their rivals—thereby confirming that the duties were punitive in intent. The *Freeman* —by this time undisguisedly a Castle paper, lampooned in the opposition press as the '*Slaveman's Journal*'—had less than four columns of advertisements, three of them from government sources and consequently exempt from the duty; its sufferings were less severe.

Advertisers gradually returned, though not before the newspaper owners had been severely shaken. On 13 February 1786, they petitioned the commons for the removal, or at least the reduction of the duties, setting out their losses. Returns called for by the house showed that the revenue from the increased stamp duty was actually less then it had been at the earlier rate, and although the revenue from the advertisement tax had doubled, the increase was far from being proportionate to the increase in the tax.[1] The attorney general, Fitzgibbon, made the ingenious defence that the tax did good by discouraging landlords from advertising auctions at which land was sold by 'cant' to the highest bidder, which was the cause of rack-renting, and to which all the peasants' misery might be attributed. In any case, he said, it was salutary for advertisers to be compelled to express themselves more concisely in order that they might be charged less duty—provoking an opposition speaker sarcastically to inquire why, in this sudden administrative enthusiasm for the promotion of *belles lettres*, the government should have reserved to itself the right to be verbose by exempting proclamations from the tax.

It is not easy to determine the extent to which taxation affected the press. Any increase in duties, whether on newsprint, on copies, or on advertisements, increased the running costs of the newspapers, and impaired the quality of the service they provided by compelling owners to cut down their expenses. The newspapers catering for the less well-to-do section of the community were the hardest hit, because their subscribers were less able to bear the extra cost and would be more likely to give up taking a newspaper, and to read the free copies provided in coffee rooms. The advertisement tax, too, weighed more heavily on the opposition than on the Castle press. In its general tendency, any increase of duties operated decidedly, if not always visibly, against the independent newspapers.

(iii) *Newspapers and the judiciary*

To consider the Irish judicature in this period as a power separate

[1] *Commons jn. Ire.*, xii, appx. lxiii.

from legislature and executive is to mistake the legal fiction for the fact. Judges, whatever they ought to have been in theory, were in practice virtually an arm of the administration. Corruption was unnecessary; the defence of the government was natural and often unconscious. They were bound to the will of the government partly by inclination, partly by their desire for preferment. Promotion through the judicial hierarchy was dependent on the administration's pleasure; and a man who had reached the top of his profession, a chief justice, could still hope by keeping in favour to rise in the peerage.[1]

John Scott, for example, had been a young man of no particular family or fortune. After obtaining some reputation in the patriot cause he had been won over by a far-seeing viceroy, who had realized that he was both talented and purchaseable.[2] Proving himself a clever advocate he became successively attorney general, a justice of the king's bench, and chief justice: and plain John Scott became Baron Earlsfort in 1784, Viscount Clonmell in 1789, and the earl of Clonmell in 1793. All this was merit's reward, but the merit lay in serving ascendancy, not in the impartial exercise of justice.

Other judges sat in the court of king's bench, but Clonmell was the strongest personality, and he did very much as he liked. As it happened, he liked dealing with press cases, and from 1784 to his death just before the end of the century, he was the judge in the majority of trials in which newspapers were concerned.

There were many ways in which the courts, dominated by such a man, could discriminate against the press. They could impose abnormally heavy sentences. Magee's month in jail may seem light in retrospect, for a time when petty larceny was punishable by death. As a special concession, too, he was allowed to transfer to the New Jail rather than the Marshalsea which 'was so extremely overcrowded that no apartment could be had that was not occupied by six, eight or ten persons'.[3] And he was able to continue working. A paragraph appearing in the Dublin newspapers on 29 January ran:

> Magee entreats his friends to be so obliging to confine their kind visits from 12–3, as he finds it peculiarly necessary to rescue a few hours each day for the arrangement of a business which seems at present to involve his . . . fate.

Still, it came as a shock to the public and to the profession that so

---

[1] Cf. Curtis and McDowell, *Irish historical documents*, p. 204.
[2] *Grattan memoirs*, ii. 141.
[3] *Freeman*, 29 Jan. 1785.

well-known a citizen as Magee should be in jail at all. The courts, too, could revive obsolescent procedures, or allow actions against newspaper proprietors which might be within the letter, but were not in the spirit of the law. 'Informations', either lodged by individuals, or '*ex-officio*' by the law officers against proprietors, were commonly used, because they made it unnecessary to put the case to the grand jury, who might refuse to allow the action to proceed further. The newspapers might find when the case came up for trial that the same judge who had up-held the 'information', would be on the bench to try the case. Nearly every action against newspapers were begun in this way, though they denounced the system as contrary to magna carta. Several months could elapse between the lodging of the information and the prosecution itself, during which the newspaper was left in ignorance what was happening, and unable to comment on the case without risking a charge of con-tempt of court. Often the threat of prosecution alone seems to have been enough, the law officers holding the charge over the owner's head as a security for the newspaper's good behaviour.

Procedures of doubtful legality could also be adopted. Magee was 'attached'—committed to jail on a judge's order; and for a while, 'at-tachments' threatened to undermine the judicial system by circum-venting trial by jury.[1] The writer of a well-reasoned pamphlet on attach-ments and informations, who remarked the dangers to the freedom of the press in the transference of the power of punishing from a jury to magistrates chosen by the crown, cited as an example 'the new process of attachment and information in the court of king's bench, so materi-ally narrowing, superseding and in many cases annihilating the trial by jury'.[2] The subject was exhaustively debated in the Irish commons in February 1785 and soon afterwards the English advocate Erskine, in a letter published by many Irish newspapers, said the judges could not entertain attachments 'without such a gross usurpation and abuse of power as would make me think it my duty, were a member of the Irish parliament, to call them to account by impeachment'. The precedent, he declared, 'if acquiesced in, would be fatal to liberty in both coun-tries.[3]

All these expedients reflected the courts' bias in favour of the prosecu-tion, in state trials. If 'attachments' had not been known, the law officers and the judges would have sought some other way around the normal process of law, because only in trial by jury lay the only source of weak-

---

[1] Cf. *Curran's speeches*, ed. T. Davis, p. 8.
[2] Vindex, *A treatise on attachments and informations* (P), 1785, p. 3.
[3] Lecky, *Ire.*, ii. 400.

ness in the government's array of forces against the press. Juries had still to be drawn from the class of men who had been Volunteers, few of whom had any sympathy with the administration. For actions against newspapers, therefore, the Castle found it expedient to avoid juries, as far as possible, either by attachments or by proceding for contempt of court. So well aware were they of the risk that no newspaper owner stood his trial before a jury, in this 1784-5 period. The essential safe-guard of press freedom had been rendered valueless.

3. INTERLUDE, 1785-8

Although the Stamp Act of 1785 provoked anger in the press, it was not comparable to the rage that had seized the newspapers at the time of Foster's press bill. With the examples of Matthew Carey, Dowling, Magee and Bingley before them, they had been forced to realize that the administration could only be opposed within the limits it prescribed; and by the summer of 1785 it had come to dislike opposition of any kind. Newspaper proprietors had learned that nothing less than abject apology and retraction could save them from vengeance if the Castle's annoyance was aroused.

When, on 23 March 1786, Dowling was ordered to attend at the bar of the house of commons for some misrepresentation printed in the *Volunteer's Journal*, he humbly submitted that he had meant no dis-respect and threw himself on their mercy. The attitude of the commons showed how little they had cause, by this time, to fear the press: they allowed the word 'wilful' to be struck out of the charge, and contented themselves with reprimanding Dowling and discharging him. Three days later the printer of the *Hibernian Journal*, up on a similar charge, was released without reproof. A member suggested that to avoid such mis-understandings in future, official note-takers should be appointed; and the attorney general remarked with pleasure how decorous the press had become.[1] Even the *Dublin Evening Post* was quiet for so long that in September 1786 the administration rewarded Magee with a proclama-tion. The next issue praised the ministers' excellence, and the care with which they watched over the people's liberties. They excelled, it added as an afterthought, in creating peers and granting pensions: and were watch-ful 'as a kite over a partridge'.[2] The proclamations were discontinued.

[1] *Ir. parl. reg.*, vi. 157.
[2] 14 Sept. 1786.

But such boldness was rare. For the most part the opposition press was by then cowed. Deprived of its chief stimulus, controversy, it rapidly went into a decline.

The *Dublin Evening Post* and the *Hibernian Journal* survived; but by the time the regency crisis began to exercise men's minds in the winter of 1788 the *Volunteer's Journal*, the *General Evening Post* and the *Morning Post*, opposition Dublin newspapers, had disappeared. So had the *Belfast Mercury* and, most significant of all, the government's *Volunteer Evening Post*. A member of parliament had referred to it as a 'paper which nobody ever sees',[1] and how small its circulation must have been can be gauged by the fact that during 1787 it sometimes carried no commercial advertisements at all. But it is unlikely that the government would have let it drop unless they were so well satisfied with the general meekness of the press that the possession of two newspapers of their own appeared superfluous.

Newspapers rarely forecast their own dissolution: nor, usually, did they print obituaries of deceased contemporaries. The reasons why the *Volunteer's Journal* and the others ceased publication can only be guessed. The absence of domestic agitation in the years from 1785 to 1789 must have been one contributory factor; newspapers with a cause for which to fight can surmount difficulties that would put down the ordinary commercial venture at once. But there was material enough for agitation, if the press had dared to use it; tithes, religious disability, and the administration's corruption and incompetence.[2] The newspapers could have continued to focus public attention on the anomalies of representation and to urge parliamentary reform. But they had been frightened. As an opposition member had said during the debate on Foster's Press Bill, 'the connection between liberty and licentiousness is so intimate that it is very difficult to correct the one without wounding the other . . . licentiousness is the speck on the political eye which ought to be touched with a very delicate hand lest, in attempting to remove it, you destroy the body on which it appears'.[3] Jail sentences, fines and taxes had expelled faction from the press in Ireland: they had gone far towards making the press impotent in the process.

Outwardly there had been little material change in the position of the newspapers. Foster's bill, which had attracted so much attention, made little real difference. But the tranquillity after the summer of 1785 was illusory. By taxation and by subsidy the executive had secured a greater

[1] 2 Feb. 1787 (*Ir. parl. reg.*, vii. 83).
[2] Lecky, *Ire.*, ii. 462.
[3] 10 Apr. 1784 (ibid., iii. 158).

measure of control over the newspapers. The legislature had shown that when challenged there was hardly any limit to its coercive powers. The judicature had found ways in which to twist the law to the Castle's purpose; they could be used again. The outlook for the press, should it attempt to stage a revival, was unpromising.

Chapter II. 1789–1803

1. BEFORE THE REBELLION

In the winter of 1788 an event occurred which raised once more the hopes of the opposition in Ireland. George III fell a victim to the first of his attacks of insanity; and the question whether or not his eldest son should be invested with the regency was of vital interest to Grattan and his followers, in view of the prince's known sympathy for their cause. The regency crisis weakened the oligarchy, because the men who had most to gain from the maintenance of the existing structure of Irish society would be unwilling to commit themselves too deeply against the opposition, in case a regency was established. The press, therefore, was able to recover its power to comment and criticize, with less to fear from reprisals—an independence it still retained when the foundation of the society of United Irishmen brought a new force into Irish political life.

The government reacted as before. After 1789 it becomes less easy to decide whether a sentence on a printer for a breach of privilege is the spontaneous reaction of either lords or commons to an infringement of their rights, or an expedient adopted by the attorney general to avoid bringing the case before the ordinary courts. Executive, judiciary, and legislature had grown closer, and it is hard to disentangle the threads. For a few months in the winter of 1794–5, when the liberal Fitzwilliam was lord lieutenant, there was discord; for the rest of the period, the Castle, the courts of justice, and the houses of parliament pursued a common purpose—the maintenance of the oligarchy's interests.

The under secretary—Edward Cooke held the post almost throughout the period—was in charge of routine business concerning the press: but often the chief secretary, or even the lord lieutenant, was consulted. Cooke's actions may have often been the result of unrecorded consultation with, or orders from, his superiors; so, also may have been those of parliament. The euphemism which attributed all executive actions to 'the Castle' had practical justification. The assumption could be made that the law officers of the crown obeyed the Castle's general and, often, particular instructions, when action was taken against the press, though in fact the attorney general was called upon less and less. Purchase began to take the place of prosecution as the main instrument of government policy. Proprietors whom the government had reason to fear were first approached with an offer of financial assistance; prosecutions were threatened or initiated mainly as an added inducement to come to terms.

The sources from which the government drew the money to buy support were the secret service fund, and the money voted annually to the government for the printing of proclamations. Again, the government were not always conscious that they were buyers—or, the newspaper owner that he was for sale. Proclamations were naturally given to a friendly newspaper; its owner felt that it was only just that if he helped to sustain the government, he should be recompensed for his trouble. Dublin journalists were not then, as they were by the time Charles Gavan Duffy started work among them, ready to take a cynical attitude. They rarely, if ever, allowed themselves to be seduced into public support of a government which they continued personally to detest. Where a change of allegiance was made it was accompanied by a change of heart, the journalist concerned managing to convince himself of the virtues of the administration before, or at least at, the time of conversion. Whether or not these conversions were only job-deep can only be gauged by a study of the journalists' personalities—a safer indication than their expressed beliefs. An independent press attracts men of ability and integrity, even if the rewards are meagre, by promising them an opportunity for self-expression. If they have continually to trim, to avoid subjects that may give offence to the government or other influential interests, they will tend to leave journalism to men who are prepared to prostitute their talents, or who are capable of persuading themselves that any cause which offers them prospects is a cause worthy of their support. Their advocacy of that cause may then be in a sense sincere; but it cannot, strictly speaking, be termed disinterested. Where such men breed in the press, it is neither free, nor healthy. Their praise conceals the flattery of the sycophant, and their condemnations reflect the malice of the renegade.

The character of the newspaper-owners during this period provides an unusually good barometer to the state of the press, because the owner was usually so absorbed in his paper that it tended to become the expression of his personality. A journalist, writing in the 1790s, described his life:[1]

[1] W. P. Carey, *Appeal to the people of Ireland* (P) (1795), p. 11.

To preserve my interest with my old advertising friends, and to obtain new, I had a daily round of visitations to make through the principal streets of business. To collect money due for advertisements I had also a number of calls out in the day. As I had neither editor nor writer, all the literary labour devolved on me. Besides essays to write, I had to run over the London, the Dublin, and the Irish country papers; to digest the packets, to make extracts, and to furnish articles of domestic intelligence, and of general observation. I had also to run to the coffee houses to pick up the news of the day; to attend the theatre in the season, in order to give an account of the performance, and the parliament house, to take down debates. When I add to this that I had to correct the proofs, to write the letters to country correspondents, and to act as my own clerk, it will appear that my hands were pretty full.

This was an extreme case. Most of the newspapers had small staffs; but they were *very* small, and the owner, even if he did not have to do all the work, usually kept the direction of the paper in his hands, and infused it with his personality. From the character of the owner it is possible to appreciate the nature of the newspaper, and vice-versa; the studies are complementary.

(i) *The Castle newspapers*

The extent to which newspapers supporting the government were influenced by the hope of reward, by timidity, or by sloth, is not always easy to decide. Certain newspapers, however, were linked to the government by an informal contract: in return for their promise of support, their owners were given direct or indirect subsidies. The existence of these arrangements soon became known and the newspapers would thereafter be termed contemptuously 'Castle prints' by their rivals. They were not necessarily subject to day-to-day direction from the Castle: but the Castle's indirect control was none the less implicit in the contract.

(a) FRANCIS HIGGINS: THE 'FREEMAN'S JOURNAL'

At the time of the regency crisis the proprietor of the *Freeman's Journal* was Francis Higgins,[1] who had risen to be one of the most influential citizens of Dublin. Higgins had become a justice: he had served for a time as city coroner: he had been elected to the Dublin city commons— a forerunner of the corporation—as one of the representatives of the hosiers' guild, of which he had subsequently become master; and he had

[1] For Higgins's career see Madden's *Irish periodical literature*, vol. ii; Fitzpatrick's biography *The Sham Squire* and the *Dublin Evening Post* during the summer of 1789.

bought out the interest of the former owner of the *Freeman* of which he was now in sole charge.

Towards the end of March 1789, a series of tortuously allusive squibs began to appear in the *Dublin Evening Post* directed against 'Frank Paragraph, proprietor of a prostitute print', alias 'Shamado', or 'The Sham'. Higgins had made an enemy of John Magee, the *Post*'s owner, who in revenge proceeded to dig up the story of Higgins's past. By research among the files of Higgins's own paper, Magee was able to disinter the story how twenty years before, Higgins, then a penniless potboy at a public-house, had imposed upon a wealthy Dublin merchant, representing himself as a man of means, and securing the merchant's daughter for a wife. The judge at the trial for fraud that followed dubbed Higgins 'the Sham Squire', the name by which he was to be known to his contemporaries and to posterity. Whatever punishment he received, it did not long keep him out of mischief; a few weeks later he had been convicted of assault, and sentenced to a year's imprisonment. At some later stage he had taken up employment as a government agent, obtaining a post on the *Freeman* and there working secretly in their interest, until such time as he was able to take over the paper and come out openly on the Castle's side.

This was the tale that Magee retold, fragmentarily, in the columns of the *Evening Post* during the spring and early summer of 1789. At first he contented himself with publishing insinuations; later he gave the jury's true bill from the 'Squire' trial. Higgins announced that, as he was taking legal action, he would not rebut the falsehoods; later he admitted their truth, attributing the incident to youth's venial folly.[1] Magee then revealed the story of the second trial, adding unsubstantiated allegations of an even more scurrilous nature—that Higgins had seduced his jailer's daughter; that, on his release, he had worked as chucker-out in a gambling den, possessing himself first of his employer's wealth, by cheating him at his own tables, and subsequently, of his employer's wife; that his employer had been driven mad; and that his wife died later from a disease contracted from Higgins, who had deserted her as soon as he had secured possession of the gambling den which, Magee complained, was still a source of shame and irritation to respectable Dublin citizens.

Higgins's past had not been such that he would have cared to attempt

---

[1] *Freeman*, 20 May, 4 July 1789. Fitzpatrick was unable to obtain a file of the *Freeman* for 1789: and he was inclined to accept the *Evening Post*'s charges without verification. Higgins did not put up much of a defence in the *Freeman*, but the nature of the charges made defence difficult.

a refutation of all these charges in detail, even if most of them were un-founded. He preferred to enlist the help of his friend, Lord Earlsfort, who by this time was chief justice of the king's bench, to silence Magee; but not before the name of Higgins had been trailed in the gutter for more than six months. The revelations do not appear to have affected his position; nor the connection with his name of some irregulari-ties in his suit against Magee. In March 1790 Arthur Browne, member for Trinity College, who had been one of Magee's counsel, inquired about the discovery of certain erasures and alterations in the court records of the case. The attorney general promised to investigate: nothing further was heard of the matter that session. The following February, Browne succeeded in reopening the inquiry. A witness brought before the bar of the house of commons admitted being present at Higgins's house while the alterations were made. The combined efforts of the chief secretary, the attorney general, the solicitor general, and other government speakers were required to hush up the scandal, by persuading the house to take no further action.[1] It is possible that the disappearance of Higgins's name from the list of justices in that year was connected with this incident; but the *Evening Post*, which, unless it was being sarcastic, would hardly have wished 'to silence misrepresentation', gave it out that Higgins had sent in his resignation some time before on the grounds of ill health.[2]

For the rest of his life—he died in 1802—Higgins devoted much of his time to acting as a government agent. He wrote frequently and at length to the under secretary, Cooke, at the Castle, giving details of the activities of United Irishmen, obtained by his 'managing' of spies and informers, including Francis Magan, the betrayer of Lord Edward Fitzgerald. The details of the 'setting' of Lord Edward are described in some detail in his letters to Cooke; there is more than a hint of black-mail in his management of Magan, and in general they confirm that the man whom the Castle accepted as their ally and adviser-in-chief in the press was without scruples and without mercy.[3]

The *Freeman* did not recover from the decline that set in when it be-came a Castle paper. Throughout the period it remained with little circu-lation and less influence. To judge by Higgins's complaints that he was neglected in favour of his rival Castle papers, the government realized its worthlessness; certainly the obscurity into which it had sunk was

---

[1] *Ir. parl. reg.*, x. 382: xi. 57.

[2] *D.E. Post*, 15 Dec. 1791.

[3] Reb. papers, 620/18/14. About 150 of Higgins's letters to the under secretary, Cooke, have been preserved in the Irish State Paper Office.

admitted in the correspondence, which followed Higgins's death, on the subject of its future.[1]

To sustain Higgins and his paper, the government had to provide a subsidy, amounting at times to over £1,500 a year, from the proclamation fund, in addition to the £300 a year pension that was paid to him, and excluding payments to him for his services as an agent.[2] For this support, they received no thanks. Higgins was rarely without imagined grievances against the government, and in his determination to see them remedied, he made himself an intolerable nuisance. In person and in correspondence, he plagued under secretary Cooke incessantly, pestering him for interviews, begging, cringing, whining and backbiting. Cooke did his best to avoid him. Higgins's letters were full of complaints that he had been denied admission to the under secretary; on one occasion he threatened to bring his bed to the Castle and sleep outside Cooke's door, to make sure of seeing him. Letter after letter detailed his services, and complained that he had never received a penny for them.

The Castle had secured, in the *Freeman*, a newspaper with a great past reputation. They were to find that reputation was, if anything, a liability. Goodwill in a newspaper is an uncertain asset; the better the paper has been beloved, the more swiftly will readers vanish when its principles change. The government, throughout the period, had the credit value only of the *Freeman's* name, to set off against the galling realization of the paper's small circulation, the cost of its maintenance, and the annoyance of Francis Higgins's importunities.

(b) JOHN GIFFARD: 'FAULKNER'S DUBLIN JOURNAL'

Faulkner's Dublin Journal remained stolidly conservative, avoiding controversy or comment, until 1788, when Thomas Faulkner, who was suffering from ill health, allowed the lease to be taken up by John Giffard.

Giffard's early career reads like a parody of the youth of Francis Higgins. Educated at a charity school, and afterwards apprenticed to an apothecary, he too managed to wed an heiress, styling himself 'Surgeon' Giffard, presumably for the benefit of her family. Later he returned to his apothecary's trade in Dublin, earning money on the side by reporting parliamentary debates for the newspapers. In this capacity, he attracted the government's attention. They offered to employ him; Giffard, al-

[1] John Pollock to the Castle, 27 Mar. 1802 (Reb. papers, 620/63/9).
[2] *Cornwallis correspondence*, iii. 320.

though he had earlier been a member of the popular party, accepted. In 1784 the *Dublin Evening Post* called him a 'Castle scribbler', and Napper Tandy roundly accused him of selling himself to the government.[1] Like Higgins, he used his guild membership to further his ambitions, becoming one of the apothocaries' members in the city commons at whose meetings he spoke often, tending to 'dwell copiously on his honesty and purity';[2] and vilifying reformers and Catholics at every opportunity.

The administration asked him to take over *Faulkner's Dublin Journal* in 1788 when they felt the need of support over the regency crisis. Seeing in its owner's ill health a chance to win the oldest Dublin newspaper to their side, they suggested to Giffard that he should, with their backing, take up the lease.[3] The negotiations were naturally kept secret, but the change in the character of the *Dublin Journal* was immediately noticed, provoking interested speculation in the opposition press. 'Mr. Giffard', the *Morning Post* announced, 'is said to be the proprietor; there was some doubt of it, until it appeared that the government purse was opened'.[4] As soon as it became obvious that the paper's new connections were known, Giffard threw off restraint and abused the 'factious and disaffected' opposition journals for their support of the claims of the prince.

Giffard himself, secure in his new favour, rapidly developed into a notorious bigot and braggart. Soon after he had taken on the *Dublin Journal*, a complaint was made to the government by the advocate John Philpot Curran, that 'a man of the name of Giffard, a conductor of your press, a writer for your government, your notorious agent in the city, your notetaker in the house of commons' had threatened him with violence.[5]

The reference to Giffard as 'your notorious agent in the city' was justified; Giffard was at least as energetic in the Castle's service as Higgins. From 1792, he acted as a go-between for under secretary Cooke and the spy Collins, the first of the systematic informers.[6] Collins posed as an extreme United Irishman, and managed to retain the society's confidence while he was sending accounts of their activities to Giffard, who forwarded them to the Castle. These services were sufficiently highly

[1] *Freeman*, 10 June 1784.
[2] *General Evening Post*, 22 June 1784.
[3] Mrs Ward to R. Peel, 14 Oct. 1816 (B.M. Add. MS (Peel) 40259 f. 156); (Hardwicke) 35758 f. 128: Off. papers, 528/199/24.
[4] *M. Post*, 2 Feb. 1789.
[5] Madden, *United Irishmen*, iv. 87: H.M.C., *Fortescue*, i. 568.
[6] *Analecta Hibernica* (1949), xvii. 3.

thought of for Giffard to be chosen in 1794 as sheriff of Dublin—given the post, his enemies alleged, because someone was needed who could be relied upon to pack an amenable jury for the trial of Hamilton Rowan.

By this time Giffard had altered the character of the *Dublin Journal.* In 1793, he was prosecuted—unsuccessfully—for a libel on the duke of Leinster.[1] The following year the *Dublin Evening Post* begged Giffard, in his capacity as sheriff, to deal with Giffard, the editor of the *Dublin Journal,* who had accused the *Evening Post* of propagating atheism. (In its next issue[2] the *Evening Post* avenged itself by caricaturing Giffard as 'the dog in office', a nickname which was to cling to him as 'The Sham Squire' clung to Higgins.) In 1794, too, Giffard earned public execration by taking the names of citizens celebrating the verdict of not guilty after the trial of the United Irishman, Dr Drennan. Such anger did he arouse, that a substantial minority of the city commons opposed the vote of thanks to the previous year's officers when he retired from being sheriff[3]—a vote normally passed *nem. con.,* as a formality. Giffard, attributing this opposition to 'the filthy scurrility of the *Morning Post,* and the wild ravings of the *Evening Post*', set about gaining his revenge. A week later he had a ballad hawker into court for selling 'The last speech and dying words of the Dog', along with the printer, Patrick Byrne. Both of them escaped on legal technicalities.[4] The proprietor of the *Morning Post* was less fortunate; for printing a libellous description of Giffard's conduct in his year of office as sheriff, he was sentenced to fifteen months' imprisonment.

The following year, Giffard was himself arrested on a charge of assaulting James Potts, the owner of *Saunders' News-Letter.* The evidence was too damning for an acquittal, and in spite of a plea that he could not be spared from 'military duties', he was sentenced to six months' imprisonment. After a month of the sentence had been served the lord lieutenant remitted the rest, an action which roused the *Evening Post* to publish an article reprobating the practice of pardoning criminals, which encouraged men to believe that influence could aid wrongdoers to escape just punishment.[5] The sentence was commuted to a fine; its payment, the *Evening Post* later claimed, was not enforced. In 1799, Giffard was found guilty at a court martial of conduct disrespectful to his com-

---

[1] *Hib. J.,* 13 Nov. 1793.
[2] *D.E. Post,* 10 Apr. 1794.
[3] *F.D.J.,* 18 Oct. 1794.
[4] *D.E. Post,* 20 Oct. 1794.
[5] Ibid., 20 Aug. 1795. Giffard's trial is reported in *Walker's Hibernian Magazine* for August 1795.

manding officer in the Dublin militia, and sentenced to a reprimand. Again, the lord lieutenant intervened, ordering that the reprimand be given 'in a slight manner'.[1]

It is to Giffard that tradition assigns the coining of the phrase, 'protestant ascendancy': and until his death, twenty years after the union, he was to be the Protestant ascendancy's most vocal advocate. The historian Madden had an interview with him on one occasion, and 'carried away a very lasting impression of his insolence, coarseness, and vulgarity'—an impression that appears to have been widely shared. Sir Jonah Barrington alone had some good to say of him; but Barrington's opinion might have been less favourable had he known that Giffard had denounced him in letters to the Castle.[2] Grattan's picture of Giffard is the one that survives:[3]

> the hired traducer of his country—the excommunicated of his fellow citizens—the unpunished ruffian—the bigoted agitator: in the city a firebrand —in the field a coward. And so obnoxious is he to the very party he wishes to espouse, that he is only supportable by those dirty acts the less vile refuse to execute

Under Giffard's control, the *Dublin Journal* lost some of its old air of commercial prosperity. But its circulation did not fall away as catastrophically as the *Freeman*'s, and its influence, if anything, exceeded its circulation, because it was read even by those to whom his views were anathema. In their assaults on the Castle press, the opposition papers almost invariably concentrated their fire upon the *Dublin Journal*. The reason was that Giffard retained some degree of independence. In the 1790s he had one serious clash with the Castle—during the brief period of the liberal Fitzwilliam's viceroyalty in 1794–5. Fitzwilliam's arrival put Giffard in a difficult position. The press generally was exultant: Cooke, writing to Fitzwilliam's predecessor,[4] had to admit that: 'all the newspapers are let loose, and hallooed against your excellency's government and its supporters'. The *Freeman* sourly commented on the sudden courtliness of papers that had earlier held republican sentiments: could it be that they were thinking of becoming 'proclamation prints'? But the *Freeman* did not dare to offend the new master by absenting itself from the chorus of welcome. Even the *Dublin Journal* published a poem

---

[1] Sankey, *Proceedings of a general court martial . . . upon Capt. John Giffard* (P), 1799.

[2] 1802 (Reb. papers, 620/62/8, 18): Barrington, *Recollections*, p. 181.

[3] Gwynn, *Grattan*, p. 368.

[4] I.S.P.O., Westmoreland correspondence, Fane, 127.

in his honour, but Fitzwilliam was not impressed. Within a month of his arrival, Cooke wrote again to Westmoreland:[1]

> Poor Giffard who had the management of the *Dublin Journal* is no longer employed. He had £300 a year for his labour; and in the faith of government he took a lease of £500 a year for seven years, government paying £300 of the rent. I hear this dismissal has been at Curran's instance. He cannot well go into opposition with his paper as he has an employment at the custom house, and poor fellow, he will be ruined.

Giffard later confirmed Cooke's account 'Fitzwilliam dismissed the *Dublin Journal* and me as a writer'. There was no diminution in the amount of government advertising in the paper; presumably only the direct subsidy was withdrawn. The incident appears to have enhanced the newspaper's popularity. The reason probably was that at the time, the bulk of the middle-class Irish Protestants—the class from which were drawn most of the Volunteers and many of the United Irishmen—had no love for the oligarchy: and they were inclined to favour some concessions to the Catholics. But they wanted to make the concessions in their own time. If any suggestion arose of conciliation as an executive policy to be pursued by a liberal viceroy, they might be stampeded by an anti-popery campaign. From their fears the *Dublin Journal*, as the most outspokenly Protestant newspaper in Ireland, probably reaped the benefit. As soon, however, as the *Dublin Journal* allowed its ties to the Castle to draw it against the current of middle class Protestant opinion, readers left it. At the time of the Union, which Giffard advocated, the influence of the *Dublin Journal* again declined, never to recover.

Giffard, for his rather doubtful allegiance, levied at all times a heavy annual tribute on the state. How heavy the expense was, was disclosed in April 1799, when the paper fell foul of the house of commons, who committed the printer—not Giffard—to custody for a few days. An inquiry set on foot by the injured house revealed that the *Dublin Journal* was being subsidized to the extent of over £1,000 a year by government proclamations.[2] Giffard's correspondence with the Castle shows that he was actually receiving considerably more. For his services as a writer the Castle had given him a pension of £300 a year, by way of compensation for taking him away from his original profession as apothecary. Of the £500 a year that he had to pay the Faulkners for the lease of the *Dublin Journal*, the Castle had undertaken to contribute £300. With the £1,000 a year he received for printing the proclamations, Giffard's total income was brought up to £1,600 from journalism alone. In addition,

[1] Ibid., Fane, 120.
[2] *Commons jn. Ire.*, xviii. appx. lcccxiv.

he had a lucrative 'place' in the Customs, and the captaincy of a militia troop, both in his case virtual sinecures.[1]

In defence of the expenditure for printing proclamations in the *Dublin Journal*, the argument was put forward that the public must be informed when emergencies arose, and that the oldest-established newspaper in Ireland would be a natural place to look for them.

The manner in which proclamations were printed in the *Dublin Journal* shows that the argument was specious. An offer of a reward for the apprehension of the printer of the *Union Star* appeared in almost every issue of the *Dublin Journal* from July 1797 to March 1798, in spite of the fact that the offer was to expire in January 1798, and that the *Union Star* was in fact suppressed before the end of 1797. It is possible that the *Dublin Journal* continued to print the proclamation *gratis*, to fill up space. More probably, it was published with the connivance of the Castle, in order to keep up the level of the *Dublin Journal's* subsidy.

The comparative prosperity of the *Dublin Journal* before 1800 meant that the government to some extent were spared a repetition from Gifford of Higgins's importunities. Giffard did, indeed, urge his and his family's claims, on occasion; but it was not until some years later that the declining fortunes of his paper made him a plague to the Castle with his requests for assistance. On the other hand, the Castle was kept in a constant state of worry and irritation by his unreliability. In 1794, years before Grattan had called attention to the dislike which was felt for Giffard even by his own party, Dr. Drennan was amused at the embarrassment which Giffard was causing to the Castle. It was not the only occasion on which the Castle had reason to regret their purchase.[2]

(c) WILLIAM CORBET: THE 'HIBERNIAN TELEGRAPH'

The third Dublin newspaper to come under Castle control in the period was the *Hibernian Telegraph and Morning Star*. The *Morning Star*, when it first appeared in 1793, had been an opposition newspaper, with United Irish sympathies: but it came into the hands of William Corbet and, renamed the *Hibernian Telegraph and Morning Star*, it renounced its former opinions. Corbet, according to a letter he wrote to the under secretary, Cooke, in 1790, had been in the Castle's service for

[1] B.M. Add. MS (Hardwicke) 35758 f. 128: Off. papers, 528/199/24.
[2] 30 Oct. 1794 (*Drennan letters*, p. 216): *Castlereagh correspondence*, iii. 9.

some time.[1] Like Higgins and Giffard, he combined his newspaper work with activities as a government agent, particularly in connection with their dealings with journalists. He was instrumental in securing the conversion of William Paulet Carey in 1794, and later, in persuading Brenan, the editor of the *Press*, to betray his colleagues. For this work, he received payments from the secret service fund.[2]

Corbet never attained the notoriety of Higgins or Giffard: but his career and—so far as can be judged from his letters—his character, were of the same pattern. His usefulness to the Castle began and ended with his work as their agent: his newspaper was a failure. The expenses of maintaining the *Hibernian Telegraph* can have been little less than those of the *Freeman* and the *Dublin Journal*; and internal evidence suggests that if the *Freeman's* circulation was small, the *Hibernian Telegraph's* must have been almost non-existent. It subsisted almost solely on Castle proclamations. Accounts which Corbet furnished to the Castle during 1797[3] show that he was receiving at least £500 a year from the proclamation fund: a typical entry being:

> For declaring the parish of Taughboye, All Saints, etc., in the barony of Raphoe in a state of disturbance (90 lines, 28 insertions at 24/4) . . . £34. 2. 6d.

—twenty-eight insertions of a piece of information that would not in any case have been read (it was a standing joke at the time that nobody read proclamations), even if the *Hibernian Telegraph* had circulated to more than a handful of readers. Opposition newspapers paid no attention to it, sufficient proof of its obscurity. Advertisers ignored the paper: on occasions during 1799, it contained no advertisements at all, though it would have a page or more of proclamations. Only once did it attract any public attention. In February 1797 the printer was ordered to attend at the bar of the house of lords for a libel on Lord Aldborough. Aldborough was himself in disgrace at the time, and the lords contented themselves with the formal reprimand usually given on such occasions to remind printers that to publish the proceedings of the house was in itself a breach of privilege. The printer escaped, not without a denunciation by Aldborough, who expressed the opinion that the press was controlled or prostituted, and printers awed by fear or power from reporting matters fairly.[4]

After this incident, the *Hibernian Telegraph* retired into the shadows.

[1] Off. papers, 512/54.
[2] Cf. Gilbert, *Documents relating to Ireland* (secret service accounts and payments).
[3] Reb. papers, 620/35/164.
[4] *Lords jn. Ire.*, vii. 509 (13 Feb. 1797).

This did not deter its owner from being almost as persistent in urging his claims upon the government, as Francis Higgins. In his letter to Cooke in 1790, he had claimed to be 'though behind the curtain, the real editor of the *Phenix*'; his labours, he said, in setting up that paper had impoverished him, and he requested assistance, the difficulties 'rendering expedition of a peculiar object to me'. In the rebellion period, he was constantly in trouble. First, he was too successful in ingratiating himself with the journalist Brenan, whom he had been instructed to win over to the government's side; Brenan fleeced him unmercifully. Then, Corbet found that he was heavily in debt to the stamp commissioners. No sooner had he persuaded the Castle to pay them than they informed him that his debt was larger than they had thought; and he had to make fresh demands upon the Castle. Finally—the crowning ignominy—Corbet learned that Marsden, the new under-secretary, had decided to take away government patronage from him, on the grounds of his intimacy with a notorious scoundrel—the journalist Brenan.[1] Although renewed pleas secured the survival of the *Hibernian Telegraph*, it remained without circulation or influence, brought out by a man who was a constant source of annoyance and expense to his employers.

(d) W. P. CAREY: THE 'GENERAL EVENING POST'

A fourth Castle newspaper, which appeared in Dublin towards the end of the year 1795, was William Paulet Carey's *General Evening Post*. Carey's case differed from those of his predecessors in the field, in that he began his journalistic career in opposition to the government, and was even, for a time, a member of the Dublin Society of United Irishmen.

Over the names of 'Junius Hibernicus' and 'Scriblerius Murtagh O'Pindar', Carey (a brother of the Careys of the *Volunteer's Journal*) had written many anti-government squibs for the short-lived *Town, or Dublin Evening Packet*, a Dublin newspaper that had been published in the days of the regency crisis. In 1791, he founded a paper of his own, the *Rights of Irishmen, or National Evening Star*. He was an able writer and an industrious editor: the new paper was a success at a time when at least one other paper set up in Dublin by the United Irishmen, with greater resources behind it, failed. The *Evening Star* paid more attention to seeking the solution of religious divisions than was usual in the opposition of the day. On the front page, a Protestant, a Presbyterian, and a

[1] Reb. papers, 620/61/140: Off. papers, 517/106/30.

Catholic were shown shaking hands. Carey kept the paper lively and controversial; he was soon in trouble with the administration.

How little serious cause for offence the *Evening Star* had given could be judged from the excuse taken in November 1792 to prosecute Carey, a paragraph copied from a Belfast newspaper giving an account of the rejoicings in Belfast after the French victory at Valmy. The attorney general pronounced this to be a seditious libel. A month later, a second prosecution was threatened, for the publication of the 'Address to the Volunteers' by the Dublin United Irishmen, for which Hamilton Rowan, Dr. Drennan, and the proprietors of the Belfast *Northern Star* were all awaiting trial. Carey, feeling that his position was growing impossible, thought it advisable to disappear for a while. He hoped to be able to carry on the paper from hiding, but this proved beyond his powers, and he had to sell out.[1]

The new proprietor, Randal McAllister—also a United Irishman—was himself soon in trouble. In March 1793 he was summoned before the house of commons for a squib in the *Evening Star*, which had defined parliament as a market where honour and virtue were sold to the highest bidder. The house voted to commit him to the Newgate prison for libel. Reporting the debate, the Belfast *Northern Star* commented that the *Evening Star* had had to cease publication on account of the numerous attacks made upon it by the administration.[2]

Deprived of his source of livelihood, Carey was an obvious prey for government agents. When, a year later, he gave evidence at the trial of Dr Drennan for the publication of the 'Address to the Volunteers' he was no longer the Carey of the United Irishmen, the tickler of viceroys' noses. He was in the box as a witness for the crown.

While he was in hiding, Carey had had time to meditate. He was married, with seven children, which made his position more difficult. And he knew what the administration could do when they took a dislike to a newspaper, as they had to his brother's *Volunteer's Journal*. His imagination conjured up the prospect of a life of fines, imprisonment, the pillory, and whippings at the cart's tail through the streets of Dublin. He therefore put his case to the Dublin United Irishmen, hoping that they would urge him to leave the country and agree to pay his bail if it should be estreated: he did not wish the men who had put it up to

---

[1] Carey's apologia, the pamphlet *Appeal to the people of Ireland*, is substantially accurate. Unless otherwise indicated, material on his career up to 1785 has been drawn from it, checked where possible from other sources such as the informer Collins's reports of the proceedings of the United Irishmen (*Analecta Hibernia*, 1949), and an MS memoir in the Madden papers, T.C.D.

[2] *N. Star*, 4 May 1793.

be out of pocket. The society was not sympathetic. With a number of its officers in prison, it was unwilling to increase its commitments. To add to his difficulties, Randal MacAllister went bankrupt.[1] Carey had allowed him to buy the *Evening Star* with a promissory note, which was accordingly worthless. Shortly afterwards a man was sentenced to a year's imprisonment and a fine of £1,000 for distributing a seditious paper in County Louth. Carey found to his alarm that he had been the paper's original printer. The United Irishmen for their part grew suspicious of him, guessing (probably with reason) that articles criticizing the society which had appeared in the *Evening Star* had been written by Carey himself; and they took that excuse to expel him from membership.

The government, through Giffard and the spy Collins, had been watching the progress of the dispute. They wished to obtain evidence with which to convict Dr Drennan of the authorship of the 'Address to the Volunteers', and when the society expelled Carey, Corbet of the *Telegraph* was instructed to win him over. Carey was told that if he would help to secure Drennan's conviction his past would be forgotten, and he would be handsomely compensated for the loss of his newspaper.[2] The terms agreed were £1,000 down and a pension of £100 a year for life, plus a contract of about £750 a year for government printing, with protection—an absurdly high price to pay for evidence against one man. But the government could rarely secure any reputable citizen to give evidence in court; men who were willing to pass information did not as a rule care to admit the fact in public. Carey would need substantial compensation for the public hatred of a turncoat; he would run the risk of injury, and possibly assassination, at the hands of the United Irishmen. A proviso in the agreement stated that if life should become impossible for him in Ireland, he should be given equivalent assistance in England.

Carey's evidence proved valueless to the prosecution. In the witness-box, his duplicity was unravelled by Curran,[3] and he cut so poor a figure that not even Lord Clonmell's efforts from the bench on behalf of the prosecution could persuade the jury to find Drennan guilty. In the circumstances it was not surprising that the government's reward owed to Carey was paid with reluctance. He had promised to revive the *Evening Star*, counting on government support; this project fell through, because the £1,000 was not paid in a lump sum, but doled out in instalments of £50 a time. The annuity was not paid at all.

[1] R. B. McDowell, in *I.H.S.*, ii. 39 (March 1940).
[2] Reb. papers, 620/49/94.
[3] *Trial of William Drennan* (P), 1794.

At the time the bargain was struck, Carey had been told that although everyone from the viceroy down had approved the terms, a written agreement was out of the question: if it was discovered, the whole group of them would be prosecuted for suborning a witness. Lacking this documentary evidence, he could do no more than protest at the delays. The arrival of Fitzwilliam as lord lieutenant was promptly seized upon as an excuse to tell him that, as everything at the Castle had been turned upside down, he could expect no more money from the administration. Carey threatened to go to court, in spite of the pledge to secrecy. The threat appears to have carried weight; shortly afterwards the Castle offered to buy his pension for £400 down—a little more than half the real market value of £100 a year at that date. After some haggling, Carey secured £500, though he had to sign a receipt that all his claims against the government had been discharged.[1]

With this money Carey set up his new paper, the *General Evening Post*, in November 1795: and thenceforward his career conforms to the established pattern—with this exception: that as Carey was not in a position to act as a government agent, he gave the Castle nothing but trouble for their money.

The *General Evening Post* remained as obscure as Corbet's *Hibernian Telegraph*. It would contain anything up to seven (out of sixteen) columns of proclamations: but ordinary commercial advertisements were few. The expense to the government must have been considerable. At a time when he had reason to minimize the amount of support he had received from the Castle, Carey himself admitted that he had obtained £1,000 from Westmoreland's administration, £500 from Fitzwilliam's, and £1,000 from Camden's.[2] And he was even more annoyingly persistent than his colleagues, in pestering the Castle for more assistance.

In June 1796, he wrote the first of many supplicatory letters to the Castle, complaining that he had not been given proclamations. The deficiency was remedied; but a few weeks later Carey wrote again, enclosing a balance sheet which showed that even with the proclamations he was losing money. 'I have no hope, no friends, no reliance but what I first place in government, and what I now rest in your humane consideration of my case'.[3] His plight moved the government—if his own story is correct—to give him a further grant of money, though they again demanded a signed receipt to the effect that he had no further

[1] Reb. papers, 620/49/94.
[2] Aspinall, *Politics and the press*, p. 411.
[3] Reb. papers, 620/24/125. Off. papers, 507/13/35.

financial claims upon them. Carey was then informed that the proclamations would be withdrawn from him. As he was filling as many as six columns of the paper with them, regardless of relevance, this would have ruined him; but a direct appeal to the lord lieutenant obtained a pension of £50, and a promise of £400 worth of proclamations for his paper each year.[1] Proclamations were given to him during 1797, in spite of Higgins's warnings to the Castle that he was printing sedition on the sly.[2] Cooke, however, must have been worried about the paper's small circulation; and, ignoring Carey's plea that circulation had risen since he altered the nights of the week on which the *General Evening Post* appeared, in order to avoid direct competition with the *Dublin Evening Post*, he decided before the end of the year that the proclamations were to be withdrawn.[3] This brought the paper to an immediate end.

The government were then to learn that allowing one of their worthless newspapers to disappear did not put an end to the embarrassments it caused them. There remained the problem of what was to be done for its owner. Carey continued to be the most persistent of mendicants. He despatched memorials to Cooke, to the lord lieutenant, and even to Whitehall,[4] setting forth his grievances in detail. Eventually in 1799 he resorted to an earlier expedient, promising to cease his importunities if the Castle rescued him from the bankruptcy he feared was imminent. Cooke impatiently scribbled on the back of his letter that documents existed to prove that every claim had been settled long before. The lord lieutenant, however, must have taken pity on him; in the secret service accounts for 1799 there is an entry:[5]

'4 June. Mrs. Carey

In full discharge of Mr. Carey's demands . . . £100.'

William Paulet Carey provides a good example of the fate of an able and intelligent journalist, who is persuaded to sacrifice his integrity. In the early part of his career he showed unusual promise: in later years, when he recovered his equilibrium, he was to become a respected connoisseur in London, attaining the posthumous distinction of two columns in the *Dictionary of National Biography*, which makes no reference to his early life, except to mention rather incredulously that he was 'said to have been' a United Irishman. The middle years, where he allowed himself to become a Castle pensioner, were melancholy for himself, and profitless to his employers.

[1] Ibid., 620/49/94.
[2] 7 Feb. 1797 (ibid., 620/18/14).
[3] Ibid., 620/49/94.
[4] Ibid., 620/40/165: 56/60: 39/163.
[5] Ibid., 620/56/24. Gilbert, *Documents relating to Ireland*, p. 30.

(e) THE PROVINCIAL NEWSPAPERS

The scattered information that remains about the Irish provincial press at this time suggests that, where newspaper owners allowed themselves to be brought over to the government's side, the story of their papers conformed closely to the established Dublin pattern.

The most influential newspaper outside the capital had long been the *Belfast News-Letter*. Although the *News-Letter* became conservative, compared to the rest of the independent press, after 1782, the historian Madden is unjust in calling it 'steady in its anti-liberal, anti-Catholic and anti-national sentiments'. The *News-Letter* took up quite a friendly attitude to the French revolution, up to the time of the king's trial. Henry Joy, the editor and part proprietor, was a friend of Lord Charlemont, with whom he corresponded frequently,[1] and his policy reflected Charlemont's liberal, but not revolutionary, cast of mind. Under Joy, it certainly was not a government newspaper.

The *News-Letter's* conversion into an unqualified supporter of the administration followed the familiar course.[2] Henry Joy found the revenue from his paper diminishing, a decline which he blamed on the war, but which was more probably due to the competition of the *Northern Star*, set up in Belfast by the United Irishmen early in 1792. The *News-Letter*, put up for sale, found purchasers in two Scots newspaper owners who appointed George Gordon, another Scot, as editor. Unable to check the *News-Letter's* decline, Gordon approached the Castle for help. In the meantime, the *News-Letter* warmed to the administration, so that Gordon, writing direct to Cooke a few weeks later, was able to detail the assistance he had given to them—not, he hastened to add, with any prospect of reward in mind, though a reward would be an incitement to further efforts on the government's behalf, and would help to make those efforts successful. At the same time Gordon canvassed influential persons to put the *News-Letter's* case to the Castle, which they did.

The Castle, convinced of the *News-Letter's* good intentions, agreed to allow Gordon to print the proclamations, thereby guaranteeing his paper a steady income for so long as it continued to give satisfaction. But Gordon found that to advocate the administration's cause was to court losing his subscribers. He explained to Cooke that he was deliber-

---

[1] H.M.C., *Charlemont*, rep. 13, appx. viii.—see index. Madden, *I.P.L.*, ii. 207.

[2] For references, see R. B. McDowell in an article on 'The Irish government and the provincial press' in *Hermathena*, liii (May 1939). and Aspinall in his *Politics and the press*, pp. 109–12, both deal with the case of the *Belfast News-Letter* in detail, extracting their information mainly from letters in the Rebellion papers.

ately avoiding adulation of the government, and might even occasionally print language foreign to his real sentiments, in order to retain his custom. For a time he maintained the precarious balance successfully, even to the extent of inserting an article so demonstrably loyal that he could send it to the Castle, in the hope that Cooke would order a reprint. But soon afterwards, the deception ignominiously collapsed. The murder of a northern loyalist so enraged the commander-in-chief of the army in Ulster that he insisted on Gordon publishing what amounted to a general condemnation of the citizens of Belfast. The citizens were furious, many withdrawing their subscriptions. An apology from Gordon, in which he maintained that he had been compelled to insert the commander-in-chief's strictures because they had been brought to him and paid for as an ordinary commercial advertisement, only succeeded in infuriating the commander-in-chief as well. Gordon found it prudent to depart for a while from the city, and later, to fly the country.

He continued to pester the Castle for assistance. So, too, did his employers. The more the paper's fortunes declined, the greater was the need for subsidies; and they wrote often to Cooke, and later to his successor, begging for better terms. Possibly because they were further away, and less well able to harass the Castle into acceptance of their demands, the owners of the *News-Letter* received less generous treatment than their Dublin colleagues. The meagre indemnification for their losses that was paid to them, and an allowance of £200 a year from the secret service fund, was little compensation for the loss of the proclamations, which were taken from the *News-Letter*, presumably because of more pressing demands elsewhere. But the calls on the secret service money were equally clamant, and the *News-Letter's* owners had great difficulty in extracting their pension, which was brought to an end by Cooke's successor in 1802.

The *News-Letter* probably owed its survival to the suppression of its rival the *Northern Star* in the spring of 1797: thereafter for a time it had no competitor in Belfast. The reaction, too, in the North against the excesses of '98 must have brought back old readers. Otherwise, during this period it conformed to type.

Most of the provincial newspapers followed the *Belfast News-letter's* example, and came over to the government side. Usually the change of heart was accompanied by a profession of principle. Madden cites the example of the *Waterford Herald*, which up to 1794 had paraded liberal principles, suddenly making a solemn denunciation of disorder, and affirming its loyalty to the constitution; shortly afterwards 'the unmistakable evidence of venality was to be found in its columns of government proclamations, Gazette notices by order of the lord lieutenant and privy council frequently occupying two of the four sides of the newspaper'. Madden's deduction is confirmed by a later petition from the proprietor of the *Herald*, Isaac Heron, to the Castle, in which he admits that he had experienced acute financial difficulties in 1793.[1]

By 1796 Heron was calling for more proclamations, which, he thought, were 'not nigh sufficiently promulged'—the illiterate did not see them. He kept the Castle informed about the state of the public mind in Waterford, warning them that the *Northern Star* was being read in the coffee-houses:—'surely it should not escape instant death?' 'The apostate Driscol's Cork paper is equally wicked', he went on, 'and ought to be destroyed.' For his support, Heron was able to claim £10 in 1795, £293 in 1797.[2] The government's satisfaction was not shared by all the local loyalists. A venerable dean, writing to the Castle in 1797, complained that the *Waterford Herald* was dangerous. A rival paper that had been set up was now defunct; the dean was prepared to offer his services to found another one in the government interest, and he hoped that he might be appointed to take charge—'for appointment I presume it may be denominated, if the proclamations, etc. are to be granted to the new paper as they were to the late'. Possibly this letter moved Cooke to withdraw government support from the *Herald*; for when Heron wrote presenting his account in 1800, the last charge was for 1797, and he gave his address as 'From Prison', complaining that his desire to serve the government had brought him into debt.[3]

Finn's Leinster Journal had for years been steady in opposition— 'very violent and democratic', Lord Ormond and Ossory termed it, writing to the Castle in 1797. But it had mended its ways and was now 'completely proper'. Finn had allowed himself to be converted, but had told Lord Ormond, in return, that when it changed its policy it would lose support. It did; and Lord Ormond and Finn were jointly petitioning the Castle for assistance. Finn later told the Castle that a claim he had put in for £1,700 had been accepted by the administration, but that the capital sum had not then been available. Instead, he was promised £300 down and an annuity of £200. The first half-yearly instalment had been paid, but nothing more. These facts, attested by Lord Ormond and by the bishop of Meath, were later put before the lord lieutenant, reinforced by a plea that a large family depended on the pen-

---

[1] Reb. papers, 620/23/89.
[2] Ibid., 620/57/142.
[3] Ibid., 620/32/177. 620/57/142

71

sion for support. In 1805 Finn was still petitioning the Castle, complaining that nothing had been done about his claims.[1]

George Grace started a newspaper in Clonmel in the late '90s—to counteract the rebellion, he later claimed, but it may have been to take advantage of the £800 a year from the printing of proclamations that the Castle bestowed upon him.[2] Another Clonmel proprietor, Power, wrote to the under secretary, Marsden, in 1803, thanking him for proclamations, and for finding his son a 'place' in the city. 'I have one favour more to beg,' he concluded, 'your permitting me to send you a vessel of Blackwater cyder of such quality as not to be had in Dublin'.[3] Even if the owner's loyalty was not originally purchased—proclamations might be asked for provincial papers without a venal design—the procuring of proclamations appears invariably to have had a fatal effect on the newspaper's independence. No proprietor could afford to risk the loss of so substantial a source of income. Support of the administration reduced newspapers' circulation to the point where they had to have the proclamations in order to survive, as proprietors found who attempted to support the government without the assistance of proclamations or pensions. Early in 1798 Henry Morgan set up the *Cork Herald* as a rival to the proposed *Harp of Erin*, which the United Irishmen were starting. The chief secretary was asked to lend assistance. It did not materialize. By June, Morgan confessed to a friend in Dublin that he was in desperate financial straits. He went to Dublin to remind Cooke of a promise of help, petitioning the lord lieutenant with requests for immediate assistance in the form either of proclamations or of a loan of £250. 'If not, the post which may bring me the answer . . . will at once put an end to the *Cork Herald*.' By the end of the year the *Herald* was defunct.[4]

This appears to have been an exceptional case. Normally, the government would rarely fail to assist any newspaper that came to terms. A letter of Castlereagh's shows that by the rebellion year this was, in fact, the government's deliberate policy: 'the principal provincial papers', he told Whitehall, 'have been secured, and every attention will be paid to the press generally'.[5] By the summer of 1798, not a newspaper of any importance remained in the provinces that had not been either frightened or seduced into support of the administration.

[1] Off. papers, 520/132/1: 529/201/9. Reb. papers, 620/57/106. McDowell, in *Hermathena*, liii. 183.
[2] Ibid., 536/262/32.
[3] Ibid., 524/153/16.
[4] McDowell in *Hermathena*, liii. 143–4.
[5] *Cornwallis correspondence*, ii. 448.

By the time of the '98 rising the pattern of the government press in Ireland was well established. Castle newspapers, and their owners, shared many common characteristics. The most significant was that they were not read. Giffard's relative independence made the *Dublin Journal* an exception; where a newspaper committed itself entirely to government direction, its circulation and influence normally contracted. Circulation figures are not available, but it is probable that the *Freeman*, the *Hibernian Telegraph*, and the *General Evening Post* mustered only a few hundred readers between them. They were dull even by the standards of the time, filled as they were with proclamations and news copied straight from the English papers. Irish news rarely occupied more than a few paragraphs, and there were few general articles or features. As a result these newspapers were despised. Their owners were execrated. Of the four Dublin owners, three had achieved an unenviable notoriety, Higgins as an adventurer, Giffard as a bigot, Carey as a renegade: all three were to be marked out for assassination in the 1797 broadsheet, the *Union Star*. Only Corbet remained in comparative obscurity; and there is nothing to suggest that this was because he was any different in character from the others. That such men should be employed in its service, was a fair reflection of the character of the Castle press.

The situation was fairly summed up by John Shea, a Dublin printer, who wrote to the Castle with a project for a new paper in 1794. 'There are at present two papers in Dublin which profess to hold these (constitutional) principles. But they are so sunk in public opinion that their circulation is very confined. And indeed they have been so long the object, if not the byword of party contempt, that it is believed every measure to restore their credit must prove fruitless'.[1] Admittedly Shea, as the prospective editor of the new paper, had an interest in damning the old; but the evidence is that his contempt for the *Freeman* and the *Dublin Journal* was justified. The same criticism could apply to every Castle newspaper.

Shea made some constructive suggestions. 'Government papers', he said, 'must avoid panegyrics, and should at least make a show of criticism of the administration.' Otherwise 'instead of removing prejudices, their sure effect is to strengthen them'. The Castle proved incapable of learning this lesson. Criticism from a newspaper that owed its existence to their support would have been thought the basest ingratitude—had any newspaper owner the hardihood to be critical. As Shea said, this simply meant that the Castle newspapers attracted few readers, and the govern-

[1] Reb. papers, 620/26/97, 142.

ment had to subsidize them. The situation arose that the smaller the circulation of the newspapers, the more the government had to pay to keep them alive. If the *Dublin Journal* cost the government over £1,500 a year with direct and indirect subsidies, the amounts paid to the *Freeman* and the *Hibernian Telegraph* must have been at least as great.

The growing cost of the Castle's efforts to control the press can be gauged from the increase in the proclamation fund. In 1795 it stood at £4,100. The estimate for the year ending 25 March 1797 was £7,000; and, on top of this sum, the printers of the official *Dublin Gazette*, who were in charge of the distribution of the proclamations to other newspapers, estimated that there would be a deficit on the current year's (1796) account of £3,400—bringing the total vote up to five figures. The excuse that was given was the great increase in the number of proclamations occasioned by the war. But if the importance of the war had really made the proclamations so necessary, they would not have been published in newspapers with negligible circulations. Over £7,000 a year continued to be set aside for the proclamation fund annually after 1796.[1] This included neither payment for the advertisements inserted in the press by individual government departments, whose total cannot be estimated, nor subsidies paid direct to newspaper owners and to individual journalists from the secret service money, accounts of which have not survived, nor pensions given for services rendered to the government, nor sinecures and places given as additional rewards. It is impossible, in the absence of these records, to do more than guess at the sum the government spent each year upon its newspapers: all that can with certainty be said is that it was ludicrously disproportionate to the services which those newspapers rendered.

(ii) *The commercial newspapers*

A few of the Dublin newspapers that had been in opposition to the administration, or at least neutral, in the 1784 struggle, had been sufficiently well established to survive the slump that followed. From the time of the regency crisis they were to find themselves in much the same position as they had been in 1784, tempted on the one hand by the prospect of increasing their circulations through taking an opposition line, and on the other, by the chance of securing subsidies by support of the government. Or—if the proprietors looked at it from another angle— they had the choice of running the risk of prosecution by attacking the men in power, or of losing the bulk of their circulation by defending

[1] *Commons jn. Ire.*, xv. appx. dii: xvi. appx. ccxcvi: xvii. appx. xxvii.

them. They could attempt to remain neutral; but where strong passions were aroused, neutrality would become a difficult, and not always a safe policy—as their owners were soon to be made aware.

The history of these established independent papers during the 1790s gives, in one respect, a more accurate picture of the difficulties which confronted the press in this period than that of their more partisan contemporaries. They were not tied to a cause. They were ordinary, commercial newspapers, and their course was none the less revealing because it was often unspectacular.

(a) JOHN MAGEE: THE 'DUBLIN EVENING POST'

Alone of the Dublin newspapers, the *Dublin Evening Post* had retained a substantial circulation and influence through the lean years after 1785. It remained well filled with advertisements, avoiding political entanglement. When in the spring of 1789 it reversed this policy, and became polemical, it was not to take sides in the regency dispute. The cause it took up was John Magee's personal vendetta against Francis Higgins, which Higgins himself attributed to a desire for vengeance, because he had appeared as prosecuting attorney in an action against Magee for illegal lottery practices.[1] Diatribes against the 'Sham Squire' filled the *Post*'s columns during 1789, to the exclusion of other controversy.

Even if Magee's charges were true, they undoubtedly constituted a scurrilous libel, and Higgins, however little he cared to parade his past before a jury, could not but bring him to court. Had Magee been left to the normal processes of law, he could have been dealt with firmly and expeditiously, and the matter might have been forgotten. But Lord Earlsfort, the chief justice, detested newspapers. The case quickly ceased to present the appearance of a libelled man seeking restitution, and became instead a conspiracy to crush the *Evening Post*.

The case against Magee was heard before Earlsfort on July 4. Magee himself was not present; he had been confined a prisoner in a spunging house on an order by Earlsfort himself. One of the sheriffs asked whether they should bring Magee up; to which Earlsfort replied that they could bring him if they liked, but he would give them no direction. The court proceeded in the defendant's absence. A jury was empanelled and the prosecution opened their case. An application for a writ of *habeas corpus* was refused, on a technicality. Another application was turned down

[1] *Freeman*, 11 July 1789.

because the advocate had not been briefed by Magee. Finally, counsel for Magee's father-in-law managed to obtain the writ, and Magee was brought to court. He denied the validity of the trial on various grounds, and was returned to the spunging house. The prosecution completed their case. No defence was offered. The jury, after listening to Earlsfort's charge, retired for half an hour and then came back to ask whether they might find defendant guilty only of printing and publishing? Earlsfort said they might not. One of the jurors ventured to suggest that Magee's trial had not been entirely fair. Earlsfort replied that his guilt must be obvious to any sensible man; and the jury thereupon found the prisoner guilty. Any other verdict, Earlsfort told them, would have disgraced them and their country.[1]

A different result from the trial would have made little material difference to Magee's position; he was already condemned to an indefinite period in jail on *fiats* granted by Earlsfort against him. A *fiat* was an order by a justice to hold a suspected criminal to bail, to any amount which the justice might think fit—an obsolescent legal process that had once been used in very serious cases, or when a strong *prima facie* case could be made for specific damages.[2] The amount of bail required from Magee on these *fiats* was over £7,000; £4,000 claimed by Richard Daly, the manager of the Theatre Royal, who asserted that his theatre's profits had dwindled by that amount owing to libels in the *Post*; £2,000 claimed by Higgins; and other suits for smaller amounts. Earlsfort accepted the aggrieved parties' valuation; and Magee, who could not raise the huge sum required, went to prison,[3] to plot revenge.

Earlsfort had just bought a new estate near Dunleary; he had spent great sums on the house and grounds, of which he was very proud. During August 1789 advertisements appeared in the *Evening Post* of a series of fêtes, 'la Bra Pleasuras', to be held in the fields beside the estate. Various entertainments were promised: Earlsfort himself, one advertisement announced, 'will condescend to exhibit the elastic properties of legal power, and the ductile extensibility of judicial privilege'. Magee also gave the populace, who were to be well filled with liquor brought in for the occasion, an idea of what was required of them: 'on this occasion, the private back door, leading from his worship's back garden into Fiat Lawn, is to be widened into a triumphal arch'.

[1] The reports of the trial in the *D.E. Post* and the *Freeman*, July 5–6, vary in emphasis but are reasonably consistent in detail.

[2] A number of pamphlets were published in the period 1789–91, giving the arguments on *fiats* propounded in speeches by barristers, etc.—see bibliography.

[3] *D.E. Post*, 17 June 1789: Fitzpatrick, *The Sham Squire*, p. 90.

If Lord Cloncurry's memory is to be trusted, the hint was taken. At the fête, of which he claimed to have been an eye-witness:[1]

> Several thousand people, including the entire disposable mob of Dublin, of both sexes, assembled as the guests at an early hour. A variety of sports were arranged for their amusement . . . until at length, the crowd having reached its maximum density, the grand scene of the day was produced. A number of active pigs, with their tails shaved and soaped, were let loose, and it was announced that each pig should become the property of anyone who could catch it and hold it by the slippery member. A scene impossible to describe immediately took place; the pigs, frightened and hemmed in in all other directions, rushed through the hedge which then separated the grounds of Temple Hill from the open fields; forthwith all their pursuers followed in a body and, continuing their chase over the shrubberies and pastures, soon revenged John Magee upon the noble owner.

After the fêtes, Magee's relatives tried to take out a statute of lunacy against him, through a case before the house of lords. When Magee found that he was only to get one day's notice in which to prepare his defence, he felt that the administration had prejudged him; but the lord chancellor, Fitzgibbon, who detested Earlsfort, dismissed the case, saying that even if all the charges were true they only amounted to acts of extravagance and indiscretion.[2]

Another judge of the king's bench, Yelverton, released Magee from imprisonment at the end of October, on a surety of £400 'to keep the peace for five years towards Lord Viscount Clonmell'—the title which Earlsfort had been given in the meantime. Within a fortnight he was again in a spunging house on more of the original *fiats*, and Clonmell sent him back to jail for contempt. On the 19th he came up again before Clonmell, who remarked with a judicial air that his arguments deserved close thought, and that therefore his trial could not come up before the following term; meanwhile Magee would be released on bail. No sooner was he out in the street than he was rearrested on *fiats* issued by Clonmell. As there were nearly 100 informations laid against him there was no difficulty in getting him back to jail whenever Clonmell felt so disposed. One charge against him was for a reflection on the court of king's bench, and for this he was sentenced to six months' imprisonment.[3]

Magee at last realized that Clonmell was quite prepared to keep him in jail indefinitely; and the *Evening Post* capitulated. By the end of the year 1789 it had returned to such quiet respectability that Magee was

[1] *Cloncurry recollections*, p. 58. Barrington's version is more restrained.
[2] *Morning Post*, 3 Oct. 1789.
[3] See Dublin newspapers, Oct. 1789–Feb. 1790.

forced to publish a denial of a rumour that he had given up his interest in the paper. It avoided comment of any kind, and became for a time, entirely innocuous.

Daly, however, pressed his claim, and the case of Daly *v.* Magee came up at the end of June 1790.[1] Damages were laid generally at a total of £8,000, the plaintiff having discovered fresh libels since the original *fiat* had been issued. The defence claimed that this was illegal: Clonmell overruled them. The articles complained of were scurrilous, but by this time Magee's treatment had won him general sympathy, and in spite of strong judicial direction the jury awarded only £200 damages, and 6d. costs. This was discouraging for Higgins, whose civil suit was pending. The *Freeman* was not doing well, to judge by the fact that it could only obtain a single column of advertisements; the *Evening Post* filled three-quarters of its space with advertisements, at the time. Although the *Freeman* reminded Magee, when he was released in July after twelve months, off and on, in prison, that the actions were still pending, the *Evening Post* gives no further clue to its proprietor's relations with Francis Higgins: the case must have been settled out of court.

Although the state was not directly concerned in the actions against the *Evening Post*, Clonmell's use of *fiats* involved the government, owing to the prevalent impression that the judges were the Castle's servants, acting under its orders. The subject was debated in the Irish commons early the following year; when a number of opposition members spoke. George Ponsonby denounced a system whereby a bare affidavit was sufficient to put a man in prison, in default of bail for a very great sum assessed by the plaintiff, especially when the plaintiff did not need to bring an action for three law terms; the Turks, he said, would not submit to it. Arthur Browne supported him, pointing out that in England *fiats* were only permissible for small amounts and for specific damages. He alleged that numbers of printers had been run down by *fiats* whom the public had never heard of; Magee had been more sturdy, therefore his suffering had made more noise. A man might be kept in jail for eighteen months on a *fiat*, only to be acquitted. The name of *fiat* was becoming as ominous as *lettre de cachet*. The legal question might be difficult, 'but, thank heavens, questions of liberty are simple'. It was no defence that *fiats* had been a practice in the past—so had Ship Money; used unscrupulously, *fiats* would mean the end of the liberty of the press. Even one of the pillars of the ascendancy, Sir Henry Cavendish, spoke against *fiats*; and the attorney general, although he

---

[1] *The trial of John Magee for a libel against Richard Daly* (P), 1790, gives a full account.

claimed that the judge's action was based on precedent, made little effort to justify their use. He asked the house not to press the point, until he had given it his full consideration.[1]

A year later, Ponsonby reopened the discussion, moving that Clonmell had acted illegally in granting the *fiats* against Magee. The attorney general spoke at such length that a later speaker found most of the house asleep.[2] The motion was rejected, but the documents of the case were placed before the committee of the house dealing with courts of justice; and although nothing specific was done, the court of king's bench did not dare to employ *fiats* again.

The use of *fiats* not only endangered the freedom of the press; it brought the law into contempt, and the courts into detestation, as the lord lieutenant himself admitted in his correspondence.[3] Grattan used the treatment of Magee to illustrate the way in which the liberty of the subject was being undermined in Ireland.[4] Magee was not the sterling patriot that some later writers have pictured him: he was unbalanced— already, perhaps, suffering from the mental instability that was to bring him in the end into an asylum. But his case showed—more clearly, perhaps, than a straightforward trial for sedition would have done—on what uncertain ground the freedom of the press in Ireland was founded. *Fiats* were only one expedient: the law could provide others in their place. And the administration could find more judges of the type of Lord Clonmell.

The *Evening Post's* popularity was naturally confirmed and increased by its owner's treatment: and, in spite of the studied moderation which it employed after the contest with Clonmell was over, it did not entirely lose its hold. In the absence of any rival patriot newspapers in Dublin, the *Evening Post* was even selected, along with the *Northern Star*, as the paper in which the society of United Irishmen published their proceedings, as late as 1794. But it was never itself strictly a patriot paper. The *Northern Star* was to accuse it in 1796 of time-serving, saying that a panegyric on Fitzwilliam on his departure was occasioned by spite, because Fitzwilliam's administration had offered it better opportunities to secure government patronage; its liberal tone may have been dictated by commercial considerations.

To other observers, the *Evening Post's* professed moderation was only

---

[1] P.R.O., H.O., 100/21: *Commons jn. Ire.*, xiii. pp. 179, 184–5: Ponsonby, *On fiats* (P), Dublin, 1791.
[2] 22 Mar. 1791 (*Ir. parl. reg.*, xi. 367).
[3] 26 Apr. 1790 (H.M.C., *Fortescue*, i. 518).
[4] 19 Jan. 1792 (*Ir. parl. reg.*, xii. 15).

a cloak for sedition. In the summer of 1797 the house of lords seized the opportunity to sentence William Gilbert, who had succeeded Magee, to imprisonment in Newgate for three months, with a fine of £200, for 'having had the insolence to print a false account of the proceedings of this house in the *Dublin Evening Post*'. Such breaches of privilege were normally dealt with by a formal reprimand, or, at most, by a few days in custody. The *Evening Post*, significantly, did not dare to comment upon, let alone criticize the decision: but newspaper reports of the debate reveal the reason for the sentence. Gilbert's defence was that he was not proprietor. He was only acting for Magee, who had become insane; and he had no financial interest in the paper. The excuse might well have served; but in the house was a man who had an old score to settle with the *Evening Post*. Clonmell assured the lords that Gilbert was accumulating vast wealth out of the irresponsibility of the *Post*; not, indeed, directly for himself, but for his son-in-law, heir to the property. They were dealing not only with an offender against their privileges, but with a disseminator of blasphemy and sedition. 'Its publications have been uniformly, I say systematically, directed against the principles of morality and piety.'[1] The sentence on Magee's successor was some compensation for the annoyance Clonmell had suffered from Magee.

Thereafter the *Evening Post* became extremely circumspect. It lent the government support throughout the year of the rebellion; and although its opposition to the Union shows that it was not then in the strict sense a Castle paper, it soon afterwards came close to losing all independence, as the *Freeman* had some twenty years before. In 1801 a member of the staff of the paper, H. B. Code, made proposals to the government, which were accepted, that he should act as their agent on the *Evening Post*. Like Francis Higgins, Code had formerly been a member of the hosier's guild; and as soon as Higgins heard that Code was working on the *Evening Post*, he informed the Castle that Code was a renegade United Irishman who in his earlier days had been employed on the *Press*, and who had given public readings of 'The Rights of Man'. He had then been employed for a time on the *Freeman*, from which he had been dismissed for bad behaviour; yet here he was in 1801, Higgins complained, boasting that he had been promised a £300-a-year 'place' by the administration![2] By this time Code was well established, a frequent visitor to Cooke's private house—Cooke thought it would be safer for him not to be seen going into the Castle.[3] He worked himself on

[1] *F.D.J.*, 13 June 1797: *Lords jn. Ire.*, vii. 611.
[2] 23 May 1801 (Reb. papers, 620/18/14).
[3] Off. papers, 544/325/9.

to the staff of the *Evening Post*, so that by February of the following year he was in a position to take instructions from the Castle how the *Evening Post* should be handled. Up to that time he had to be careful; now, he felt, he could be more actively employed, if the Castle so wished. The proposition was accepted, and thereafter he wrote frequent reports to the Castle of his work—for example, that he had kept out a speech by Grattan, or expunged material from articles that might offend the administration.[1]

By 1803, the under secretary, Marsden, was actually a contributor to the paper; and the *Evening Post*, which expressed detestation of Emmet's rebellion, appears to have played incidents up or down on his instructions. And in addition to his work for the Castle as a journalist, Code, with Corbet and Giffard, acted as one of its agents, collecting much information—not, as a rule, of value.[2]

As the *Evening Post*, under Code's editorship, drew closer to the Castle, the familiar process was repeated. Code had sense enough to realize what would happen once the *Evening Post* became known to be a Castle paper; he once confessed to the under secretary that he had felt compelled to insert an address which he had promised to keep out, in order to avoid appearing partial 'and subjecting the popular character of the paper to suspicion'.[3] The pretence could not be kept up indefinitely. The under secretary had to be told that friends of the *Evening Post* were angry at the reactionary turn it had taken; and Code asked that the Castle should arrange for some new orders to be sent for the paper from the country, in order to dupe the owners of the paper into thinking that the change of policy was good for business.[4]

The *Evening Post* was not under Code's direction for long enough seriously to embarrass its reputation; in the winter of 1803, he either left, or was sacked. But he continued to pester the government. By his own account he fell into financial difficulties, brought upon him by his work for them. When he was later being dunned for debts, he proposed to the under secretary that he should be allowed tacitly to overcharge for the reports which he, as its agent, was sending to the Castle, promising to use the extra income this would bring him towards paying off the £105 he owed. His abject begging letters were eventually stopped by the award of a 'place' in the customs.[5]

[1] Reb. papers, 620/61/119, 144.
[2] Landreth, *The pursuit of Robert Emmet*, pp. 149, 233: Off. papers, 524/153/93.
[3] Reb. papers, 620/61/124.
[4] Off. papers, 524/153/93.
[5] B.M. Add. MSS (Hardwicke), 35749 f. 110: 35750 f. 254: Cox's *Irish Magazine*, March 1813.

F

(b) THOMAS MACDONNEL: THE 'HIBERNIAN JOURNAL'

Although the story of the *Dublin Evening Post* in this period offers the greater variety of incident, that of the *Hibernian Journal* is the better reflection of the difficulties that beset a commercial newspaper. Magee was an eccentric; Thomas MacDonnel, who became owner of the *Hibernian Journal* in 1788, appears to have been a straightforward character, liberal by inclination, but easily intimidated when his livelihood was threatened.[1]

His newspaper took the prince's part in the regency crisis and later, for a time, supported the Society of United Irishmen, of which Mac-Donnel was a member. The government acted against it, as soon as an opportunity was offered. In January 1793, the attorney general called the commons' attention to what he termed a very gross libel on the house, which had appeared in the *Hibernian Journal*. It had published resolutions that had been passed by the citizens of Dublin at an aggregate meeting, 'that the house of commons is not freely chosen by the people'; and 'that the house, as at present influenced by places of emolument and pensions, do not speak the sense of the people'.

The truth of these two statements was too much to be borne by the commons; and Thomas MacDonnel was ordered to appear before them on the following day. He pointed out that the resolutions had been signed by the sheriff of Dublin. The attorney general replied that the sheriff's signature might mitigate, but did not excuse the printing of a libel. Opposition speakers argued that a newspaper could hardly hope to print a better authenticated document than these resolutions. Curran said that on the attorney general's theory of libel, the Volunteer resolutions which led to the liberation of 1782 could not safely have been printed; and Grattan thought that the expressed desire for reform was perfectly reasonable. By a large majority, members expressed their agreement with the chancellor of the exchequer, who said that even if these resolutions were not particularly mischievous, faction must be stamped out as soon as it reared its head. The number of the *Hibernian Journal* was voted libellous, and MacDonnel was ordered into custody.[2]

He was released with a reprimand two days later. Either the commons only wished to give him a fright, or the attorney general was manœuvring to detach him from his allegiance, for use against the United Irishmen. MacDonnel had received notice that he was to be prosecuted for pub-

---

[1] Matthew Carey, who worked under MacDonnel as an apprentice, found him hard and overbearing (M. Carey, *Autobiography*, pp. 3–4).
[2] *Commons jn. Ire.*, xv. 133: *Ir. parl. reg.*, xiii. 83: *Hib. J.*, 25–30 Jan. 1793.

lishing their 'Address to the Volunteers'; but the attorney general was after bigger men. He was prepared to come to terms with newspaper owners, if they would co-operate. In April, MacDonnel resigned from the United Irishmen;[1] and, like W. P. Carey, he appeared in court in the trial of Dr Drennan as a witness for the crown.

The first indication the United Irishmen had been given of Mac-Donnel's impending defection was his refusal—on the advice of the informer, Leonard MacNally—to give back the MS of the resolution for which the society were being prosecuted. It bore signatures of men whom the government would be anxious to indict; MacDonnel, therefore, could use it if necessary to save himself.[2] On being asked in court whether he was the printer and publisher of a newspaper, MacDonnel said that he did not wish to implicate himself. The attorney general immediately offered to file a *nolle prosequi*, to set his mind at rest, if he cared to give evidence required. MacDonnel agreed; the transaction was completed, there and then. Resuming his evidence, MacDonnel admitted that he had published the address, and that it had been inserted by the United Irish Society.[3] The information proved of little value to the prosecution, because Drennan was still not specifically implicated. Although the incident must have shaken confidence in MacDonnel—the *nolle prosequi* was obviously prearranged—he had not committed himself to the government side as openly as W. P. Carey.

Thereafter, MacDonnel took care to steer clear of any further trouble. He was brought up before the lords at the same time as Gilbert of the *Evening Post* in 1797, but he was able to persuade them that the paragraph about which they complained had been copied inadvertently from the *Post* into his paper, and that only a few copies were printed before he had seen it and ordered its removal. He escaped with a reprimand. Francis Higgins, in his frequent warnings to the Castle about the menace of the opposition press, rarely mentioned the *Hibernian Journal* —though on one occasion in 1798 he urged that 'MacDonnel should be punished'.[4] By this time the newspaper was innocuous, and extremely dull. Comment was shunned and home news reduced. It was even accepting a few government proclamations. The *Hibernian Journal* did not, however, become a Castle paper. Like the *Evening Post*, it opposed the Union. The *Post's* obituary of MacDonnel at his death in March 1809 bears out the impression that the *Hibernian Journal* did not sacri-

[1] R. B. McDowell in *I.H.S.*, ii. 40 (Mar. 1940).
[2] *Drennan letters*, p. 131.
[3] *Hib. J.*, 27 June 1794.
[4] 20 Aug. 1798 (Reb. papers, 620/18/14).

fice its financial independence; but that independence of thought was not a conspicuous feature of the paper during the rebellion years. In the first number for the year 1802, the *Hibernian Journal* was to be found ranged alongside the papers it had so often denounced for their sycophancy, praising 'the temperate, conciliatory, and beneficent conduct of our present wise and vigilant government'.

(c) JAMES POTTS: 'SAUNDERS' NEWS-LETTER'

After the *Dublin Journal* was taken over by Giffard, *Saunders' News-Letter* was the only Dublin paper to retain unchanged the characteristics of an earlier period. It relied mainly upon advertisements, filling up what little space remained with unedited news from abroad, and rarely reporting, and still more rarely commenting upon, home events. As the years went by, it became less easy for the paper to avoid noticing what was happening at home. Reports of parliamentary debates came to be grudgingly inserted, getting the paper's owner, James Potts, into trouble with the commons in February 1791. They accepted his excuses; he escaped with a reprimand.[1] *Saunders'* aversion from controversy was not enough to protect it from calumny. In 1795 the *Dublin Journal* began to accuse Potts of propagating jacobinism. In a sense this was true, as the deeds of the jacobins occupied a considerable proportion of the foreign news which, each morning, the printers copied out verbatim from the English papers. Newspaper readers in Ireland have never been so well served with continental news as they were in the late eighteenth century: a diligent reader of *Saunders'*—or of almost any Dublin newspaper—must have gained a really extensive knowledge of continental affairs, which may be one of the reasons why the United Irish movement owed so much to the French revolution.

Giffard's accusations infuriated Potts, as well they might: and he was momentarily roused from his policy of neutrality, into publishing a squib on 'the Dog'. The next Sunday morning Giffard accosted him, knocked him down, and horsewhipped him.[2] That so innocuous a newspaper as *Saunders'* could be accused of jacobin sympathies was symptomatic of the chronic state of fright in which the ascendancy had come to live: any proprietor who was not actively for them, they felt, must be against them. Higgins took the same line as Giffard; he warned Cooke about the menace of the paper, and alleged that John Potts (James died soon after Giffard's assault) was under the thumb of a United Irishman.[3]

[1] *Commons jn. Ire.*, xiv. 66–79.
[2] *Walker's Hibernian Magazine*, Aug. 1795: *D.E. Post*, 4 July 1795.
[3] 11 Oct. 1796: 26 May 1797 (Reb. papers, 620/18/14).

This was in May 1797; in the same month Potts was brought up before the commons, charged with publishing a report of a speech by the chief secretary that might be construed as throwing doubts on the loyalty of the yeomanry regiments. Potts's defence, that he had not seen the report, may well have been true—though it was the same defence that he had made six years before, and was, in fact, almost invariably made on such occasions. He and the reporter of the debate were ordered into custody, remaining in prison for ten days before being released, with a reprimand.[1]

Saunders' became, if possible, still more respectable after this incident; soon, proclamations again appeared to swell its advertising revenue. Higgins remained critical; but if the Potts family had any sympathy with the rebels, they took care not to allow it to appear in the paper. It remained unchanged in form and policy through the rebellion period, and later gave the Union its negative support.

*   *   *

The significance of the government's handling of the commercial newspapers lies in the reflection it gives of the times. All three were regarded by their owners primarily as sources of income, and only secondarily as vehicles for the expression of opinions. If Magee and MacDonnel were in sympathy with the United Irish cause in the early '90s, this was symptomatic less of any revolutionary ideas, than of the fact that the United Irishmen represented, at that time, the prospect of more rational and stable constitution. As the movement grew more revolutionary, and as a consequence less palatable to the bulk of the well-to-do middle-class from which it had originally drawn its support, these newspapers tended to drop out of direct connection with it, and to take up a central position between the movement and the oligarchy. That the Castle should react with prosecutions—that even *Saunders'* should be charged with jacobinism—only confirms that when a social and political structure is as unsound as was Ireland's in the period immediately before the Union, the expression of any moderate opinion—or even the failure to express positive loyalty to the administration—is interpreted as treason in disguise, and treatment is prescribed accordingly.

(iii) *The opposition newspapers*

The opposition newspapers in the period were of two types: those founded and run by the United Irishmen, and those which owed their

[1] *Freeman*, 20, 30 May 1797.

existence to the pertinacity of individuals who, although in sympathy with the movement, preferred to stay out of its main stream. Of the newspapers owned by individuals, three attracted more than momentary attention. Journalistically they were of less importance than the United Irish newspapers, but their histories are not without interest.

(a) PETER COONEY: THE 'MORNING POST'

The newspaper that attacked the administration most unsparingly during the regency crisis was a new *Morning Post*, set up by Peter Cooney in 1788; and his support of the prince's claims led early in 1790 to prosecution for libels. Cooney claimed that he had been out of town when the libels were printed—the usual defence. He added that the most serious of them had been copied from a London newspaper, and that the London paper had not been prosecuted, which was not improbable, considering the nature of the paragraph. It ran:

'The . . . was formerly a very domestic woman, but now gives up too much of her time to politics.'

This, the prosecution stated, was clearly a reference to the queen. Either owing to a misunderstanding, or to, as Cooney implied, malice, neither he nor his attorney were present when the case came up for trial. The verdict went against him by default, and he was sentenced to six months' imprisonment.[1] He was also condemned to stand in the pillory, quite a welcome break, probably, from prison life. The statute of King William III, near which the pillory stood, had been draped with black during the night; a notice proclaimed:

IN MOURNING
FOR THE BILL OF RIGHTS
AND THE LIBERTY OF THE PRESS

A large crowd of onlookers, the *Morning Post* reported, hearing a rumour that Giffard had hired men to pelt Cooney while he was in the pillory, came out to protect him and to demonstrate their sympathy. A committee was formed to receive subscriptions on Cooney's behalf, the signatories including Napper Tandy and Hamilton Rowan.[2] He served his full sentence, coming out on the same day as Magee, with whom he had shared a cell—a situation not without humour, as Magee had accused Cooney of being a satellite of Francis Higgins. During Cooney's imprisonment the *Morning Post* moderated its tone, and even accepted

[1] *M. Post*, 9–11 Feb. 1790.
[2] Ibid., 29 June 1790.

a few Castle proclamations; this was possibly owing to financial difficulties, as the paper then attracted few advertisements. Once back in office, Cooney resumed his campaign against the administration. The proclamations ceased.

Cooney was proposed for membership of the United Irishmen in 1793;[1] but there is no evidence that he was active in the society: probably he preferred his independence. The *Morning Post* greeted the new year following with the boast that while most other patriot newspaper proprietors had only talked about liberty, he had suffered for it; imprisonment, fines and the pillory had been his lot, but he would carry on, in spite of intimidation. Carry on he did, and his forthright comments upon the government's treatment of Hamilton Rowan led to threats of prosecution which might have been carried out, if Giffard had not made it unnecessary for the Castle to proceed further against the *Morning Post*.

When Giffard retired from the office of sheriff at the end of September, the *Post* printed a malicious description of his conduct while he had been sheriff, alongside a cartoon of 'a dog running out of office' with a can tied to its tail. The truth of the article made it still less palatable to Giffard; he brought Cooney up before the king's bench and had him convicted of libel. On the following day Cooney was found guilty of two further libels. Giffard, who was taking no chances, had held other charges in reserve, which were to be tried; but he expressed himself satisfied with the success of the first actions, and offered no evidence. Cooney was sentenced to terms of imprisonment totalling fifteen months.[2]

During Cooney's imprisonment the *Morning Post* continued in opposition. But it was inconsistent. On occasion it might carry as many as three columns of Castle proclamations; one issue would launch squibs at 'the Dog in Office'—the next would urge firmness on the magistracy in the course of their duty. Possibly for this reason the *Morning Post* failed to exercise any great influence, or to cause the administration concern. Francis Higgins continually urged upon the Castle the evils that resulted from allowing such a paper to continue. He sent Cooke an article that appeared in the *Morning Post* in August 1796, describing it as a disgrace to the nation, which called loudly for remedy; a few months later, he complained that Cooney did not seem to care what he published in the *Morning Post*; and he continued to draw Cooke's attention to inflammatory material in that paper, alleging that Cooney was

[1] *Analecta Hibernica*, xvii. 64.
[2] *M. Post*, 15–25 Dec. 1794.

well in with the stamp commissioners who were allowing him to sell un-stamped papers.[1] But Cooke held his hand.

On 28 March 1798, Higgins exultantly noted that the *Morning Post* had failed to appear. A few days later an advertisement appeared in other Dublin papers to say that Peter Cooney, late proprietor of the *Morning Post*, wished to inform the public that in consequence of being obliged to relinquish publication, he had, with the advice of friends, em-barked in the coal trade.[2] The sarcastic tone of the announcement and the date on which it appeared suggest that the decision was taken for financial reasons. The additional stamp duty of 1d. which had just been imposed would have had the effect of putting out of business any news-paper near the margin between profit and loss. If that was the case, its collapse would provide one of the few cases where an increase in duties had a direct and immediate effect on the press. Usually, the newspapers dragged down by increased taxes struggled on for a time, so that the cause of their eventual collapse was not fully appreciated.

(b) DENIS DRISCOL: THE 'CORK GAZETTE'

The newspaper which expressed the most advanced views of the day —occasionally beyond the horizon of the United Irishmen—was the *Cork Gazette*, which had been founded in or about the year 1790, and was edited by the Rev. Denis Driscol, a convert from catholicism. From castigating corruption and the deficiencies of parliamentary representa-tion, he went on to criticize primogeniture and pluralities, and to urge full employment.[3] The *Gazette* was more vigorous in expression than any provincial paper of its time.

Early in 1794 Driscol was prosecuted for one of his sallies, found guilty of libel, and sentenced to two years' imprisonment. The govern-ment tried to escape some of the responsibility for this prosecution by allowing it to be initiated by the Rev. F. Archer, formerly a close friend of Driscol's—he was, in fact, one of the paper's securities with the stamp commissioners. The *Dublin Evening Post*, however, was able to demolish this pretence by showing that almost every member of the jury was in government employment at the time.[4]

In February 1797, Driscol told the readers of the *Gazette* that another prosecution had begun against him; and a few months later a notice in

[1] Reb. papers, 620/18/14 (24 Aug. 1796: 11 Oct. 1796: 25 May 1797).
[2] *Hib. J.*, 9 Apr. 1798.
[3] R. B. McDowell, *Irish public opinion*, pp. 174, 201.
[4] *D.E. Post*, 1 May 1794.

the paper announced that 'after seven years devotion of his time to advocacy of sound, just and constitutional principles', he would have to cease publication. This was one of the rare occasions that a newspaper was in a position to forecast its own disappearance. Counsel for the defence had proposed that if the prosecution were to be suspended, the paper would be discontinued after a final issue had been published in order that subscribers might be warned. The prosecution agreed, reserving the right to resume the case should Driscol be mixed up in any other seditious paper in future. The court acquiesced. He was released on condition of obtaining security of £1,000.[1]

The *Cork Gazette* might have suffered the same fate in any period of history. That Driscol was allowed to publish a final issue indicated that the court was aware that this was an unusual case. Visionaries who are ahead of their time rarely make successful journalists; a newspaper can seldom afford to outstrip its public.

Deprived of his means of livelihood, Driscol sank into poverty, and was compelled to apply to the Castle for a passport in order to emigrate to America.[2] If his request was granted he may have missed the opportunity to enjoy a sardonic laugh, when the whirligig of time brought forth one of its revenges. The Rev. F. Archer had lived for some years in constant terror of his life from the United Irishmen, angered as he assumed they were by his betrayal of Driscol. In 1802, he found himself threatened with jail by the stamp commissioners for non-payment of over £100 arrears—the sum of duty owed by him as a trustee for the *Cork Gazette*.[3]

(c) WALTER COX: THE 'UNION STAR'

The *Union Star* began to appear in the streets of Dublin during the summer of 1797. It was not a newspaper, but a periodical broadside against the Castle, printed on one side only, so that it could be pasted up on walls. Varying in size from a small handbill to a full newspaper sheet, it contained patriotic slogans and lists of individuals who deserved assassination, Giffard, Higgins and W. P. Carey among them. '. . . perhaps some arm', it regularly quoted,

> More lucky than the rest, may reach his heart,
> And free the world from bondage.

[1] Judge Day to the Castle, 22 Sept. 1797 (Reb. papers, 620/32/136).
[2] R. B. McDowell, in *Hermathena*, liii. 146.
[3] Reb. papers, 620/61/80.

Needless to say, the names of the proprietor and printer were not given; and the paper was neither stamped, nor dated. Although it expressed strong United Irish principles, the *Union Star* was not produced with the society's consent; if it had been, one or more of the host of informers within the society would certainly have betrayed it. The more responsible elements in the society denounced the paper for doing harm to the cause by its advocacy of assassination; Thomas Emmet detested it, and the United Irishmen's newspaper, the *Press*, complained that it gave more assistance to the government than it did to the opposition. The suggestion was even made by the *Press* that the *Union Star* was encouraged by the Castle in order to justify reprisals.[1]

This credited the government with too much cunning. Cooke did not know who was responsible for the *Union Star*, nor where it was printed. Even Francis Higgins, for once, was on a false scent; he thought that Stockdale, the future printer of the *Press*, printed the paper, and during September 1797 he kept asking why the administration did not send round to Stockdale's in Abbey Street and catch him red-handed. In October he had to admit that Stockdale was not responsible for the paper, but his next guess was no closer.[2]

Not until mid-winter was the under secretary able to inform his superiors 'this day I suppressed the *Union Star*'. A reward had been offered the previous July for information leading to the arrest of the proprietor. In December a Dublin gunsmith, Walter Cox, presented himself at the Castle, promising that if he was given a safe-conduct he would disclose the proprietors' and printers' names. When the bargain was struck, he told Cooke that he himself was the proprietor and printer.[3]

Cox had come to the conclusion that the *Union Star* could not continue indefinitely, and that this was a good opportunity to escape unscathed. The reasoning was correct, but only up to a point. As a journalist, or as a gunsmith, he could have given useful service to the patriot cause. But after his confession he was a marked man, always closely watched, and trusted by neither side.

The *Press* had been right, in one sense; the importance of the *Union Star* lay in the help it gave to the Castle. Walter Cox was not representative of the United Ireland movement. His antagonism to the administration was apparently the product of injuries done to his family—to a personal vendetta rather than to patriotic conviction. In any case, he

[1] *Press*, 30 Jan. 1798.
[2] Reb. papers, 620/18/14 (15 Sept., 24 Oct. 1797).
[3] Cooke to Whitehall, 14 Dec. 1797 (B.M. Add. MS (Pelham) 33105 f. 262).

was too unstable and conceited a man to co-operate whole-heartedly with any rebel movement. But the *Union Star* was used by the government to provide the self-justification required for extreme measures. When Whitehall was worried at the tales which reached England of military excesses, of floggings and pitch caps, it could be sent copies of the *Union Star*, to show the nature of the adversary with which the Irish government had to contend.

Although Cox thus indirectly assisted the government, there is no evidence for the charge made in the *Press*, that the *Union Star* was a Castle paper, which has been accepted for truth by some later writers.[1] They have credited the Castle with preternatural guile. There is evidence that Cox put his pen at the disposal of the government; but he had too high an opinion of himself to play the common traitor. His ambition was to be the plague of both houses. 'He is a clever man, and deep,' Cooke had written after their first meeting. Cooke wanted to use him as a Castle agent, making this one of the conditions of his pardon; and Cox did pass on some information,[2] but none of it of a nature that would brand him as an informer. Having sense enough to see that the United Irishmen's cause was hopeless, riddled as the movement was by spies, he even urged upon Cooke the desirability of publishing everything that was known about the movement, because, he said, the United Irishmen would be deterred from taking any rash step if they realized how comprehensively they had been betrayed.[3]

At the time of Emmet's rebellion Cox was naturally a suspect; and Corbet was dispatched to bring him round by threats or bribes. Again, Cox managed to give the impression that he was helping the Castle, while actually giving them no assistance. Marsden was so impressed that he sent Cox a note with portentous secrecy:

> If the person to whom this is addressed will give the writer an interview no one whatever beside shall have knowledge of it. A line dropped into the G.P.O., will be received.

—the characteristic reply was that the person addressed had nothing to fear from publicity, and would see the under secretary openly, whenever he liked. The cause, Cox told Marsden, had degenerated, and he was quite willing to work against sedition.[4] At the same time, if the truth were known, he may have been jesting with the insurgents about the stupidity of the authorities.

[1] R. R. Madden, Helen Landreth.
[2] Reb. papers, 620/37/194.
[3] Cooke to Whitehall, 13 Mar. 1798 (P.R.O., H.O., 100/80).
[4] Reb. papers, 620/56/56a: 64/107, 149.

(iv) *The newspapers of the United Irishmen*

The personalities of the owners of the United Ireland newspapers are relatively unimportant. Efforts were usually made to set up the society's papers on a joint ownership basis, in an attempt to make them as democratically representative as possible: and even though this usually broke down in practice, the papers tended to follow the party line, rather than their owners' whims. In considering their relations with the government, there is not the distraction represented by the personalities of men like Cox and Cooney. The Castle was not dealing with individuals, whose newspapers would disappear the day that they were bribed or bullied into submission: instead, it found itself faced with the problem that new owners, new editors would promptly instal themselves in the newspaper office, the day that their predecessors were taken away to jail. The suppression of the newspapers owned by the United Irishmen could only be achieved by force.

But before force was used, all the expedients tried against the independent press in 1784–5 were revived and improved. Spies were employed to watch the newspaper offices; workers were bribed to give away their secrets: agents were set to work to seduce members of their staffs away from allegiance to their employers. Where the courts were used, new twists were found to employ against the newspaper owners. In the last resort, when other methods had failed, the military were permitted or ordered to raid the newspaper office, and to smash or carry away the equipment.

The odds against the opposition press were overwhelming; but the *Northern Star* and the *Press* survived long enough to demonstrate afresh that polemical party newspapers could exercise considerable influence, when allied to a popular cause.

(a) THE BELFAST 'NORTHERN STAR'

In October 1791 Wolfe Tone established the first society of United Irishmen in Belfast. One of its earliest decisions was to set up a rival newspaper to the *Belfast News-Letter* which, although still liberal, would be unlikely to have any sympathy with the aims of the society. Drennan, in a letter, said that he would not like to injure Joy, who had always used him civilly: but he felt that new papers in Belfast and Dublin could do good service.[1] The newsagents in country towns in Ulster

[1] *Drennan Letters*, p. 60.

were canvassed, and their replies were encouraging. A few hailed the idea with relief, one from Fivemiletown complaining that the *News-Letter* was all advertisements. Others, though friendly, were pessimistic. A reply came from Donaghadee that 'attempts of this nature heretofore have failed . . . we are all in this little town through long acquaintance quite wedded to Mr Joy, and mostly too poor to gratify ourselves with a second entertainment'; and the Limavady newsagent recalled that the *Mercury* had received little support there. From Portadown alone, however, was there positive disapproval: a second paper was dangerous, the answer ran, as it could only create anarchy and discord. Most of the newsagents who replied said that they would take copies.[1]

The *Northern Star* appeared for the first time on 14 January 1792. It was nominally owned by twelve proprietors, who had jointly subscribed the £2,000 capital. Samuel Neilson, who undertook the editing of the paper, was also the biggest shareholder. Although restrained at first, the *Northern Star* soon began to criticize the administration. Its policy was stated early in 1794, in an editorial:

> A reform in parliament was the great end of our establishment; the union of Irishmen, the means. The latter is accomplished. Let every honest man in the nation, then, avoiding levellers (if there are any) on the one hand, and trimmers (who are very numerous) on the other, rally round this one point —equal representation of all the people in parliament.

This was the line consistently adopted; the *Northern Star* urged reform but reprobated violence—in particular, abominating 'those infatuated people called defenders'—the Catholic agrarian underground organization.

By 1792, the call for parliamentary reform was, to the Castle, sedition in disguise. Even if the writers did not themselves desire rebellion, it was argued, they encouraged it by criticizing the government; and other less moderate men would be ready to take over as soon as parliamentary reform was accomplished. To some extent this belief could be justified, Wolfe Tone admitted that the necessary, if not the avowed consequence of the *Northern Star's* policy, was to erect Ireland into an independent republic.[2] The attitude of the newspaper to the events of the French Revolution, too, made its professions of moderation sound equivocal.[3] But the proprietors could argue with greater force that the constitutional imperfections which they were trying to expose would, if not remedied, bring disaster to the country; and that if newspapers were

---

[1] Reb. papers, 620/19/42.
[2] Madden, *I.P.L.*, ii. 227.
[3] See R. B. Mc Dowell, *Irish public opinion*, p. 157.

not permitted freely to voice the prevailing discontent, the leadership of the opposition would pass into the hands of the men that the government had still greater cause to fear, and civil war would be inevitable.

The men whose livelihood depended on the continued existence of the abuses attacked by the *Northern Star* were unlikely to appreciate these arguments. From the time that the paper appeared, the Castle kept a close watch on its activities. The foreman printer was induced to sign a sworn information giving the number of copies of the first six issues that had been printed without stamps.[1] In a footnote, however, he insisted on expressing his opinion that the owners did not wish to flout the law: they had been disappointed in their expectation of a supply of stamps—which had been ordered from Dublin. Before the year was out the administration had initiated a prosecution against the proprietors and the printer for publishing the Dublin United Irishmen's 'Address to the Volunteers'. While the prosecution was pending, a riot was fomented against the paper—by the military, it was believed—and a government agent was instructed to approach the proprietors to persuade them to come to terms. The prosecution was to be abandoned, provided that the *Northern Star* moderated its politics; but after a meeting of the paper's supporters, the negotiations fell through.[2] Clearly, the administration was alarmed by the *Northern Star's* popularity. It had been an immediate success, with a circulation reputed to be over 4,000,[3] a spectacular figure at the time, and the attorney general's procedure shows that he took the prosecution more seriously than most.

How easily the judicature could be manipulated by the Castle in these actions was shown in the proceedings against the *Northern Star*.[4] The original publication complained of was the number for 5 December 1792, which had contained the 'Address to the Volunteers'. In January 1793, all twelve proprietors were suddenly called upon to proceed to Dublin to enter into bail before Clonmell. To his chagrin they arrived on time. Each of them was compelled to put up £100 and find two securities of £50. When they asked with what they were charged, Clonmell was unable to tell them—incitement to arms, he thought; but the crown solicitor thought it was something to do with tithes. A copy of the warrant was refused. The prosecution was then delayed, a favourite ex-

[1] I.S.P.O., Miscellaneous undated papers, A.I. 52.
[2] R. B. McDowell, in *Hermathena*, liii. 145.
[3] R. Jacob, *The rise of the United Irishmen*, p. 178.
[4] The story of the trials of the *Northern Star* owners has been extracted from reports in the press, from two pamphlets (see bibliography) and from the accounts in Jacob, *United Irishmen*.

pedient of the crown's law officers to give newspaper owners time to consider, and perhaps repent, their temerity. No action was taken in the first legal term after the informations had been made, except to file six more informations against the proprietors, in case any of the charges broke down on legal technicalities. In July, notice of trial was served for two out of the eight charges, not including the original one. The proprietors briefed their lawyers, and an elaborate defence was prepared. Five days before the trial was due to begin the crown lawyers announced that they were not ready to prosecute. The trial was provisionally fixed for the following February. It eventually took place at the end of May, eighteen months after the charges had first been made.

The proprietors were tried not on the original charge of publishing the 'Address to the Volunteers' but for reporting the inflammatory proceedings of a Belfast club. Curran made an ingenious defence, arguing that all the proprietors could not possibly be held responsible for publication. Suppose one of them had been out of town? The court might just as well prosecute the owners of a vessel whose captain had turned pirate. It was not Curran's skill, however, that brought about the acquittal. Clonmell had discovered a legal complication, which gratified him immensely (his knowledge of law was notoriously weak). He declared that the publication was the most mischievous, flagitious, and seditious that he had ever had the misfortune to read, and he sentenced the printer to a term of imprisonment; but the proprietors were found not guilty, on the strength of his technicality.

The wisdom of the attorney general in filing the other informations then became apparent. The original charge was selected, and the proprietors again brought to trial, in November 1794—this time, before a northern jury. Curran's defence was masterly. Either by a trick or by collaboration, the witness from the stamp commissioners, who was there on behalf the prosecution, was induced to bring in his pocket a copy of the *Belfast News-Letter*, dated the day before the 'Address to the Volunteers' had been printed in the *Northern Star*. Curran called upon him to produce it; the witness hesitated—it was cleverly staged if prearranged—but was eventually compelled to show the paper, which contained the 'Address'. The *News-Letter* had by this time become so notoriously a government paper that people had forgotten that in 1792 it had been less well disposed towards the administration; and to have prosecuted one paper and not the other seemed clear evidence of partiality. The jury, although they found defendants guilty of publishing, gave it as their opinion that there was no malicious intent. This, the bench refused to accept; the jury were told that they must give a general verdict, guilty or not guilty. The jury retired, consulted, and returned a verdict of not guilty.

The administration then found new ways to harass the *Northern Star*. Bird, alias Smith, a spy whose duplicity bordered on insanity, was employed to ingratiate himself with Neilson and the staff of the paper. Bird had been in jail in England, and had escaped to Ireland by breaking parole; the facility of his inventiveness made him useful to the Castle.[1] On his evidence a warrant for the arrest of the proprietors was issued in September 1796. Bail was refused, and Neilson had to make arrangements for the paper's continuance as best as he could from a Dublin jail—by post, as he was at first denied visitors.[2] Early in February 1797, Colonel Barber, in charge of the military, received instructions from the Castle to make a further raid, and this time to take possession of everything to be found in the office, types, machines, and papers, and to arrest all concerned with the paper. These instructions were carried out on February 3, when the brothers Simms, who had taken over from Neilson, were arrested and sent to Dublin. They petitioned from jail that the paper should be put in the hands of Thomas Corbett. This was exactly what the Castle had determined to avoid. Cooke sent word to Barber to prevent anyone from reviving the paper without a regular printer—his idea being that if a printer applied formally for registration in the usual way, he could deal with him through the stamp office. Thomas Corbett appeared before the stamp commissioners, saying that he had been authorized by the proprietors to take on the production of the paper. The commissioners refused, on the grounds that there was no proof that he had any such authority. The Simms's tried to send written confirmation of Corbett's appointment; but this was intercepted by the Castle.[3]

Nevertheless, the *Northern Star* reappeared. In spite of pleas by the government's supporters in Belfast—one of them begged that the *Star* men could be sent to Botany Bay without trial, by act of parliament; in spite of inducements held out to the staff of the paper—when he was giving them notice, Colonel Barber boasted, he had hinted that he could be of great service to anyone who cared to quit the paper; in spite of harsh treatment accorded to the proprietors in Newgate, where bail was still refused; and in spite of the removal of the types, a rumour began to circulate in Belfast that publication was about to be resumed.[4] On

[1] Reb. papers, 620/34/28: 620/37/277.
[2] *Drennan letters*, p. 241.
[3] Reb. papers, 620/28/199–271: 34/35.
[4] Reb. papers, 620/28/233–319.

February 24, the *Northern Star* reappeared. An editorial explained that publication had been recommenced without stamps, but in accordance with the spirit of the laws, as their representative had been waiting on the stamp commissioners for a fortnight. The next issue announced that the commissioners had given way, and Corbett was now the legal printer and proprietor. Although in great difficulty owing to poor equipment, inexperienced staff, and lack of money,[1] the revived *Northern Star* ran for some weeks, its language, according to a Castle agent, growing 'worse and worse'. Dr Drennan's sister, writing to him at the end of March, expressed fear that the newspaper would soon be sacked for the third time. On 19 May 1797, a party of the military entered the office, without a warrant, and finally destroyed it.[2]

By this time rumours of the situation in Belfast had reached England, where the opposition began to ask why the freedom of the press was being so abused. Whitehall anxiously called for an explanation. It received two. The chief secretary wrote that the destruction of the *Northern Star* was an outrage not to be justified, and that the soldiers concerned in it had been punished. The lord lieutenant's version was that the raid was a justifiable reprisal. The men could not be punished, because no one would come forward to identify them.[3] A letter from General Lake, officer commanding the troops in Ulster, described what had actually happened:[4]

I have extreme satisfaction in telling you that upon my return to town after an absence of 4 hours, I found the Monaghan Regiment, in consequence of the printer of the *Northern Star* having refused to insert their resolution in that paper, had attacked the office, destroyed the types, press, etc., but unluckily before they had completed the business, Colonel Leslie arrived and took them to the barracks, but as luck would have it, the moment they were gone the recruits of the artillery with some of the old hands rushed into the place and did lay about them most lustily, and almost totally demolished the whole of the machines.

This time the *Northern Star* did not reappear. Neilson remained in prison for eighteen months without trial. A memorial written and signed by him and some of his fellow-prisoners alleged that they were kept in a dungeon, subsisting on 3d. worth of milk a day.[5] He was released only after the informer Bird had confessed that the charges against him were entirely without foundation. A few weeks later he was rearrested, and

[1] *Northern Star*, March 1797.
[2] Reb. papers, 620/29/131; *Drennan letters*, pp. 253–6.
[3] March 1797 (P.R.O., H.O., 100/70: H.M.C., *Fortescue*, iii. 385–7).
[4] N.L.I., Lake MS, Letter 79.
[5] T.C.D., Madden MS, 1469 Q.I.

his banishment, with the other rebel leaders, removed him from the country. Efforts by other Belfast men to set up a new paper on the same lines after the union were twice frustrated by the administration who, forewarned by the proprietor of the *Belfast News-Letter*, told the stamp commissioners to refuse them registration.[1]

In his memorial to the French Directory in 1798, the United Irish leader MacNeven expressed the opinion that had the *Northern Star* reappeared, the outrage would have promptly been repeated, the suppression of the paper being a necessary part of the government's policy of keeping different portions of the country in ignorance of what was happening elsewhere, the better to prevent concerted action.[2] His diagnosis was correct, except in so far as it attributed to the government entire consciousness of this aim. The instinct of self-preservation was sufficient to compel them to put down the *Northern Star*. The suppression was too inefficiently handled to suggest, even if the official correspondence did not disprove, that it was planned. When the interests of the oligarchy were so directly threatened, the forces working for the destruction of the opposition newspapers became so strong that planning ceased to be necessary.

(b) THE DUBLIN 'PRESS'

For some reason the United Irishmen found it difficult to set up a newspaper in Dublin of the calibre of the Belfast *Northern Star*. A Dublin *National Journal* appeared at about the same time as the *Northern Star*; but it only survived a few weeks. Drennan in his correspondence mentions that many difficulties were encountered in the preliminary stages; and when it came out, he complained that the paper was bad, and the printing often inaccurate. After publication was suspended, he explained that it was because the Catholics objected to the editor, and could not make up their minds who should be his successor.[3] Another view was expressed by William Paulet Carey, who thought that the *National Journal* failed because of the difficulty of running a paper in support of an association:[4]

to use a common phrase, what is every man's business is no man's business. A literary committee may possess talents, yet jealousy, vanity, and indolence prevent it from successful exertion. There must be an acting-editor of

[1] Aspinall, *Politics and the press*, p. 61.
[2] *Castlereagh correspondence*, i. 304.
[3] *Drennan letters*, pp. 60–89.
[4] W. P. Carey, *Appeal to the people of Ireland* (P), 1795, p. xix.

abilities to conduct the business, and no man of spirit will ever submit to the caprice, the control, and the censures of the number of persons who will deem that they will have a right to interfere in a matter which their money goes to support.

The *Northern Star* faced the same problem; but the editor of the *Northern Star* was also the largest shareholder, and therefore had the powers he required. To judge by Drennan's account of the setting up of the *National Journal*, Carey's explanation is probably correct. Twenty owners were to put up £50 each, in equal shares. The editor, Drennan explained, was to be free from interference; but where twenty owners, of various religious beliefs, were on the board, the editor's position was unlikely to be easy.

Whatever the reason, the Dublin United Irishmen did not have a paper of their own until 1797, unless the *Morning Chronicle*—whose prospectus, ominously, was sent by an agent to the Castle—was set up by members of the society. Parliamentary reform was advocated, and articles were reprinted from the *Northern Star*; at least it was sympathetic to the movement. It disappeared, however, within a few months. Again, the failure may have been caused by poor commercial sense. The prospectus had had the word '*Evening*' crossed out, and '*Morning*' inserted; and the fact that in August the publishers announced that they were reverting to their original plan, and changing their paper's title from the *Morning Chronicle* to '*The Chronicle and Evening Star*', suggests that they may have made a tactical error, and realized the fact too late. The public were still accustomed, in spite of Cooney's efforts in the *Morning Post*, to regard morning papers primarily as commercial, advertising journals, and to look to the evening papers for polemics.

When the *Northern Star* was put down, the United Irishmen were left without a newspaper that could be relied upon to support their cause; and during the summer of 1797 plans were again made to found one in Dublin. Owing to the need to make prosecution as difficult for the Castle as possible, the men behind the venture did not proclaim themselves. Arthur O'Connor and Thomas Emmet were apparently the chief sponsors; a compositor on the paper who lived to work on the *Nation*, later recalled that Lord Edward Fitzgerald had an interest; and Leonard MacNally informed the Castle that Valentine Lawless, the future Lord Cloncurry, was 'principal' shareholder.[1]

The first number of the *Press* appeared on 28 September 1797. The Castle had been warned a fortnight previously by Higgins that the United Irishmen were setting up a new paper, with the help of the

[1] Fitzpatrick, *Ireland before the union*, p. 71: *Secret service under Pitt*, p. 196.

printer Stockdale; and before it appeared, he had added that it was to be called the *Press*, but was already jocularly known as the *Newgate*, from a determination to carry on from there, if need be. Peter Finerty, Higgins continued, who had worked for a while under Corbet in the government's *Hibernian Telegraph*, was to be the nominal proprietor. Higgins lamented that the administration was doing nothing to prevent the paper from being set up, which would be easier than to put it down once it had started.[1] His information, on this occasion, was correct. When the *Press* appeared, Finerty's name was registered as printer and proprietor. He was not yet of age, but the United Irishmen were no doubt pleased to have someone willing to accept the risk of prosecution and imprisonment on their behalf. From the start, the *Press* set out to emulate the *Northern Star*. The first editorial led off with a panegyric on the liberty of the press, concluding, with a more business-like air, 'a system such as no newspaper has gone to the expense of heretofore, has been adopted for procuring the earliest intelligence'. It quickly settled down into vigorous, though at first not violent, criticism of the administration.

The Castle, as quickly, set about its destruction. Incommoded by the elaborate precautions taken to hide the identity of the men behind the paper, their first need was to unmask them. Finding that the editor, Charles Brenan, was in debt, the Castle secured his imprisonment, the better to persuade him to betray his colleagues. Why Brenan should have obtained employment on the paper remains a mystery. His reputation had earlier been blackened in the *Dublin Evening Post*, at the time of Higgins's dispute with Magee. Magee's story was that Brenan, annoyed at some allegations in the *Evening Post*, had gone round to Magee's home, armed with an oak bludgeon stuck with splinters of broken glass. Magee was away—which, a terrified household had been informed, was as well for him; and Brenan had stormed around the house, smashing ornaments and disabling a man who sought to restrain him.[2] Even allowing for exaggerations in Magee's story, it was surprising that the *Press* should have employed Brenan. Corbet of the *Hibernian Telegraph*, set to work on him, soon brought him round. Brenan wrote to his employers saying that unless they paid his debts, he would be compelled to give the government all the information he had about the *Press*. O'Connor refused, and the Castle obtained their information, including MSS in the handwriting of contributors.[3] Mean-

[1] Reb. papers, 620/18/14 (15–21 Sept. 1797).
[2] *D.E. Post*, 30 July–6 Aug. 1789.
[3] Reb. papers, 620/35/2: 61/140.

while, other agents were employed to discover what was happening behind the scenes in the *Press* office. Contributors were spied upon. One of them, sending in an article, apologized for not sending it through the post; if he went to the post office with a letter addressed to the *Press*, he would be a marked man. For all his precautions, his contribution found its way to the Castle.[1] The *Press* complained that newsvendors selling the paper, and citizens buying it, stood in risk of assault; and that innocuous-looking paragraphs were reaching the office for insertion in the paper, which contained concealed libels, to give an excuse for prosecution. Leonard McNally, the better to watch the *Press*, bought a share in the paper with £50 provided by the government.[2] And on November 2, little more than a month after the paper's first appearance, Major Sirr arrived at the office with a warrant to arrest Finerty, who was taken off to the Newgate.

While Finerty was in prison, attempts were made to persuade him to follow the course taken by Brenan. His parents, he complained at his trial, were induced to reason with him on behalf of the government: and it was suggested to Cooke that the offer of proclamations for the *Press* might help to bring him round. But he remained steadfast, reacting to the news of his colleague's treachery by writing that 'villain, ruffian, knave would henceforth be superseded by the word Brenan, as more expressive of baseness'.[3] After remaining eight weeks in jail, he was brought up on a charge of printing a seditious libel—a report of the trial of William Orr. William Orr had been sentenced to death for administering the oath of the United Irishmen. Soon after his trial, two of the jurors confessed that they had been made drunk in the jury room on whiskey that had been passed in through the window, to induce them to agree to a verdict of guilty. Nevertheless, Orr was executed. Lecky, who deals exhaustively with the case,[4] comes to the conclusion that since justice must not only be done, but must be seen to have been done, the administration erred. The administration, however, having committed themselves to the fact of Orr's guilt, could not allow it to be challenged in a newspaper. Curran, for Finerty, said that although the press was theoretically free to criticize, every newspaper in the country was being put down or bought by the administration. He tried to make the prosecution produce figures of how many newspapers were in Castle pay; the court ruled against him. The attorney general rested his case on

---

[1] Ibid., 620/32/182: 33/67.
[2] Landreth, *The pursuit of Robert Emmet*, p. 67.
[3] *Trial of Peter Finerty* (P) (1798), p. 117: Reb. papers, 620/33/113, 137: 34/51.
[4] Lecky, *Ire.*, iv. 103 ff.

the assertion that if the *Press* story excited sedition, that was enough. Finerty was found guilty and sentenced to two years' imprisonment, a fine of £20; he had also to find security for £1,000 for seven years, and to stand in the pillory.

For the moment, it looked as if the *Press* would cease publication. One issue was missed; then, on December 29, Arthur O'Connor registered as nominal proprietor with the stamp commissioners, as Higgins had already warned the Castle that he would. By his own account, O'Connor had been the real owner since the beginning. Circulation soared as soon as the *Press* appeared over his name.[1] The paper grew more violent, printing horror stories of pitch caps and floggings and murders by the military. Arthur O'Connor sailed for England early in the year, and he cannot have directed the day-to-day policy: but Thomas Emmet, the brothers Sheares, Thomas Russell, and Dr Drennan all contributed. So did young Tom Moore, who was just seventeen, though his mother was so horrified when she heard about it that she made him promise never to write for the paper again.[2] The growth of the influence of the *Press* was reflected in the volume of its advertising. The first issue of sixteen columns had only one column of advertisements; in a few weeks the number had risen to five. A sudden relapse to three, and subsequently less, during December, was explained by an article complaining that advertisers had been intimidated; the price to subscribers had to be increased to compensate. Gradually the advertisers overcame their fears; by February 1798 the paper had more advertisements than ever before.

The government and its supporters grew more nervous as the *Press* grew less restrained. The Castle was besieged by self-appointed agents offering suggestions (for reward) how the paper could be put down, ranging from straightforward military assault, to an ingenious scheme whereby exact replicas of the *Press*, printed by the government and containing recantation of past errors, could be sold on the streets an hour or so before the *Press* itself appeared. Higgins told Cooke that the Government had only to levy the maximum fine of £20 for each unstamped copy sold—newspapers whose circulation rose rapidly often ran out of stamps, and risked selling unstamped issues—and the *Press* would face bankruptcy. Higgins also warned Cooke that Pasley, one of the sheriffs of Dublin, had actually intervened to protect the *Press* office from an assault, and to permit the paper's circulation. 'J. C. Beresford can make Pasley more steady', Higgins ominously concluded: Beresford

---

[1] Madden, *United Irishmen*, iv. 31.
[2] Moore, *Memoirs*, i. 55.

was a notorious sadist who delighted in flogging suspected rebels. The Castle took the trouble to compile a list of all the English subscribers to the *Press*, who included a duke and two earls;[1] but they took no positive action until in February, the *Press* found an opportunity to irritate them more effectively than by straightforward denunciation. Bird, the Castle spy, had disappeared, and Giffard's *Dublin Journal* accused the United Irishmen of his assassination. Bird, however, began to send letters to the *Press* denouncing fellow-informers, confessing that he had trumped up the charges against the proprietors of the *Northern Star* at the government's instigation, and threatening to expose the whole government spy system.

By this time the Castle's methods were so well known that the prospect can hardly have caused them much embarrassment; but that the *Press* should be able to jeer at them about Bird must have been galling. A few days later, notice was given that charges that had been pending for months against Arthur O'Connor were to be tried the following day. O'Connor, however, was out of reach, in England. At the end of February, the printer, Stockdale, a United Irishman of long standing, was arrested and brought before the house of lords. He was charged with printing an article reflecting on Lord Glentworth, for which he was sentenced to six months' imprisonment and a fine of £1,000. Even the lord chancellor, Clare, expressed the opinion that this was excessive.[2]

To the Castle's annoyance, the *Press* reappeared early in March. O'Connor being by this time under arrest in England, they had felt confident that the publication would cease. On the lord lieutenant's recommendation, a warrant was made out to put an end to the *Press*; he had previously complained of its 'unheard-of boldness', and now expressed himself pleased at any excuse to 'suppress a paper which was causing incalculable mischief'.[3] Within a week, however, a new owner came forward, to revive the paper. William Dowdall had been secretary to Grattan, who thought him a handsome young man of good education and considerable possibilities, and who deplored his conversion to more extreme opinions.[4] The news of his intention to resume publication of the *Press* was brought to the Castle. A squad of the militia were immediately despatched to the *Press* office, where they found the paper half printed. They seized the incomplete copies, broke up presses and types

---

[1] Reb. papers, 620/18/14: 35/24.
[2] *D.E. Post*, 24 Feb. 1798.
[3] Fitzpatrick, *Secret service under Pitt*, p. 196: P.R.O., H.O., 100/75/183.
[4] *Grattan memoirs*, v. 226.

with sledge-hammers, and entirely destroyed Stockdale's printing equipment.[1]

The administration reinforced the lesson of its destruction by continuing to harass the men who had been connected with the *Press*. Finerty was released from jail after serving a year of his sentence; but when he applied for a passport to take up a job he had been offered in England, it was at first refused by Castlereagh.[2] Later, when Finerty found occasion to report some uncomfortable truths about the disastrous Walcheren expedition, Castlereagh had him prosecuted, and he was again given a long term of imprisonment, in England. Stockdale served his full sentence, and although the house of lords remitted his fine, an entry in the secret service money book[3]—

'William Corbet, per agreement by Mr. Pollock relative to Stockdale . . . £100',

indicated that their benevolence may not have been entirely disinterested. Stockdale's services to the Castle, whatever they were, did not prevent him from being imprisoned on suspicion at the time of the Emmet rebellion. Dowdall fled to England after the raid on the *Press*, but he was soon arrested and sentenced, along with Arthur O'Connor, Neilson, and the other United Irish leaders, to banishment at Fort George.

The *Press* was not a great newspaper. 'Vulgar for the vulgar', was Drennan's description, and Tom Moore's recalled it as being more distinguished for earnestness of purpose and intrepidity than for literary talent. But its influence was greater, considering its brief existence, than that of any earlier Irish newspaper, except perhaps the *Freeman* in its heyday. 'I can answer for the experience of my own home', Tom Moore wrote in his memoirs, 'for the avidity with which every line was devoured'.[4] It was not the last of the United Ireland newspapers to succumb: the *Harp of Erin* in Cork had still a few days more of life. But its suppression marked in effect the final decision of the government to tolerate no longer the publication of newspapers that could not be brought to heel.

(*c*) THE CORK 'HARP OF ERIN'

An advertisement in the *Press* on 6 February 1798 announced that a

[1] A printed account of the raid, which Dowdall tried unsuccessfully to publish as an advertisement in the Dublin press, is to be found with the last number of the *Press* in the B.M. file at Colindale. See also *Drennan letters*, p. 251.

[2] Reb. papers, 620/47/41: 52/233.

[3] *Hib. J.*, 27 Aug. 1798: Gilbert, *Documents relating to Ireland*, p. 66.

[4] Moore, *Memoirs*, i. 55.

newspaper called the *Harp of Erin* was about to be set up in Cork. This was not news to the Castle; they had already been warned about the *Harp* by the sponsor of a rival newspaper, the *Cork Herald*,[1] who suggested to the chief secretary that he might use his influence with the stamp commissioners to prevent the *Harp* from appearing. Securities for both papers were tendered on the same day; the *Herald's* were accepted, the *Harp's* refused.

The first issue of the *Harp* eventually appeared on March 7. Arthur O'Connor was later to claim that his brother Roger was the editor and did most of the work: according to Jonah Barrington, the brothers Sheares were the real editors. The paper continued on the same lines as the *Press*: 'The *Harp*', its motto ran, 'is new strung, and will be heard.' It was not destined to be heard for very long; the printer, Daly, was arrested on March 20, and the types and MSS confiscated. An attempt to revive it was frustrated.[2]

Details of the suppression of the *Harp* are lacking. By that time the *Dublin Evening Post*, which in the past could have been relied upon to have some comment, referred only to the fact that some arrests had been made in Cork. 'The *Harp*', jeered the *Freeman*,[3] 'is unstrung', and went on to praise the authorities for their vigilance, but gave no further details. It can be assumed that the authorites, learning their lesson from the resilience of the *Northern Star* and the *Press*, had by this time decided to put down and keep down any journalist who might seek to bring out a newspaper friendly to the cause of the United Irishmen.

*   *   *

The changes in the climate of Irish opinion during the 1790s are faithfully reflected in the story of the opposition newspapers. In 1790, the standard was high enough to impress an English visitor who was touring Ireland:[4]

> The newspapers here in general are spirited and well supported. To them are attributed the advantages which Great Britain has already conferred on [the Irish]. It was the press which diffused the spirit of volunteering throughout the kingdom. No writings are admired in the newspapers which are not highly seasoned with patriotism and reflections on the government.

[1] Reb. papers, 620/38/8.
[2] Ibid., 620/36/34, 46: *Barrington recollections*, p. 321 (n.): Madden, *United Irishmen*, iv. 15.
[3] *Freeman*, 29 Mar. 1798.
[4] Charles Bowden, *A tour through Ireland*, p. 65.

The impression he gives is of a vigorous and healthy press exercising its natural functions. The opposition newspapers at that date, and up to the time of their suppression, gave a larger proportion of home news, and very much better and more extensive commentaries on that news, than did the Castle press. They were able to do so not by reason of greater resources—taxation kept profits small—but because their advocacy of popular causes attracted more readers, and writers who would work without fee. Their contributions, verbose and turgid by later standards, were at worst an improvement on the endless columns of unedited foreign despatches that filled the Castle papers.

The higher the standard of the opposition press, the more strongly ministers had reason to fear it. Their resentment of criticism tended to be in proportion to its justification. Comment alone was suspect: criticism was soon equated with sedition. In one sense, the oligarchy had reason for their alarm. Reform of the constitution could only be carried out at their expense, and so strongly were they entrenched that reform would virtually mean revolution. The example of 1782 had shown that revolution could be bloodless and constitutional. But since that time the word has taken on a different connotation: it brought to men's minds the course of events in France. The oligarchy could point to the menace that might lie behind the projects of the most well-meaning of reformers. Even if the leaders of the United Irishmen were at first genuinely determined to proceed only by constitutional methods, might they not, when the time came, be superseded by extremists—the Lafayettes replaced by Robespierres? In its very detachment from the people of Ireland, the Castle was encouraged in this belief by the reports of informers and spies, who had a financial interest in making the reformers sound more dangerous than they were. The fears of an Irish 'Terror' were real.

The oligarchy must have felt these fears were justified when the United Irishmen followed the course expected of them, as the movement took on its underground, rebel character. But that it did so must be attributed to the oligarchy's intransigence. The reformers, denied constitutional redress and persecuted for adopting similar methods to the Volunteers, were driven to the threat of violence as a last resort. Prosecutions of the leaders of the movement and of the newspapers supporting them embittered the United Irishmen, so that they lost their early moderation, becoming increasingly savage in their antagonism to the government; intemperance in the *Northern Star* and the *Press* was the reflection of natural feelings denied a natural outlet. The maintenance of the oligarchy's power proved incompatible with toleration for the newspapers.

When newspapers felt their freedom was being circumscribed they became irresponsible: and their irresponsibility provided the pretext the Castle required to justify their final suppression.

There is no evidence that the government pursued a comprehensive planned policy of destruction at least until 1797. The patriot newspapers were the victims of the fears that jacobinism inspired—fears which produced a state of mind inimical to press freedom. Frightened men then, as always, could produce ready rationalizations to justify their actions—that the press should be allowed liberty, but not licence: and that opposition was one thing, sedition another. This feeling was shared by all members of the oligarchy, so that executive, legislators and judiciary needed no formal plan to secure uniformity.

Judicial summings-up of press cases in the period tended to echo the case for the prosecution. Judges acted as servants of the administration —consciously, in some instances. Clonmell in his diaries more than once admitted as much. In 1790, referring to his treatment of Magee, he wrote—'last month I became a viscount, and for want of circumspection in trying a case against a printer, I have been grossly abused for several months. I have endeavoured to make that abuse useful towards my earldom.' Later, he justified his connection with the court of king's bench on the grounds that it was the best means of keeping himself in power, and in connection with the government of both countries.[1] His function, he considered, was to serve the government: and the view of most of his colleagues on the bench was not substantially different.

Majorities in both houses of parliament were as willing servants of the administration. Newspapers were still in theory not permitted to report proceedings at all, so that any reference to debates could in theory bring down punishment on the newspaper concerned. In practice, printers or owners were only punished for references considered derogatory: but as each house was judge in its own case, the net could be cast wide. The right of the houses to decide the extent of their own privileges was never contested. A pamphleteer writing in 1792 was in no doubt that they were above the ordinary law of the land—they could not even be discussed in the courts.[2] Accusations against newspaper owners of breach of privilege might lead to no more than a delivery of a formal reprimand; but the case of Gilbert of the *Evening Post* in 1797 showed that the lords were prepared to impose sentences as heavy as any that might be heard in the court of king's bench. The *Press*, warned by his fate, for a time refused to print parliamentary debates at all (ostensibly

[1] Fitzpatrick, *Ireland before the union*, pp. 33–8.
[2] *Observations on . . . privilege* (P), 1792.

because they were tedious) because it feared reprisal—rightly, as it turned out, when Stockdale was sentenced for a breach of privilege in 1798.

Assured, therefore, of the co-operation of the courts and of the houses of parliament, the executive had not needed to work out a detailed plan of campaign against the opposition newspapers. They disappeared because the combination of powers against them was too formidable to withstand. In so far as this victory enabled the oligarchy to keep its power and privilege intact, it must have been well satisfied. But the oligarchs' policy was to be as disastrous for them as it had already been for the country. By gagging the press they had helped to make armed rebellion inevitable; the rebellion, by making it clear to the British government that Ireland could not safely be left with even the limited degree of independence she had attained, made inevitable the Union, and with the Union the power of the oligarchy vanished. They would have done well to ponder the words of John Philpott Curran who, in one of the most characteristic of his perorations, had sombrely warned the court at the trial of Hamilton Rowan what they might expect if the government continued with their repressive policy.[1]

> What calamities are the people saved from by having public communications left open to them? I will tell you, gentlemen, what they are saved from, and what the government is saved from. I will tell you also, to what both are exposed by shutting up the communication. In one case, sedition speaks aloud, and walks abroad. The demagogue goes forth; the public eye is upon him; he frets his busy hour upon the stage; but soon either weariness, or bribe, or punishment, or disappointment bears him down or drives him off, and he appears no more. In the other case, how does the work of sedition go forward? Night after night the muffled rebel steals forth in the dark, and casts another and another brand upon the pile, to which, when the hour of fatal maturity shall arrive, he will apply the flame. As the advocate of society, therefore, of peace, of domestic liberty, and the lasting union of the two countries. I conjure you to guard the liberty of the press, that great sentinel of the state, that grand detector of public imposture; guard it because when it sinks there sinks with it, in one common grave, the liberty of the subject, and the security of the crown.

2. '98 AND THE UNION

During the early part of the year 1798, the administration began to investigate how they could substitute cure for prevention in handling what they took to be a diseased press.

[1] Charles Phillips, *Recollections of Curran*, p. 185.

On February 24, a committee set up by the house of commons reported that Foster's Act had proved insufficient and should be amended. The attorney general introduced the amending bill, which was rushed through the commons in three days, in spite of complaints from the opposition that they had no time to consider it properly. The only substantial amendment they secured was a reduction of the sureties required from the proprietors of newspapers, from £1,000 to £500. 'Lord Charlemont's members', as the lord lieutenant referred to them,[1] pointed out that nobody would come forward to undertake the precarious business of running a newspaper if £1,000 was demanded, especially as he had to obtain sureties for the same amount to back the paper; and the chief secretary conceded the point. The only other concession the opposition obtained was that the Act's duration should be limited to two years. The lords' amendments made the bill more draconian. They added a clause that made the printer's name on a newspaper *prima facie* evidence that he was the printer, which, it was pointed out, gave a good opportunity to anyone who had a grudge to work off against a printer that he disliked. Another clause they inserted enabled a grand jury to decide that a newspaper was a nuisance, and to seize and hold its press and types and destroy them; and as soon as printers were charged, they could be compelled to give security not to print any more copies of the paper until after the trial, which might be months ahead.

Other clauses of the bill tightened up the regulations concerning the registration of newspaper owners. The staffs of papers, as well as the printer and publishers, were to be registered with the stamp commissioners. Heavy fines—up to £100 a day—were laid down for breaches of the regulations. Magistrates were given power to issue search warrants, and to seize and hold presses pending trial. Printers and proprietors found guilty of seditious libel were to be disqualified from printing or owning a newspaper again.[2]

A second bill,[3] a few days later, ostensibly granted new duties to the crown—and in practice completed the subjection of the press. One innovation was that no printing press might be set up without a licence. The ways in which a printer could disqualify himself from the ownership of his newspaper were increased—for example, if he stayed away from the country for more than three months. The bill sought to ensure that the name of the printer on each copy of the newspaper would in future be 'really and truly' the printer. Most important of all, a further penny per

---

[1] Camden to Whitehall, 6 Mar. 1798 (P.R.O., H.O., 100/75/154).
[2] *Irish statutes*, 38 Geo. III, cap. 7.
[3] Ibid., cap. 18: and see P.R.O., H.O., 100/80/107.

copy was added to the stamp duty; an excise duty of 2d. in the lb was placed upon all newsprint of home manufacture; and the duty on imported newsprint was increased to 3d.

The opposition press by this time had been cowed, and these two acts were accepted with little comment. The *Hibernian Journal* tried to discredit the belief, if it existed, that the duties were for revenue, by producing an article which showed that the stamp duty was always increased after the administration had cause to be annoyed with the newspapers. The first law for the registration of printers' names had come after the publication of a scurrilous periodical, the *Monitor*, in 1773: the stamp duty was increased from ½d. to 1d. in 1785, after the appearance of the *Volunteer's Journal*: and now it had been raised to 2d., as a result of the *Press*.[1] But the *Hibernian Journal* left it at that: and the *Dublin Evening Post*, announcing an increase in its price, made no comment at all. The *Freeman* alone felt safe to express what must have been the prevailing opinion among the newspapers. Although it took care to flatter the chancellor of the exchequer and to admit there was every justification for repressive measures, considering the licentiousness of the press, it murmured, 'we behold with concern the general operation of the measure'.

'Concern' can hardly have described the newspapers' feelings. The *Freeman* was better off than some of its rivals, at the time. It was getting about a page of proclamations, which were to remain free of tax, and were consequently more lucrative than the same quantity of ordinary advertisements. Nor can the change have seriously worried *Saunders'*, which relied for its income on filling its pages with small advertisements; the advertisement tax had not been raised. For the *Dublin Evening Post*, though, the combined weight of the new impositions must have been serious. The extra penny per copy on the stamp duty, the yearly licence for the printing press, and the increased excise on paper, meant that the price to readers had to be put up to 4d.; and 4d. represented a sum which the class of person who took the *Evening Post* may have preferred to put to better uses. As matters now stood the administration took up to half of the newspapers' gross revenue—takings, not profits—and the temptation to accept the tax-free proclamations must have been strong. The production of a newspaper was so hedged around with restrictions by the new Press Act, that it had in any case become a wearisome business. To found a new paper would require more capital, and the men who were putting up the money would want to be certain that the paper's policy would give the administration no offence.

[1] *Hib. J.*, 26 Mar. 1798.

'Offence', under the new Acts, could have meant immediate suppression and confiscation of press and materials.

The only opposition that was tolerated in the months following the rebellion, was to the project of a legislative Union between Great Britain and Ireland. The *Hibernian Journal* and the *Evening Post* both condemned the idea; and new papers were actually founded with the aim of supplementing their efforts. The *Anti-Union*—a periodical tract, rather than a newspaper—ran for a few weeks at the beginning of 1799, suspending publication, by its own account, only because the Union had been postponed. The *Anti-Union's* last editorial promised that the publication would be resumed if the need arose, and in December the first number appeared of the *Constitution, or Anti-Union Evening Post*. It was on a larger scale than its predecessor, and could smite the Union's supporters with some vigour, nearly landing itself in trouble on at least one occasion with the house of commons.[1] The *Constitution*, nevertheless, was pallid by contrast with the *Press* or the *Northern Star*. Opposition to the Union was probably permitted only because the Castle did not wish to arouse popular anger. They could not easily have found a jury who would convict; outside the purchased members of the legislature, the Union had negligible support among the ascendancy. But the former vitality of the press by this time had been so sapped that it could not take advantage of its opportunities. The *Constitution* itself correctly gauged the situation:[2]

> It is a melancholy proof of the efficacy of the terror and that influence which the administration of this country have exerted since the agitation of the Union question, that scarcely one public print in Ireland has boldly ventured forth to interpose, between the minister and the constitution, the shield of a free press. All—or almost all—have been tamely acquiescent—their *poverty*, if not their *will* has consented, and if they have not assisted the assassin, they have stood by, indifferent spectators, while the crime was perpetrating.

In the hundredth number the proprietors of the *Constitution* informed their advertisers, who by that time were sufficiently numerous to confirm the newspaper's boast of a big circulation, that as the king's assent was to be given that week to the Act of Union, it would cease publication.

The later history of some of the men most closely connected with the paper suggests that its future would not, had it continued, have been very secure. Moore, the publisher of the *Constitution*, was an old-established bookseller, and had been a United Irishman. The reports of the speeches

[1] *Commons jn. Ire.*, 1800, xix. 53.
[2] *Constitution*, 3 May 1800.

made by the opposition in the debates on the Union were sent to him for publication, in spite of a warning that he was not to be trusted. Acting on Castlereagh's instructions, Cooke bought the MSS from Moore, and they were burned.[1] John Shea, the printer of the *Constitution*, had already proposed himself to the Castle as a potential conductor of a new government journal; and if he was not working for the Castle at the time that he was printing the *Constitution*, he was to enter its service very shortly afterwards.[2] He was chosen as the printer of a new government journal, which came out for the first time in 1803. With the aid of subsidy the *True Born Irishman* was sold for $\frac{1}{2}$d., directing its feeble energies to antagonize the labouring classes against France. Its design was to persuade 'labouring men of Ireland' that they would be even worse off under Bonaparte:

> *British Laws for my guard*
> *When my cottage is barred*
> *'Tis safe in the light as the dark, Sir!*
> *If the squire should oppress*
> *I get instant redress*
> *My orchard's as safe as his park, Sir!*

The paper's quality can be gauged from its 'authentic accounts' of Bonaparte's private life, including the case of a servant girl in Yorkshire, who was with child by him. The patronizing air would undoubtedly have made it irritating to the persons towards whom it was directed, had they been able to read it; but as a class they were illiterate.

[1] *Grattan memoirs*, v. 179: Gilbert, *History of Dublin*, iii. 34.
[2] Reb. papers, 620/26/142: B.M. Add. MS (Peel) 40232 f. 248.

Chapter III. 1804–12

1. HARDWICKE'S ADMINISTRATION

The revival of the opposition press in Ireland after the rebellion years was delayed partly by the caution of the newspaper owners, who were unwilling to risk prosecution, and partly by the character of the administration. Hardwicke, sent over as lord lieutenant to enforce a repressive policy, revealed himself to be tolerant and temperate, and his government was not unpopular. Consequently, he won the approval of such newspapers as the *Dublin Evening Post* even after that paper had purged itself of government connections, and resumed a cautious independence. Only the extreme Orangemen, who resented the policy of toleration, were inclined to be critical.

At the same time that the *Post* was eulogizing 'the good Lord Hardwicke' and his 'wise government', it was accusing Giffard's *Dublin Journal* of nursing a secret hatred for the lord lieutenant.[1] Giffard had become the mouthpiece of the Dublin Orangemen, and his fulminations against the Catholics, at a time when Hardwicke was anxious to conciliate them, soon brought the two men into conflict. In 1805, Hardwicke had Giffard removed from his place in the customs, for his part in the presentation of a strongly worded Orange petition from the corporation of Dublin to the king. Giffard, protesting, said that when the Fitzwilliam administration had withdrawn support from the *Dublin Journal*, they had not touched his customs place. He was too old, he said, to learn a new trade, and the *Dublin Journal*, which he held in trust for the government, was not very profitable; he hoped that Hardwicke would not harden his heart against him.[2] Hardwicke would not relent. A few months later, when Judge Johnson was arraigned in England for a libel, in which he had referred to the Trojan horse, 'comparing that wooden machine with the head of Lord Hardwicke', Giffard, who went to give evidence on the judge's behalf, seized the chance to accuse the

[1] *D.E. Post*, 13 March 1804.
[2] B.M., Add. MS (Hardwicke) 35728 f. 128.

lord lieutenant of turning him out of the customs job 'because he was a Protestant'.[1]

Apart from the *Dublin Journal's* quarrel with the government, the press in the last months of the Hardwicke administration showed little sign of change. Francis Higgins was dead, and the patriot writers dispersed; otherwise, however, the same journalists tend to appear, in much the same circumstances as in the rebellion years. H. B. Code continued to supply the Castle with information: so did William Corbet, of the *Hibernian Telegraph*. The government gave financial assistance to newspapers that promised support; George Grace established the *Clonmel Herald* on these terms during Hardwicke's viceroyalty.[2] The older subsidized newspapers printed proclamations, and their owners drew pensions. Prosecutions ceased, but that was owing less to the Castle's forbearance than the absence of anything that could be termed seditious. The press, during the first five years of the Union, remained torpid. Only in the last few months of Hardwicke's stay in Ireland did a few signs appear that the independent press was beginning to shake off this lethargy. The *Evening Post* was still friendly to the government. It could say, shortly before Hardwicke left, that the people of Ireland were satisfied with the administration, and affectionately attached to the resident nobility and gentry. But it was gradually adopting a more critical line, urging Catholic claims, and expressing resentment at restrictions on press liberty. By the time of Hardwicke's departure, the *Post* had so far recovered that Dr Drennan enclosed a copy in a letter to his sister-in-law, 'by which you will see the spirit that is unextinguished in Ireland'. His correspondence also mentions favourably another newspaper, the *Evening Herald*, which came into existence in Dublin in Hardwicke's last months there.[3]

2. 'ALL THE TALENTS', 1806–7

The fact that the independent newspapers, the *Evening Post*, the *Hibernian Journal*, and the *Evening Herald*, had been well disposed to a tory government, and were likely to be still more friendly towards the liberal ministry of 'All the Talents' formed in England in 1806, might have encouraged the duke of Bedford, who succeeded Hardwicke as lord lieutenant, to sweep away the whole structure of government subsidies, leaving the press to its own resources. The absurdity of the system was soon brought home to him. He complained in his correspondence

[1] *D.E. Post*, 28 Nov. 1805.
[2] Off. papers, 534/243/3: 553/413/29.
[3] *Drennan letters*, pp. 354, 368: Madden (I.P.L.) MSS 277.

that Giffard had assailed the Catholics with violent invective. Everybody knew of Giffard's connections with the Castle: the Catholics, Bedford wrote, were not unnaturally irritated, contrasting him unfavourably with Hardwicke, who had not allowed Giffard to escape without punishment for a similar offence.[1]

Instead of putting an end to the subsidies, however, the Castle reverted to an old expedient. They decided to set up a new paper of their own, and to endow it with such advantages that, unlike its predecessors, it would be a commercial success. The *Correspondent* appeared in November 1806. It was set up by compact with Bedford, the government promising a subsidy of £1,200 a year—£500 a year from the secret service money, £400 from proclamations, and the rest from some unspecified source.[2] Within a few weeks the proprietors had obtained a still more valuable concession. In December the editor wrote to the under secretary asking permission to see the copies of the English newspapers which arrived by express. This privilege was thereupon granted, exclusively, to the *Correspondent*.[3] These 'expresses' were brought from London to the Castle by government courier; they were several hours quicker than the ordinary mail, which meant that the *Correspondent* could often be a day ahead of its rivals in printing the British and continental news that filled most of the Dublin papers. This concession was a decidedly more effective method of aiding the Castle press than the grant of proclamations, and far more of a threat to the opposition newspapers than prosecutions. The government also increased the proclamation fund from the £7,000 at which it had stood since the Union, to £10,500.[4] From these actions the independent newspapers received the first instalment of a lesson they were painfully to relearn many times during the century: that the whig for all his resonant professions of principle was in practice no better, and sometimes much worse, a friend to the freedom of the press than the tory.

3. RICHMOND'S ADMINISTRATION

(i) *Arthur Wellesley, chief secretary, 1807–9*

Early in 1807 the ministry of 'All the Talents' fell, and the new tory government in April replaced Bedford by the duke of Richmond, who brought Arthur Wellesley with him as chief secretary.

[1] 20 Mar. 1807 (H.M.C., *Fortescue*, ix. 121).
[2] B.M., Add. MS (Peel) 40242 f. 267.
[3] Off. papers, 530/218/38: 534/240/24.
[4] *Parl. papers*, 1810–11, vi. appx. cl.

For some newspapers the position was immediately clarified. The *Dublin Journal* promptly returned to the fold. Giffard was rewarded by the restoration of his place in the customs; when this appointment was criticized—room had to be made for him by dividing customs and excise into two separate jobs, in order to give him an appointment worth £600 a year—Wellesley justified his action by stating Giffard's fitness, his long and faithful service, and 'the opinion we entertained that if he had been guilty of an indiscretion, three years' deprivation of office was a sufficient punishment'.[1] Conversely, the *Dublin Evening Post* returned to opposition. Its support for the government had not brought it rewards enough to tempt its proprietor—John Magee, son of Higgins's enemy—to trim; and when Bedford left in April 1807, it compared his departure to Fitzwilliam's in 1795, the inference being that the *Post* would have little sympathy with his successors.

After the death of Higgins the *Freeman's Journal* had come into the hands of Philip Whitfield Harvey, who had a government pension of £200 a year.[2] Under him it had continued to support the government, ineffectively, in obscurity. Harvey lost no time ingratiating himself with Wellesley, to judge by the fact that the *Correspondent* soon complained that the *Freeman* was given the expresses. Harvey managed, too, to obtain a government subsidy.[3] At the same time he was keeping in with past patrons, writing to Hardwicke to say that the *Freeman* was printing full reports of his speeches, and defending him from the malice of the *Dublin Journal*.[4] Harvey had picked up some of Higgins's craft. When he bought up a new Dublin paper, the *Evening Packet*, in 1807, he assured the Castle that he was doing it not for personal gain, but to render service to the government. The paper had begun in dangerous hands— it had belonged to the former printer of the *Press*, Stockdale—but he would keep the paper in its old politics for a while, to avoid antagonizing its readers.[5]

As soon as they heard of the impending change of government the proprietors of the *Correspondent* wrote to the Castle, announcing their apprehension that they might be adversely affected. With their £1,200 a year subsidy, and exclusive right to extract news from the expresses, they did not care to lose government favour; and they begged the lord lieutenant to persuade his successors that they were worthy of support.

---

[1] *Wellington civil correspondence* (1807–9), p. 361.
[2] *Commons jn. Ire.*, xix. appx. dxvii.
[3] Off. papers, 539/290/91.
[4] B.M., Add. MS (Hardwicke) 35606 f. 317.
[5] Off. papers, 532/240/25.

Although formally regretting the departure of Bedford, the *Correspondent* began to smooth its path to the other side by professing distaste for political acrimony. It greeted the new lord lieutenant effusively on his arrival, but its connection with Bedford took some time to live down. A few weeks later the editor complained that the agreement whereby he was to receive the expresses exclusively had been broken; they had been given to the *Freeman*. He promised good behaviour in future, if the privilege should be restored, hinting that the government might find the *Correspondent* less to their taste if the preference for the *Freeman* continued. After the proprietors had apparently reinforced this plea with a direct approach to the chief secretary, an order was given that the editor of the *Correspondent* should again have exclusive access to the expresses.[1]

With the restoration of this privilege the *Correspondent* began to thrive, and by September 1807 could claim to have the largest circulation of any Dublin newspaper—over 2,500 copies a day. This prosperity was significant, as it provided the first instance of a Castle newspaper becoming a thriving commercial success. Subsidies, time had shown, were not enough; a Castle newspaper must be given some more positive journalistic advantage over rivals, if it was to flourish. The better news service that the *Correspondent* was able to supply, from its access to the expresses, attracted a substantial section of the newspaper-reading public, in spite of their distaste for its policy.

The opposition press quickly realized the danger. In September 1807 the *Evening Herald* began to warn its readers that a bad administration must always gag independent newspapers, and 'it matters little to the public if that effect be produced by the strong arm of power, or the more insidious means of undue partiality'. The *Evening Post* demanded to know why, if the expresses were paid for out of the public purse, the *Correspondent* should be the sole beneficiary. The *Correspondent*, delighted with itself, solemnly denied the receipt of any Castle favours —it was first with the news, an editorial claimed, by virtue of its efficiency.

Finding the public apathetic, the independent newspapers transferred their case to a court where they might hope for a more sympathetic hearing. The following March an Irish member, Henry Parnell, who had been a treasury commissioner in the ministry of 'All the Talents', asked questions about the expresses in the house of commons, saying that one paper's circulation had dropped by 5,000 copies a week as a

[1] Ibid., 534/240/10, 24; *Wellington civil correspondence*, p. 108.

result of the monopoly. Wellesley replied that the cost was about £20 a day, and admitted that the *Correspondent* was the only newspaper to benefit. The *Evening Post* reminded its readers how the *Correspondent* had denied the fact that Wellesley now admitted. A few days later Parnell again referred to the practice, which 'went directly to the suppression of the liberty of the press in Ireland'. Wellesley's answer was that the *Correspondent*, as the only *daily* evening paper in Dublin, was the obvious choice; only one London paper came by express, so that only one Dublin paper could benefit. To this ingenious argument, Parnell replied that all the editors could see the paper in one place, if it was put at their disposal.

The following month Parnell drew the commons' attention to an older abuse. When the chancellor of the exchequer for Ireland moved the annual grant of £10,500 to pay for the printing of government proclamations in the Dublin *Gazette* and other papers, Parnell moved the omission of the words 'and other papers'. He told the commons that the Castle used these proclamations merely to gain a hold on the press. Editors used them unscrupulously for revenue: he instanced a case of a newspaper that had just published a proclamation giving warning of a plague that had broken out in Gibraltar in 1805, and another, giving details of a temporary enactment that had expired before the proclamation appeared.

Wellesley replied that proclamations were not distributed with any intent to influence newspaper proprietors; they were also given to the opposition press, and if out-of-date proclamations were published, they would not be paid for. John Wilson Croker said that one Irish editor had told him that he often used old proclamations: ' 'Tis not very interesting, to be sure,' he had said, 'but then, it all serves to fill up the paper.' Parnell, however, persisted in his argument that the proclamations were used to purchase support. If they were occasionally offered to the opposition newspapers, he maintained, it was only as a bribe to tempt them over to the other side.[1]

The opposition papers did, in fact, receive a few proclamations. The *Post* carried as many as two columns full of them, on occasions during the summer of 1808. But it continued critical, correctly forecasting that the favour would extend only while parliament was sitting, and that Wellesley would restore favours to the government press as soon as parliament was prorogued. The most influential Cork newspaper, the *Southern Reporter*, received no proclamations, although it paid nearly

[1] 15 Mar., 27 Apr. 1808 (*Parl. deb.*, x. 1088: xi. 84).

£1,400 a year in stamp and advertisement duties; yet the proprietor of the *Cork Evening Post* was able to strike a bargain with the government, receiving the promise of proclamations on condition that it gave the government its full support.[1]

Wellesley's arguments were no more than political face-saving. His correspondence shows that it was he who, in February 1808, secured the monopoly of the expresses to the *Correspondent*. On his departure from Ireland he had a qualm of conscience—or possibly he feared that he might later be taken to task. Writing from London, he asked the under secretary, Saxton, to see Webb, the *Correspondent's* proprietor, 'and tell him that I prevented the paper from going over to him because I did not think it proper that anything for any individual should be sent by the express'. However, even then Wellesley was prepared to make an exception in the case of the London *Sun*, which, he said, might still be given to the *Correspondent*.[2]

In another letter, Wellesley set out the principles that guided his treatment of the press. Harvey of the *Freeman*, alarmed that the change of chief secretary might injure his paper, had written to him asking him to direct that the private subsidy to the *Freeman* should be continued.[3] This allowance, Harvey said, was smaller than of old; he had also lost money on his *Evening Packet* because government assistance had not come up to his expectations, and if the subsidy for the *Freeman* were to cease, the *Freeman* would cease with it. Wellesley was at Portsmouth, on his way to the peninsula, when he wrote to Saxton, enclosing Harvey's letter:

which recalls to my mind the measures which I had in contemplation in respect to newspapers in Ireland. It is quite impossible to leave them entirely to themselves; and we have probably carried out reforms in respect to publishing proclamations as far as they will go, excepting only that we might strike off from the list of those permitted to publish proclamations the newspapers, both in town and country, which have the least extensive circulation, and which depend, I believe, entirely on the money received on account of proclamations. I am one of those, however, who think it will be very dangerous to allow the press in Ireland to take care of itself, particularly as it has so long been in leading strings. I would, therefore, recommend that, in proportion as you will diminish the profits of the better kind of newspapers, such as the *Correspondent* and the *Freeman's Journal*, and some others of that class, on account of proclamations, you should increase the sum they are allowed to charge on account of advertisements and other publications.

[1] 30 Oct. 1807 (Off. papers, 534/240/40).
[2] *Wellington civil correspondence*, pp. 108, 593.
[3] 5 Apr. 1809 (Off. papers, 539/290/91).

Mindful of his troubles the previous year, Wellesley went on to warn Saxton that it was absolutely necessary to keep the newspaper charge down to the annual parliamentary vote of £10,500 a year, and that the accounts must be of a kind that could be put before parliament.[1]

(ii) *Wellesley-Pole, chief secretary, 1809–12*

Arthur Wellesley was succeeded, after a brief interval, by his elder brother, William Wellesley-Pole, a man of some sense, as a letter he wrote to the lord lieutenant soon after his appointment showed:[2]

> A peremptory order should be given to place, without a moment's delay, the payments to newspapers for proclamations and advertisements upon such a footing that the vote of parliament cannot be exceeded. By adopting this plan you will lose what is called the support of some newspapers. But I very much doubt whether any benefit is derived from the enormous expense which has been incurred by purchasing the newspapers. Most of the papers (indeed I may say all but the *Dublin Journal*) in the pay of the government give but an hollow support, and take lines directly hostile to us upon almost all the questions of importance . . . I do not think that the press in Ireland can do the same mischief to the government that it does here (England). If the government is conducted with purity and close attention to the public interests in Ireland, the newspapers cannot materially affect the administration. The great political questions are already settled in the minds of all parties, and no newspaper writing can have any effect one way or the other.

The reasoning was sound, but it was based on a false premise—that the great political questions were settled in the minds of all parties. In the minds of whig and tory, perhaps they were: but whigs and tories together represented a tiny fraction of the population of Ireland. In the minds of those to whom British party labels meant little, two great questions remained to be raised, when opportunity offered: Catholic emancipation and the repeal of the Union.

The divergence of opinion between Wellesley-Pole and the two most influential Castle newspapers, the *Freeman* and the *Correspondent*, arose on the subject of Catholic claims. Much had been promised to the Catholics to secure their acquiescence in the Union. Since 1800, they had become aware that they had been deceived. The appointment of Pole, notoriously unsympathetic to them, confirmed their fears, preparing the way for agitation on a national scale. So long as the more moderate elements headed the movement it aroused sympathy among

[1] *Wellington civil correspondence*, p. 647.
[2] N.L.I., Richmond MS, 73 f. 1704a.

Protestants—except for the Orangemen, for whom Giffard continued to cater in the *Dublin Journal*. The owners of the *Freeman* and the *Correspondent*, finding popular sympathy running strongly against the government, began to hedge, incurring Pole's displeasure. Within a few weeks, they found themselves cut adrift from the Castle, independent in spite of themselves.

(a) THE REVIVAL OF THE OPPOSITION PRESS

The effect on the press of Pole's administration was remarkable. The opposition newspapers had once again a cause for which to fight: and as the months passed without the Castle taking any action against them in the courts, they began to grow bolder. The *Evening Post*, in particular, became steadily more vehement, until in August 1810 it published the most outspoken indictment of the government that had appeared in an Irish newspaper for many years, blaming Pitt for setting a fashion for government treatment of the press: 'what oppression could not accomplish, seduction attempted, and bribery too frequently had the looked-for success'. This fashion, the *Evening Post* said, the Irish ministry had copied: they were trying to undermine the Irish press by taxation, bribery, and fraud.[1]

The *Evening Post's* example was followed by the *Evening Herald* and, more circumspectly, by the *Hibernian Journal*. After Harvey had lost his government subsidy, he still had his pension to consider, and it was some time before the *Freeman* ranged itself with the opposition: but by the autumn of 1810 Walter Cox, who had reappeared in journalism as owner-editor of a magazine, remarked that it had become 'another character since it flung £1,200 Castle ballast overboard to become patriot'.[2] The *Freeman* claimed that the breach with the Castle was the result of Pole's treatment of the Catholics, which was indirectly true. Harvey did not, however, commit himself too deeply to the Catholic cause, preferring to steer a middle course, reprobating extremists of both colours, orange or green. Only against the chief secretary himself did the *Freeman* really let itself go, lashing out in the new year of 1811 at the 'political coxcombs whom Mr. Pole pays from the honest earnings of an impoverished people', and at the 'dulness, flippancy, insolence and servility' of the government press.[3]

The most unexpected convert to the opposition was the *Correspondent*.

[1] *D.E. Post*, 9 Aug. 1810.
[2] Cox's *I. Mag.*, Oct. 1810.
[3] *Freeman*, 2 Jan. 1811.

The proprietors were faced in 1809 with an ultimatum: either they must give the government unqualified support, or they would cease to receive support from the government. The owners were placed in a dilemma. The *Correspondent* had won its popularity through exclusive access to the expresses. If the government withdrew its countenance its advantage over rivals would disappear. If, on the other hand, the owners ranged themselves behind the Castle they might lose the bulk of their subscribers, so unpopular had the government become. The owners must have felt that they were strong enough successfully to defy Pole and, if the worst came to the worst, to walk without the assistance of Castle crutches. They reasserted their independence. Within a few weeks government favours were withdrawn.[1]

The *Correspondent* did not succeed in shaking off the pompous, pontifical tone which as the leading government journal it had assumed, so that its acquisition was of doubtful value to the independent press. In company, however, with the *Evening Post*, the *Evening Herald*, and the *Freeman*, it formed one of a strong team. They were assisted by a small flood of associates—weeklies, monthlies, magazines, and *ephemeridae*. The Dublin *Messenger* appeared in the autumn of 1808, the first weekly to be published in Dublin for some years—a symptom of the feebleness of the press in the rebellion and post-rebellion period, because weeklies were common and popular in England. It was run by the editor of the *Freeman*, F. W. Conway, who devoted it to the service of the Catholic Board, a task which it performed ably enough to infuriate the Castle press on several occasions—notably when it eulogized Shelley on his visit to Dublin in 1812.[2] As experience was beginning to show, newspapers published in the Catholic interest stood their best chance of survival if they came out no more often than once a week. Few Catholics could afford to pay fivepence—to which price newspapers had risen—for a daily; but the *Messenger* at sixpence a week was for a while prosperous.

Of the periodicals, the most influential was the *Belfast Magazine*, which was founded by Dr Drennan in 1808, and largely written and edited by him for the next five years. It represented an attempt to return to the serious politics of the *Northern Star*, and it won the admiration of O'Connell and the southern Catholics. 'This invaluable publication has perished', he wrote in 1815, 'to the deep injury of our country and the sad reproach of our national spirit and gratitude'[3]—a tribute he

[1] B.M., Add. MS (Peel) 40201 f. 293: Off. papers, 538/284/8.
[2] McCarthy, *Shelley*, p. 296.
[3] Madden, I.P.L. MS 263.

would not have paid to any of its Dublin contemporaries. The most celebrated of them was Walter Cox's *Irish Magazine*, which first appeared in 1807, and for a few months kept within reasonable range of its sub-title, 'a repository for neglected biography'. When Pole was in office Cox could not resist the temptation to join the chorus raised against the Castle, and the *Irish Magazine* was filled with scurrilities and horror stories, notably a series of Goyaesque illustrations of the half-hangings and pitch-cappings of '98.

Other less notable periodicals appeared and disappeared. A *Ghost of the Free Press*, whose 'first apparition' (and probably last) was observed in 1810, likened the government to a gang of robbers who gagged before they stole: a *Dublin Satirist* which ran from 1809 to 1811, filled its pages with laboriously disguised near-pornographic libels: and half a dozen other magazines were founded during the period of the Pole administration, most of them innocuous and none of them long-lived, but in their birth an indication of a new spirit. 'You have been yourself the remote agent,' an anonymous pamphleteer told Pole in 1811, 'the vital and master-spring which communicated impulse and energy and effect to the Irish press.'[1]

(b) THE CASTLE NEWSPAPERS

A few weeks after his arrival, Wellesley-Pole had to admit that there was only one newspaper that he could call an ally—the *Dublin Journal*. He expressed his appreciation at Giffard's fidelity in the most practical manner. Giffard wrote to him in 1810 to remind him that he had promised that the *Dublin Journal* would be supported 'more liberally than the strict regulation', and also that the government would foot the bill for the distribution of the newspaper to all public boards. Pole, who was away at the time, asked to be reminded of the matter on his return.[2]

Grateful as it must have been for a friend in the press, the Castle cannot have failed soon to realize that Giffard was a nuisance, that his newspaper was hated, and that its circulation was insubstantial. Casting around for more effective support, Pole came upon William Corbet's *Hibernian Telegraph*, which still survived with the aid of government subsidies; though it was so little considered that the manager of the Theatre Royal had discontinued the normal practice of sending two

[1] *A list of the Catholic committee . . . interspersed with strictures on . . . the Castle Press* (P), 1811.
[2] Off. papers, 541/304/17.

complimentary tickets to the editor, and the government's help had not kept Corbet out of debt.[1] Corbet was ordered by Pole to discontinue the *Telegraph*, and to set up a new paper, the *Patriot*, in its place, 'on an extensive scale'.[2] His office was to be close to the Castle, where he could easily be reached in case of emergency. Liberal financial assistance was promised and exclusive access to the expresses. The first number of the *Patriot* appeared in July 1810. Its title proved an ineffective disguise: the *Evening Post* immediately commented 'we suspect the wolf, though dressed in sheep's clothing', and a few days later referred to it as the '*Patriot, ci-devant Telegraph*'.[3] Once recognized for a government paper, the *Patriot* would have required much greater editorial talent than it had at its command to prosper; and the accounts that Corbet presented to the Castle a year later showed that it was not a success.

The accounts also show the extent of the government's assistance to the *Patriot*. In the first six weeks of its life, over £250 worth of copies had been distributed free around the country on Pole's orders, and batches of the paper had later been given free for a while to coffee-houses and military messes. The circulation had risen, but very slowly, and there were still considerably less than 1,000 copies bought of each issue, in spite of the advantage of the early news from the expresses. The weekly profit on the newspaper came to only £5, and Corbet claimed that he was about £730 out of pocket, having received nothing himself from the government, although they had given him £500–600 a year for the *Telegraph*.[4] The Castle had been poorly recompensed for its expenditure.

Another compact that the government entered into with a newspaper owner was even less successful. John Shea saw his opportunity to re-enter his old profession, approaching Pole in 1810 with an offer to run a newspaper in the government interest, in return for the grant of the proclamations. With their help his *Weekly Advertiser* ran for several years—in deep obscurity, if Watty Cox is to be trusted—before sliding its owner into petulant bankruptcy.[5] The only other periodical in which the government had an indirect interest was that oddest of Irish periodical curiosities, Brenan's *Milesian Magazine*, which was intended as a monthly, but in practice delivered its sixteen numbers erratically over a period of thirteen years. Dr Brenan was an eccentric, smarting under the grievance that his cure for the childbirth fever then killing off an

---

[1] *Report of the trial of Jones v. Corbet* (P), 1810.
[2] B.M., Add. MS (Peel) 40201 f. 293.
[3] *D.E. Post*, 28 July, 7 Aug. 1810.
[4] Off. papers, 545/335/4.
[5] Ibid., 541/304/13: 568/483/66.

alarming number of Dublin mothers—the application of turpentine—had not been accepted by the Rotunda hospital authorities. Tradition has it that the small pension he enjoyed was given for the services to the government by his paper, in the early numbers of which the Catholic leaders were quite effectively lampooned: but the *Milesian Magazine* appeared too infrequently to be of real service to them.

Cox, in his *Irish Magazine*, mentions an obscure and short-lived Castle newspaper set up in 1811, the *Dublin Evening Express*: but the only recruit upon whose acquisition the government could really congratulate itself was the *Hibernian Journal*, which had lived on in quiet prosperity until Thomas MacDonnel died in 1809. After his death it continued for a while independent, earning the praise of the *Evening Post* the following year; but early in 1812, a letter—the first of a cascade that was to flow into the Castle from him and his son—arrived from J. B. Fitzsimons, who with a sleeping partner, Warren, had bought the *Hibernian Journal* and installed his son Edward Fitzsimons as editor. Fitzsimons—who had a government pension of £200 a year paid to him for unspecified services in 1805—wrote to say that Warren was preventing him from publishing the paper in the way Fitzsimons would have liked—which, the under secretary was left to assume, would be to the Castle's liking, too. Warren had sent around a clerk to vet all MSS before publication: 'Now, Sir, when I tell you that the clerk is a *Roman Catholic*, I think it will appear only right that Warren should be directed to discontinue him!'[1]

Later in the year, after the *Hibernian Journal* had been sued for a libel on a prominent member of the Catholic committee, Fitzsimons wrote a further letter to the under secretary, saying that Warren had treacherously wished to admit the libel, and hinting that the government might deal with him.[2] The trial had revealed, among other things, that Fitzsimons was insolvent, that he had inserted the libel, that both he and his son were Castle placemen, and that he was already receiving a government subsidy for the paper. Warren was so demonstrably a sleeping partner that he was only sentenced to a nominal fine of £5;[3] thereafter he disappeared from the scene, and the Fitzsimonses ran the *Hibernian Journal* entirely in the Castle's interest. They took control too late to be of much help—or hindrance—to Pole: but before he had left Ireland, they had succeeded in losing most of the newspaper's readers. Watty Cox credited it with a circulation of 'twenty-two', a few more than he

---

[1] Ibid., 548/299: 548/366/19.
[2] 14 July 1812 (ibid., 548/366/14).
[3] M. Maley, *Report of two trials for libel* (P), 1812

allowed the *Dublin Journal*. The jest—to judge by the catastrophic decline in the paper's advertisements—must have been too near the truth
to amuse the Fitzsimons.

Friendly and unfriendly newspapers alike, the press in Ireland gave
Pole little but worry. A letter[1] written in 1812 by F. W. Conway, who for
nearly half a century was to be one of the most influential of Irish
journalists, gave an idea of the situation just before Pole left—though
allowance must be made for the fact that Conway had an interest in
writing down the government papers, the better to push his claims for a
post on one of them (he had just been sacked from the *Freeman*). 'Besides their dulness and want of character', he wrote, 'the court prints
are without circulation'. It was fortunate, he thought, for the government, that they were; the *Dublin Journal's* references to the 'Wafer God
of the Catholics', and to St. Bartholomew's Day, would cause trouble,
if anyone read the paper. He blamed the under secretary for allowing
Giffard too much rope. As for the government's second paper, the
Hibernian Journal, which employed ribaldry against the Catholics—if
Bonaparte wished to down the Castle, he could want no better ally!
The third, the *Patriot*, had been dangerous, but after a change of editor,
it had become 'as quiet and harmless and dull a production as any in
His Majesty's Dominions. Such is the government press'.

Conway spoke less critically of the opposition papers. He named the
Freeman at the head of them—presumably because he had been connected with it, as he admitted the superior circulation of the *Evening
Post*. The *Herald* had been dangerous, but lately was more moderate.
The *Correspondent*, Conway thought, was 'a ponderous and conceited
production which would soon go to the bottom'. But distorted and
prejudiced as the opposition might be, Conway expressed himself convinced that they were not so mischievous to the government as its own
press.

(*c*) DEBATES IN THE COMMONS

Not only did Pole have the irritation of dealing with the recalcitrant
newspapers; he was embarrassed by the same awkward questions that
had faced his brother in the house of commons. To what end was the
expenditure of all the government money on the press? Hearing that
Sir John Newport—who, as chancellor of the exchequer for Ireland in
the ministry of 'All the Talents', knew about the details of that expenditure—was about to bring up a motion on the subject in the house of

[1] Conway to R. Martin, 22 July 1812 (B.M., Add. MS (Peel) 40228 f. 230.

commons, Pole investigated the accounts in 1810, and found to his alarm that the sums paid to the newspapers in 1808 had been nearly double the sum allotted to them by parliament—£10,500 had been granted, and over £20,000 paid. It was no use raiding the secret service fund to make up the sum, as that only came to £5,000 a year, most of which was marked for pensions. 'I have no doubt', Pole wrote to the lord lieutenant:[1]

> but that (the expenditure) will be struck at by Newport. I cannot imagine why Arthur gave in to this expense: Your Grace perhaps may know his motives, but I have never heard any reason yet assigned which induced me to think that the proceeding was either politic or justifiable.

It is not recorded how Pole managed to wriggle out of the embarrassments bequeathed to him by his brother; the debate in the commons, in which Sir John Newport and other opposition members complained of the amounts that were being spent on Irish newspapers, was not published. The reporters had been excluded, temporarily, from the house over another controversy.[2] The following year, the opposition's energies were diverted to the campaign against the advertisement tax. But, in March 1812, when Pole proposed the usual £10,500 for the proclamations in the vote on the Irish miscellaneous services, the argument began again. Pole said that he had effected a considerable saving; the money spent had always previously exceeded the grant, whereas he had kept expenditure down to within the £10,500. The amount was agreed; but Newport shortly afterwards moved that a detailed account of expenditure on proclamations be laid before the house, repeating the charge that they were in reality only a payment to newspapers for supporting the government. Pole retaliated by pointing out that in his first year as chief secretary, the expenditure on proclamations had been within the sum allotted; whereas when Newport had been chancellor of the exchequer, the expenditure—he alleged—had been £17,000. Pole then went on to deny that the proclamations were rewards. An opposition member protested that his brother had virtually admitted that they were.[3]

The opposition could hardly afford to press their case, knowing that the evidence of their own conduct in office could be produced against them. The subject was dropped, to the annoyance of the *Correspondent*, who said that if Newport had followed it up, he would have revealed that Mr Pole paid several thousands a year to newspapers to puff Mr

[1] N.L.I., Richmond MS, 73 f. 1704
[2] *D.E. Post*, 27 Mar. 1810.
[3] *Parl. deb.*, xxi. 1217: xxii. 1114.

Pole.[1] The *Correspondent* was, by this time, the paper that most vigorously condemned the system by which proclamations were given only to ministerial newspapers. Its memory was conveniently short—and needed to be, as within a few months it was once again gratefully to receive the proclamations.

(d) TAXATION

The administration's reaction to the renewed activity of the opposition press followed the course made familiar before the Union. Legislation was brought before parliament, which discriminated against newspapers not allied to the Castle; and when opportunity offered, individual newspapers were brought before the courts.

In 1810, the stamp duty paid on each copy of a newspaper was 2d., and the duty on every advertisement printed, 1/-. In the budget for that year John Foster, once again chancellor of the exchequer for Ireland, increased it to 2/-. He defended the increase on the grounds that the duty was 3/- in England: but this ignored the fact, as the opposition were quick to point out, that in England the 3/- represented a flat rate, whereas in Ireland the duty was graduated according to the length of the advertisement. Foster pleaded the excuse that revenue was urgently required and that the new duty would bring in an extra £30,000. Sir John Newport replied with a forecast that the increased advertisement tax would not bring a penny more into the exchequer. The independent newspapers read their own meaning into the tax. 'Are we to wonder', the *Evening Post* asked, 'that those who have swelled and fattened in the school of Pitt, should detest the press? . . . It is ridiculous to consider the item in any other light than as an attack, not merely on the liberty of the press, but on its very existence.' The *Correspondent* complained that the public did not realize how the freedom of the press was being insidiously undermined, 'not by the hands of armed power, nor by precedents taken from lawless times of tumult, but by the ignominious and not less effectual tyranny of the tax-gatherer'.[2]

As before, the new advertisement duty did more harm to the opposition newspapers than to papers which were supported by the government. The *Evening Post* filled ten out of its sixteen columns with advertisements on June 21, before the tax came in; on its first issue after the tax was imposed, a week later, the number of advertisement columns had dropped to five. The government papers, with their smaller circulations,

[1] *Correspondent*, 2 July 1810.
[2] *Parl deb.*, xvii, 208: *D.E. Post*, 19 June 1810: *Correspondent*, 3 July 1810.

had fewer advertisements, so that they had less to lose (the proclamations, on which they relied, were still not taxed). Whether or not Foster was sincere in his assertion that the increased tax was for revenue only, it did in fact operate severely against the opposition newspapers, which were compelled to put up their price from 4d. to 5d. The stamp and advertisement duties together made it difficult for a newspaper to survive without outside assistance. The *Evening Post*, with its large circulation was able to keep going: and the *Correspondent* just held out until a new administration brought it back into government favour. But the weight of taxation was a strong deterrent to any newspaper which contemplated opposition.

Henry Grattan summed up the situation in the commons in May 1811, a year after the new advertisement duty had been imposed. A petition had been received from the Irish newspaper manufacturers, protesting against the excessive duty, and government speakers had produced a variety of specious excuses to show that the tax had done no direct harm to the press. The tax might not go directly to affect the liberty of the press, Grattan said:[1]

but it may affect the circulation of the press, and if you affect the circulation you affect the liberty of the press in this way: that few men will undertake to conduct newspapers unless they are under the influence and protection of other men of influence and weight, so as to convert the press at any time to the purpose of any ministry.

A few days later, Newport explained to the commons that if government advertisements escaped duty, the advertisement tax as it stood must be injurious to the freedom of the press; nor was it any excuse to say that the tax was for revenue. So far from producing the extra £30,000 Foster had expected, the duty had only brought in £2,000 more.[2] Newport's arguments were reinforced by Richard Brinsley Sheridan:[3]

there are three ways of destroying the liberty of the press: one is by oppressive acts of parliament, another is by ex-officio informations and the banishment of printers to distant gaols; and the third is by raising the price of cheap publications. This—and this is the way resorted to in Ireland—is a mean, cowardly and circuitous attempt.

Other speakers reiterated that the duty, if it brought in little extra

[1] *Parl. deb.*, xix. 1012.
[2] *Parl. papers* 1810–11 (157) vi. 1093.
[3] *Parl. deb.*, xx. 311.

I   129

revenue, must exist to stifle the freedom of the press. Foster could produce no reply; but the duty remained.

(e) PROSECUTIONS

Poorly served by his supporters, and assailed by his opponents in the press, Pole's reasonableness gave way to irritation. Early in February 1812 he gave as one of his excuses for the proclaiming of the Catholic board that 'the government was assailed from all quarters, particularly by the factious prints, with the grossest abuse'.[1] The *Evening Post*, by this time, had sufficient self-assurance to reply: 'that the secretary has suffered by the "factious press" is not less true than that his silly egotism and ludicrous vanity appears plain and palpable—a matter of merriment with his opponents—of regret and disgust among his friends'. And the *Post* was not being outspoken from any impression that the government was thick-skinned. Only a week before, writs of attachment for libel had been issued by the attorney general against the proprietors of six opposition newspapers, the *Post* included.[2]

The actions against the newspapers were part of a general campaign of repression against the Catholic party. Largely through the efforts of Daniel O'Connell, the revived Catholic committee had extended its activities throughout the country to an extent that Pole felt himself compelled to prosecute some of its leaders for violating the Convention Act of 1793. On the breakdown of the first prosecution, the Catholics attempted to take a retaliatory action against the chief justice: and it was in this charged atmosphere that the newspapers who had taken the Catholics' part found themselves facing prosecution.

Apart from minor actions—a disgruntled Orangeman had tried to sue the *Correspondent* and *Evening Herald* for libel, and there had been an instance of intimidation of a Kerry newspaper proprietor, in what was probably a chance outburst of military petulance, rather than a calculated legal process[3]—the newspapers had enjoyed freedom from prosecutions since the rebellion years. The only journalist who had suffered in the courts was Watty Cox, who had more than once been in trouble for articles in the *Irish Magazine*. His office had been raided in 1809, and all his papers seized: the following year he had been arrested for debt: and in 1811 the attorney general had proceeded against him for an

---

[1] Ibid., xxi. 494.
[2] *D.E. Post*, 25 Jan., 13 Feb. 1812.
[3] Ibid., July–Aug. 1808.

article entitled 'The painter cut'[1] which had advocated the severance of the connection with England. The article was not particularly inflammatory, but the reputation of the *Irish Magazine* was such that the prosecution had little difficulty in convincing a jury that Cox was inciting the public to disaffection. He was sentenced to a fine of £300, to twelve months' imprisonment,[2] and to the pillory. This last punishment he appears thoroughly to have enjoyed, a large crowd, if his own account is to be believed, appearing to cheer him.

Watty Cox was so unusual a journalist as hardly to qualify for the name: and no journalist proper was prosecuted until 1812, in spite of the increasingly violent tone of the press. Perhaps Pole still clung to the belief he had expressed on entering office, that the influence of the newspapers was negligible. An administration that was bringing actions against the Catholic leaders, however, could hardly afford to ignore newspapers that were repeating and amplifying the assertions for which those leaders were being prosecuted. In the new year of 1812, newspaper owners were once again found facing trial in the court of king's bench.

The article for which the *Evening Post* was to be prosecuted was a mild complaint about the inefficiency of the police. The Castle evidently had trouble in finding an article that was demonstrably libellous, that would not at the same time involve them in embarrassment, if the true facts were produced in court. When John Magee came up for trial the jury found him guilty of publishing, but without malicious intent. The usual scene was re-enacted; the judges refused to accept the qualification, and the jury allowed themselves to be persuaded into a straight verdict of guilty.[3] The government appears to have been content with the verdict, not pressing for a conviction.

The *Freeman's Journal* and the *Evening Herald* were brought up on another charge.[4] After the Catholic leaders had taken an action against the chief justice, the *Freeman* had phrased its inquiry about the chief justice's competence, in the event of the case coming to trial, in a way that could be interpreted as casting doubts upon his competence generally. Harvey was found guilty and called up for justice, but—as his newspaper put it—'influenced by a consideration of the description of prison which is assigned to delinquents of his class (badly calculated for a constitution not regularly robust), and by a hope drawn from a determination of submitting his case to the legislature, he did not sur-

[1] Cox's *I. Mag.*, Oct. 1809: Jan., July 1810.
[2] *Freeman*, 30 May 1811.
[3] *D.E. Post*, 22 Feb. 1812.
[4] Ibid., 6 Feb. 1812.

render himself'. He went into hiding.[1] These proceedings against him were never brought to issue. A letter that Harvey wrote to Colonel Mac-Mahon, the prince regent's personal secretary, about the time the proceedings were begun, suggests that he may have escaped punishment by invoking royal protection.[2]

The *Evening Herald's* counsel put up a clever defence, arguing that the article for which his clients were being prosecuted was meant as a piece of nonsense, and then reading it out aloud in court in such a ludicrous manner that the bench of judges had to agree with him. Although the proprietors were technically guilty, the chief justice decided, he would not think that the crown would find it necessary to bring them up for sentence on the strength of so silly an article. The attorney general appears to have taken the hint. None of the prosecutions, in fact, appears to have ended in conviction.

* * *

Before the conflict could be taken any further, Wellesley-Pole underwent a change of heart towards the Catholics, deciding no longer to oppose their claims. This decision followed soon after his marriage, and coincided with the revival of whig optimism that followed the establishment of the regency, when, for a while, it seemed that a new liberal ministry of the type of 'All the Talents' was inevitable. Whether either of these events had anything to do with Pole's altered sentiments is not known. Irish hopes were dashed in the summer when Lord Liverpool became prime minister; his appointment involved a change in the Irish administration, not of a kind to arouse enthusiasm in the opposition press. The knowledge that Pole's successor would probably be still less tractable did not prevent exultation at his departure. 'The Right Honourable and Right Revered and Right Renowned Little Man has been at length removed', the *Freeman's* announcement ran, 'from the office which had been so long playing the devil with him in this country'.[3]

Pole's mistake had been in imagining that a responsible press could flourish in a country whose citizens had been deprived of responsibility. He had grasped the stupidity of a system which lavished money upon newspapers that were not read: and even if his objection was less to the immorality of the payments than to their failure to produce commensurate returns, so hard-headed an approach would not have been ill-

[1] *Freeman*, 25 Mar. 1812.
[2] B.M., Add. MS (Peel) 40196 f. 146: *George IV correspondence*, letter 27.
[3] *Freeman*, 8 Aug. 1812.

suited to the development of a free press, if Ireland had been politically more stable. As it was, Pole found himself in the position of a ruler who is robbed by the thieves whom he has released under an amnesty. Independent newspapers could not but voice the prevailing discontent, and the most serious agitation—against Catholic disabilities—was necessarily directed against Pole himself. Finding himself assailed, Pole forgot past wisdom. Government newspapers found themselves again obtaining from him the financial support to which he had objected; and prosecutions were resumed against their rivals. The policy, however, was haphazard. It inflamed, rather than intimidated. At the time of Pole's departure, the government newspapers were expensive, incompetent, and unread; and, overshadowing them, was a vigorous and self-confident opposition press.

Chapter IV. 1812–18

ROBERT PEEL, CHIEF SECRETARY

'I am very anxious to do something with the press in Ireland', Peel wrote to his prime minister in September 1812, soon after he had taken up his appointment, 'and I am not quite without hopes that we may be able to put it on a better footing.' Peel was already primed with information about the Irish newspapers. One of his closest friends was the diarist John Wilson Croker, who regarded himself as an authority on the subject, and had warned him what to expect. 'Your advice, you will perceive, was not thrown away,' Peel wrote to Croker in October 1812. 'It is easier to silence an enemy's battery than to establish an effective one of your own, at least in the contests of the press. I would give anything for your turn for a paragraph, it would be invaluable here.' The tone of the letters[1] indicate the adoption of a new attitude towards the press in Ireland. Peel was already dissatisfied with the results obtained by the unsystematic threats and cajolements of his predecessors.

The Irish, Peel thought, were not to be trusted with their own newspapers. Finding that only by autocratic methods could British rule be preserved, he was soon writing: 'I believe an honest despotic government would be by far the fittest government for Ireland.'[2] His despotism left no room for an opposition press. Left to himself, Peel might have pronounced sentence of death *sans phrases*; but he had to justify his actions in the commons. He had to pretend that all he was doing was stamping out faction and sedition, when in effect he was deliberately eliminating the opposition press in Ireland and replacing it by newspapers subsidized by his government, and pledged to its support.

Previous governments had drifted into a similar policy; but none had set about it systematically. In a period of rebellion, the closing down of the opposition presses was inevitable: no such excuse existed in 1812. Peel appears to have formulated his plans less from fear of the opposi-

[1] Parker, *Peel*, i. 114.
[2] Ibid., i. 215.

tion—he was irritated, rather than frightened, by their criticisms—than from a conviction that the press should be used almost as an instrument of government. Direct evidence is lacking of his motives, but they would be in tune with what is known of his character, if he was anxious not so much to prevent people reading opposition heresies, as to make sure that they read the orthodox version presented by the government.

Peel, it must be recalled, was only twenty-four years old when he became chief secretary. He believed that he was pursuing a sensible, sane policy in Ireland, and that if only people could be persuaded to hear his case, they would appreciate the government's attitude. There was nothing Machiavellian in his treatment of the press; his opinions were sincerely held. But his policy was none the less dangerous for that. If press freedom was to be lost, it would be no consolation to know that the executioner imagined that his actions were all for the best.

(i) *The suppression of the opposition newspapers*

Peel had two instruments with which to subjugate newspapers that opposed his policy: the courts and the exchequer.

(a) PROSECUTIONS

The Irish courts had not changed noticeably as a result of the Union: and in Lord Norbury of the king's bench they had a judge whose ascendancy prejudices excelled even Lord Clonmell's. He regarded himself as the servant of the administration, and used to write complaining that he was insufficiently rewarded for his support.[1] For journalists he had a strong dislike, intimating on at least one occasion that he would prefer them to be excluded from the courts.[2] The law in his hands was a sword to be wielded in the cause of ascendancy, as he had shown in two cases during Pole's administration. When a journalist, Michael Maley, sued the editor of the *Hibernian Journal* (which by the time of the trial was notoriously a government paper) for libel, Norbury accepted the defence that the 'editor'—a term not yet known in law—should not be held responsible for libels in the paper; and he took the opportunity to insult the press in general. He wished, he said, that no member of the bar—Edward Fitzsimons was a barrister—would allow himself to be mixed up in newspaper editorship, which should be left 'to the pandemonium of printers' devils, who arrogated to themselves the consequence

[1] Off. papers, 530/214/13.
[2] *D.E. Post*, 15 Dec. 1810.

of legislators but, on examination, were found to be only the sweepings of garrets'. Edward Fitzsimons's father, the proprietor of the newspaper, sycophantically agreed: his son, he said, only connected himself with the newspaper on the father's account—'he felt himself above it'—and assisted only to help constitution and country. The case was dismissed.

If the editor could not be held responsible for libels, the responsibility must lie with the proprietors. When Major Bryan of the Catholic Board had sued Warren, Fitzsimons's partner in the *Hibernian Journal*, for a libel, he had won his case: but as Warren was only a sleeping partner, the court had given nominal damages, which Major Bryan had refused to accept, preferring to sue Fitzsimons instead. The jury in both trials was exclusively Protestant. The bench lent its assistance to the defence by permitting such irrelevancies as a demand that Major Bryan should produce his original army commission in court. The jury, in the second trial, were told that Bryan was trying to get two lots of damages for the same offence; and the judicial summing up, while admitting the libel, stressed the probability that damages would ruin a poor man. The jury awarded Major Bryan £5.[1]

While Peel was in office the judiciary as a whole continued to act in this way, as if they were supernumerary crown counsel. So closely were they linked to the government, that Peel himself confessed qualms about them to the lord lieutenant. The lord lieutenant agreed that they had 'a great many men of high family on the Irish bench, and that it would be better to place there some who would keep us from the imputation of promoting to that bench from political motives',[2] as the newspapers had been suggesting. Seats on the bench had been distributed as government patronage. The judges themselves recognized that their post was a reward for past work and that future promotion, in rank or station, would depend on their continuing to give satisfaction. They had, in their courts, willing allies in the government's service. By informations *ex-officio*, and attachments, the crown law officers continued to avoid the use of juries, as far as possible; and where juries had to be used, they could always be packed.

*   *   *

The *Evening Post*, as the newspaper most closely identified with the Catholic cause, was Peel's first concern. During his early months in Ireland, it was easily the most influential newspaper in the country. It

[1] Maley, *Report of two trials for libel* (P) 1812.
[2] N.L.I., Richmond MS, 71 f. 1408.

claimed to have a circulation three times as large as any other evening paper, priding itself on giving plenty of home news, and not relying entirely on the London press for its information—with which, Peel complained, it was frequently first.[1] An English traveller who wrote a book on his Irish experiences singled it out for special mention for its propriety;[2] and it monopolized the surly attention of the government press. Among the newspapers named at an aggregate meeting of Catholics in July 1813, that had 'disdained more corruption, and withstood more persecution, than ever the free press has yet sustained', the *Evening Post* congratulated itself upon receiving the accolade.[3] Relying on its strength and influence, it continued to harass the government, undeterred by fear of fresh prosecutions.

A few months after Peel's arrival in Ireland, an excuse presented itself for an action against the *Evening Post*. It had informed the lord lieutenant, the duke of Richmond, that his administration was no better than that of the worst of his predecessors, and had then proceeded to describe his predecessors' corruption, baseness, cruelty, and depravity.[4] Possibly the *Evening Post* took courage from the then prevalent rumour that the government was about to be replaced by a coalition—Wellesley, Canning, and Grey—but even after that vision had faded, the gibes at the Castle continued.

In April 1813, John Magee was called upon to give bail pending his trial for a libel on the duke of Richmond; and in June he was committed to jail for another alleged libel on the police magistrates. He was fortunate not to be brought up on a third charge, of printing a libel on the prince regent. The prince had given Peel to understand that reports of a speech of O'Connell's that had appeared in the *Post* had made him 'very irritable'. Peel wrote that the prince:

wished extremely to punish the author of them. That he was well inclined to retaliate upon Mr. O'Connell by a year or two of imprisonment, and that it was difficult to make him understand that a conviction might be very doubtful, and that an attempt to prosecute would be very unwise.

Peel realized that action by the prince not only would arouse great resentment in Dublin, but also would jeopardize the success of the prosecutions already planned. He called on the prince, telling him that Magee was already in prison for one libel and would soon, he hoped, be sentenced for another. The prince was still not satisfied. Peel promised

[1] B.M., Add. MS (Peel) 40232 f. 147.
[2] Rev. J. Hall, *Tour through Ireland*.
[3] *D.E. Post*, 3 July 1813.
[4] Ibid., 5 Jan. 1813.

to obtain for him the opinions of the crown law officers in Ireland, and Richmond had no trouble in arranging that both attorney general and solicitor general should pronounce against a new prosecution—even of the printer.[1]

Nevertheless, a third prosecution was soon afterwards initiated. In August 1813 the *Evening Post* published some resolutions passed by the Kilkenny Catholic Committee, condemning the government's treatment of Magee. The crown law officers pronounced them libellous, and the prosecution was set in motion at the request of Peel, who hoped, on this occasion, to strike at bigger game than the newspaper —the men behind the resolutions.[2]

For the libel on the duke of Richmond a jury, which was composed exclusively of Protestants, found Magee guilty and he was sentenced to a fine of £500 and two years' imprisonment. A statute dating from the rebellion period, which enacted that government stamps should be withheld from newspaper owners who had been convicted of libel, was invoked for the first time; to enable the *Post* and the *Evening Herald*, both of which were Magee's property, to continue publication, Magee had to give them into the control of his brother James.[3] This took time to arrange, and the government took the opportunity to initiate further prosecutions for the sale of some unstamped copies of the *Post* that had appeared in the interim. The charges, however, were never pressed. There was no need; in February 1814, John Magee was sentenced to a fine of £1,000, and a further six months' imprisonment, for the publication of the Kilkenny resolutions.[4]

These sentences on Magee were out of proportion to the offences. The *Evening Post's* condemnation of the Richmond viceroyalty had been violent: but the sentence for publishing resolutions passed by a representative gathering of citizens in a country town, and the invocation of the act removing government stamps from the proprietor upon conviction, suggested that there was more behind the prosecutions than the simple enforcement of the law. Peel's correspondence confirms that they arose from a design to put down the *Evening Post*. It reveals that a few weeks after Peel had taken office Magee complained that the 'expresses' were being communicated to favoured newspapers and not to the *Evening Post*.[5] In this, Peel was only carrying on the policy of his

---

[1] June–July 1813 (N.L.I., Richmond MSS, 71 ff. 1411, 1474, 1478).
[2] Parker, *Peel*, i. 116.
[3] *D.E. Post*, 14 Dec. 1813.
[4] Ibid., 10 Feb. 1814.
[5] Aspinall, *Politics and the press*, p. 181.

predecessors; but the following autumn he went further, depriving the *Evening Post* of the translations of foreign despatches normally given to the press—a serious matter in a time when newspapers could not afford to employ their own translators. Having discovered the newspaper's source of exclusive information—he found that the *Evening Post* had given up the traditional Irish habit of waiting for the English papers to arrive to copy from them and, instead, was obtaining its own news through the post office—Peel wrote: 'I have now got the same intelligence through the same channel for our papers, but I do not think that sufficient. I think we should prevent the *Evening Post* from having it.' He gave orders that the transmission to it of any foreign news from the post office was to cease, saying that he would take the blame if there was any protest. The post office obeyed.[1]

Peel hated Magee's newspaper with what, for him, was remarkable vehemence. 'Most of the dissatisfaction in this country', he wrote in 1813,[2]

> arises from the immense circulation of that nefarious paper the *Dublin Evening Post*. It is sent gratuitously into many parts of the country, and read by those who can read, to those who cannot; and as it is written with a certain degree of ability, and a style which suits the taste of those upon whom it is intended to work, it does, no doubt, great mischief.

When Whitworth arrived to succeed Richmond as lord lieutenant, one of Peel's first communications with him included a tirade against the *Evening Post* for suggesting that he had been sent over to Ireland 'to implement a liberal policy'. Peel's every reference to the paper contains prejudice.[3]

With John Magee out of the way the Castle turned its attention to his brother James, who was brought up in February 1814 on a further charge of libel, for printing a speech of O'Connell's, in which O'Connell had suggested that Catholics were sometimes not sufficiently protected from Orange violence. This trial took a different course. F. W. Conway, who had become the editor of the paper, gave evidence that he had received specific instructions from James Magee to moderate the paper's tone: and although a verdict of guilty was returned, the *Evening Post* the next day congratulated itself that the solicitor general had 'distinctly held out a hope that Mr. Magee would not be brought up for judgement, if his future conduct should be found to quadrate with his present profession'.[4] The Magees, apparently, had had enough.

[1] Ibid.
[2] B.M., Add. MS (Peel) 40385 f. 137.
[3] Parker, *Peel*, i. 105, 134.
[4] *D.E. Post*, 26 May 1814.

Their weakening was not, however, wholly attributable to the success of Peel's siege. A quarrel had arisen between the Magees and Daniel O'Connell. When O'Connell had defended John Magee in the Richmond libel trial, the Magees' immediate reaction had been unqualified approval. But, as the days went by, they began to realize that it was less a defence than a reiteration and amplification of the libels in the original article. O'Connell's savage attack upon the attorney general who, as a turncoat—he had written, spoken and voted against the Union—was particularly hated, might make Saurin's name odious to posterity, but it was also likely to make Saurin implacable in his hatred of the *Evening Post*. On a motion to set aside the verdict of the trial, Magee's other counsel unhesitatingly threw O'Connell over, begging the jury not to allow the guilt of the client to be aggravated by the sins of the counsel. O'Connell was naturally annoyed. Magee, on his side, began to feel hardly used. He had voluntarily shielded the author of the libel on the duke of Richmond. Now, he realized that he was being left with the responsibility for the printing of the Kilkenny resolutions, whether he liked it or not.

The chairman of the meeting, whom the *Evening Post* had earlier called 'this distinguished honest Irishman, and incorruptible patriot', was the Captain Bryan of the *Hibernian Journal* libel actions—from which he had clearly learned a lesson. As chairman, he had taken upon himself the task of transmitting the resolutions to the *Evening Post*; but he refused to come forward to avow them. Inevitably, both sides began to feel aggrieved and recriminations began. The government took their opportunity, promising that if the Magees altered their paper's allegiance, James would not be brought up for sentence. 'Has Gregory told you of the adhesion of Magee?' the lord lieutenant asked in a letter to Peel in May 1814. 'Like other worthies he has made the *amende honorable*, and professes an inclination to efface his misdeeds by serving us to the best of his power.' Gregory explained to Peel shortly afterwards:[1]

> As to my friend, he is the most impudent filch I ever knew, having betrayed his own party, and not true to ours. He had the audacity to tell me that it was principally owing to the line of writing pursued by him that the Catholic Board was brought into disrepute.

The *Evening Post*, as a matter of course, continued to profess independence; but the Catholic party regarded it as a Castle paper. The *Post* was driven to retaliate by condemning Captain Bryan for allowing Magee to go to prison on his behalf, and O'Connell, for prejudicing Magee's case by his defence. The government were delighted with this

[1] Aspinall, *Politics and the press*, pp. 121–2.

turn. In April 1815 Peel, noticing the change for the better, gave orders that the translations should be restored to it:[1] and a year later Gregory, enclosing a copy with a letter to Peel, praised it for being the only Dublin newspaper which took the trouble to give what the Castle thought was a correct account of the trial of the Cork printer, Harding Tracey, for libel.[2] That winter the *Evening Post* began once again to congratulate itself on the superiority of its special news service. Evidently the last of Peel's restrictions had been lifted.

John Magee served out his terms of imprisonment. On 29 July 1815 the *Evening Post* noted that his sentence for the Richmond libel had expired, and the sentence for the Kilkenny resolutions begun. He was eventually released on 10 January 1816, after paying £1,500 in fines, the *Evening Post* said, and entering into heavy recognizances. The fine of £1,000 was later remitted, after negotiations between Saurin and a representative of the Magees had secured a further promise of good behaviour. Payments of £100 to the editor were recorded during 1818 and 1819; later, these amounts were increased.[3] The *Evening Post* did not take as sycophantic a line as the *Dublin Journal* or the *Patriot*; it continued to follow a moderate and fairly conciliatory policy. But it never regained the influence it had wielded when Peel became chief secretary.

Its defection left the Catholic party without a newspaper upon which they could rely. The *Evening Herald* was described by the under secretary, Gregory, in 1813, as 'the worst of all the papers'. But, on 20 June 1814—a few weeks after the Magees had changed sides—an editorial announced that the paper's name would shortly be changed to the *Sentinel*. Apparently its ownership had changed hands. The *Sentinel* came out two days later, some forty-eight hours before it was due, having in place of an editorial an open letter to the attorney general. A poster, apparently, had been put out saying that the *Herald's* last number would contain some startling revelations—secret instructions alleged to have been given by the prince regent, against the Catholics in Canada. 'Your police', the open letter ran, 'took down the placard of the *Herald*; you did other things which for the present I omit to mention—you are greatly mistaken if you think that your threats, or your police can influence the conduct of the proprietor of the *Sentinel*'. Evidently the last number of the *Herald* had been suppressed; details, however, were not given, beyond the sinister 'you did other things'. The slightly hysterical note of

[1] Ibid., p. 182.
[2] B.M., Add. MS (Peel) 40202 f. 366.
[3] Aspinall, *Politics and the press*, p. 122.

141

bravado was not to be justified; the paper proved ineffectual, and did not long survive.

The Catholic party thereupon set about founding a newspaper of their own, during the early months of 1815: Dr Brenan of the *Milesian Magazine* inserted an 'advertisement' for an editor, 'a person perfectly competent to be the ostensible proprietor of a patriotic religious newspaper. He must be in circumstances to enable him to say he has no preference for the streets of Dublin to the cells of Newgate'.[1] The *Dublin Chronicle* appeared during the summer. According to Peel, it was established by O'Connell 'when he and his colleagues had brought the editors of all other papers into Newgate for publishing speeches which they composed and corrected'.[2] It was a spirited, but never a very influential newspaper. The *Evening Post*, in December, referred to a dispute in which the *Chronicle* had charged the *Dublin Journal* with incest as 'between two papers not in general circulation', and the small number of advertisements the *Chronicle* attracted corroborated the insult.

The *Chronicle* devoted its energies more to tormenting the government newspapers than the government itself, and for some months it survived unscathed; but in May 1816 its owner, Æneas MacDonnell, was brought up before the court of king's bench. He was found guilty; the jury, however, recommended him to mercy, because the libel was 'trifling and insignificant'. As O'Connell had already commented in his defence, the speech of the attorney general had shown that the Castle were very little concerned with the article that had been made the excuse for the prosecution: what they really objected to was the *Chronicle's* continued opposition to the government. The bench ignored the jury's plea, sentencing MacDonnell to six months' imprisonment and a fine of £100. The *Chronicle* published a list of the religions of all those concerned in the case. The entire panel for both grand and petty juries, the court officers, the clerks—even the bailiffs sent round to arrest Mac-Donnell—were Protestants.[3]

The *Chronicle* did not cease to ridicule the government press—which, to the *Chronicle*, meant every other newspaper in Dublin except itself—but apart from an action against it for libel by Giffard, out of which it escaped only by a much qualified apology, it seems to have avoided further trouble until its decease, which was not long delayed—probably on account of a dispute between MacDonnell and O'Connell.[4]

[1] *Milesian Magazine*, May 1815.
[2] Croker, *Correspondence and diaries*, i. 89.
[3] *D. Chronicle*, 24 May 1816.
[4] Ibid., 20 Aug. 1817: *O'Connell correspondence*, i. 49.

Apart from the *Dublin Chronicle*, it appears that no metropolitan newspaper existed after the *Evening Post's* conversion to trouble Peel's mind with opposition. As a pamphleteer had written in 1813,[1] describing the effects of the libel actions, 'the habit of intimidation produced by these prosecutions is enough to silence the press with regard to the abuses of government'. The *Freeman* was an example. Alone of Dublin newspapers, it managed to retain some degree of independence throughout Peel's term of office; but this was at the price of extreme editorial caution. When it published the speech of O'Connell's for which the printer of the *Cork Mercantile Chronicle* was sent to jail, its editor Michael Staunton only avoided prosecution by humble self-abasement in a long *apologia* to the Castle.[2]

Harding Tracey, a Cork printer, was sentenced to two years imprisonment and a fine of £300 for the publication of this speech,[3] in which there had been allegations of corrupt practices in the courts; his release several months before the sentence had expired was probably the result less of the ill health which he had pleaded at the trial, than of ministerial admission that they had failed in their real object—the trapping of O'Connell himself.

John Lawless, who had done his best to keep the opposition press alive in Belfast, narrowly escaped a similar fate. His *Ulster Recorder* was suppressed in 1815, when it fell into debt with the stamp commissioners. He founded a new paper, the *Ulster Register*, in its place; the printer was soon afterwards convicted on a number of counts, for technical infringements of the Stamp Acts. The *Register* disappeared; but Lawless, prosecuted at the same time as his printer, managed to evade conviction.[4]

Watty Cox was less fortunate. He was still in jail when Peel arrived in Ireland. O'Connell went to the courts in 1814 to urge the termination of the sentence, his argument being that the fine of £300 was excessive, and therefore contrary to the Bill of Rights; but the judge disallowed the appeal, saying that Cox ought to have complained of the fine at the time of his sentence.[5] Peel expressed his opinion in a letter to Croker, enclosing some copies of the *Irish Magazine*, which Cox had continued to produce from Newgate. Cox rather preferred residence there to anywhere else, Peel thought; he could easily have raised the money to pay

[1] *Hints to jurors on the liberty of the press* (P), 1813.
[2] 3 May 1815 (B.M., Add. MS (Peel) 40201 f. 15).
[3] *D.E. Post*, 21 May 1816.
[4] B.M., Add. MSS (Peel) 40259 f. 263: 40260 f. 133.
[5] *D.E. Post*, 8 May 1813.

the fine, if he had wanted to.[1] There Peel was almost certainly wrong; Cox was not a man of many friends. He remained in jail for over three years, until the government released him on condition he went into exile. Writing to the author of the libel that had brought him into prison, he said he 'was obliged to submit to the government to avoid another dreary imprisonment and, as the attorney general threatened, in a remoter jail. They insist, as one of the terms, that I must leave the country: but have agreed to pay my passage to America and, when landed, to pay me £400'.[2] He sailed in 1816. Peel paid him a valedictory compliment by instancing the *Irish Magazine* in a commons' debate as an example of the menace of the opposition press in Ireland.[3] That a monthly magazine run by an eccentric was the worst he could find as an illustration showed that the objective Peel had set himself on taking up his appointment had been attained. His boast to Croker had been fulfilled: the enemy batteries were silenced.

(b) TAXATION

Legislation concerning the press, by the time Peel came to Ireland, had reached such a pitch of selective discrimination against the opposition newspapers that further government activity in that direction proved scarcely necessary. Acts passed in 1815 and 1816 revised and underlined the laws of the rebellion period, not materially altering them, except to add a further sixpence to the advertisement duty, to increase the burden still carried mainly by the independent press. So long as opposition newspapers were being published, the Castle press accepted the existence of heavy duties, knowing that they operated more severely against rivals. But as the months passed, and it became clear that an opposition press was no longer to be feared, the owners of government papers grew discontented, and before Peel's departure, they had begun an agitation for the lowering of the duties.

Henry Townsend of the *Correspondent* memorialized Peel in April 1818 on behalf of the Irish newspaper owners, to the effect that they were unfairly treated. The English stamp duty was 4d., compared to 2d. in Ireland; but the English owners received a 20% rebate, and the Irish only 1½%, and the English were very much better able to sustain the higher rate, owing to the greater prosperity of their country. The cost of

---

[1] (Undated) Croker, *Correspondence and diaries*, i. 89.
[2] Ó Casaide, *Watty Cox*, p. 22.
[3] 26 Apr. 1816 (*Parl. deb.*, xxxiv. 35).

printing, the memorial continued, was higher than in England, and there were a number of other grievances. Fines for technical breaches of the law, or failure to pay duties on time, securities required from all owners in case they were involved in seditious libel actions, and the advertisement duty, were all felt to be excessive.[1]

Peel's reply to the memorial was discouraging.[2] There might appear to be no further need for the retention of the heavy duties, once the opposition press had disappeared; but the government had to bear in mind that individual newspapers would be tempted to reassert their independence, if they could do so without incurring financial loss. Not that Peel was necessarily fully aware of the deterrent value of the heavy duties. They may have been imposed, and retained, as a product of the magnetism which attracts ministries—without, apparently, consciousness of motive—to adopt means which will indirectly operate towards the attainment of the ends that they desire.

(ii) *Aid for Castle newspapers*

On 10 June 1816 the *Dublin Chronicle* published an article purporting to give an account of the sums paid by the government to satellite newspapers:

Newspaper	Proclama- ations £	Govern- ment Advertise- ments £	Pensions £	Total £
Correspondent	1,040	400	1,200	2,640
Patriot	1,040	500	900	2,440
Dublin Journal	1,040	300	900	2,240
Hibernian Journal about the same as the *Dublin Journal*				2,240
Saunders' Newsletter, approx.				1,100
Profits from jobs held by placemen connected with these five newspapers				2,500
25 provincial newspapers at £150 each, cost of expresses, and miscellaneous items, bringing total cost to approx.				27,000

With the crumbs that fell to the *Freeman*, *Carrick's Morning Post* and, now that it was behaving itself, the *Dublin Evening Post*, and with disbursements that could not be checked from the secret service money, the total government outlay on the newspapers, the *Chronicle* concluded, must be in the region of £30,000 a year.

[1] B.M., Add. MS (Peel) 40275 f. 303.
[2] Ibid., 40276 f. 25.

The *Chronicle* was the only newspaper at that date which received nothing from the government. It had every inducement to malicious exaggeration. Yet the detailed nature of this statement of accounts suggests that it was based on inside information—procured, possibly, from some government official. Some of the figures the *Chronicle* itself admitted to be approximations, and others may have been guesswork; but much of the account is confirmed from other sources.[1] In 1813 Gregory told Peel that in addition to the proclamation money, and payments for insertion of government advertisements, the *Dublin Journal* and the *Patriot* received a subsidy of £800 apiece from the Castle, and the *Hibernian Journal* £500—'formerly more'. When Peel urged the discontinuance of the *Dublin Journal* in 1816, he said that the saving to the government would be £1,400. A year before, he had complained that the *Patriot* cost the government £1,500 a year; and by Gregory's account three years later the *Patriot* was, in fact, receiving £1,760—£500 from the secret service money, £800 from proclamations, £260 from the king's printer, and a £200 pension for Corbet. Henry Townsend, in 1815, claimed that under the terms of his agreement with the government he was to get £1,200 a year: £500 from the secret service money, £400 from proclamations, and £300 from some unidentified source: the first two sums, he said, had been paid, but there was some dispute about the unidentified £300.

(*a*) PROCLAMATIONS

Proclamations remained the steadiest source of income to newspapers which gave the government satisfaction: Parliament continued to vote £10,500 a year towards them annually, and they were distributed approximately in the proportions described in the *Chronicle*. The amounts paid to individual papers varied. An account for the years 1818–20 that was put before the House of Commons showed that only the *Patriot* had retained its full allowance of £1,040 a year. The *Correspondent* had dropped to £600, the *Hibernian Journal* to £750, the *Dublin Journal* to only £300 a year, but the total sums paid to newspapers for the insertion of proclamations was still £10,500 a year.[2]

Although the fiction was maintained that the proclamations were not distributed with any ulterior motive, they were in fact conditional on the newspaper remaining in favour. For example, they were taken away

[1] The figures are taken from B.M., Add. MSS (Peel) 40196 f. 137: 40205 f. 167: 40242 f. 267: 40288 f. 52: 40290 f. 176.
[2] *Parl. papers, 1821* (478) xx. 209: Aspinall, *Politics and the press*, p. 138.

from George Grace of the *Clonmel Herald* in 1812; Grace had supported the opposition candidate in the General Elections, and General Matthew, whom he had helped to elect, told the commons that they had been withheld for that reason.[1] By 1818, Grace had managed to convince Peel, by eulogies in the paper and a constant flow of begging letters, that the *Clonmel Herald* was a friend to the government; the proclamations were resumed. Until Peel's arrival, the *Waterford Mirror* was one of the newspapers that received the proclamations. In May 1813 the *Evening Post* referred to it as being liberal and enlightened. Evidently Gregory had already noticed the fact; a few days before he had written to tell Peel that the proclamations were being withdrawn from it, in consequence of its taking the popular side, and he also said that other provincial newspapers 'which were adverse, and had the benefit of proclamations, have been struck off the list'—the *Wexford Journal* and the *Cork Southern Reporter. Saunders' News-Letter* was the beneficiary. Its political neutrality had in the past led to government neglect. But Gregory believed that *Saunders'* circulation was greater than all the other papers put together. If any of them should have the proclamations, he thought that *Saunders'* should.[2] *Saunders'*, however, was still independent—and Peel had given orders that proclamations were not to be given to any newspaper that showed signs of independence. Evidently the proprietor and Gregory came to terms, as the *Evening Post* that summer began to detect, and reprobate, signs that the paper was departing from its traditional policy: '*Saunders'* owes all its strength to its neutrality', the *Evening Post* warned; it should not join the sycophants. But—as it usually did, in difficult times—*Saunders'* succumbed to government influence.[3]

(b) GOVERNMENT ADVERTISEMENTS

The 'government advertisements' referred to in the accounts in the *Chronicle* represented advertising by government departments. To judge by the official figures given for the year 1816,[4] the *Chronicle* was guilty of exaggeration: but the probability is that the administration's definition of what constituted an 'office advertisement' differed from the *Chronicle's*. Certainly the *Chronicle* was later able to back its contention convincingly, with evidence that two government papers in Dublin had re-

[1] George Grace, *Letter to the duke of Richmond* (P) 1813: *Parl. deb.* xxv. 813.
[2] Aspinall, in *E.H.R.*, lvi. 267: B.M., Add. MS (Peel) 40196 f. 77.
[3] *D.E. Post*, 27–30 Aug. 1814.
[4] *Parl. papers*, 1822 (588) xviii. 465.

ceived between them some £26 worth of government advertising in a single day, in the form of lists of game licences issued in various counties, a subject, the *Chronicle* pointed out, of little direct interest to Dubliners.

The official accounts in any case could not disguise the fact that the newspapers who supported the government were again the main beneficiaries; £218 to the *Correspondent*, £146 to the *Hibernian Journal*, £108 to the *Patriot*, and £58 to the *Evening Post*. The neutrals did poorly, the *Freeman* obtaining £24 worth of advertisements, and the *Morning Post* only £4. The *Chronicle* received no government advertising at all. With the provincial papers, the total cost to the country of these office advertisements came to nearly £2,000; evidently they were given out on the same principle as the proclamations—as a reward for services rendered.

(c) PENSIONS

The distinctions cannot always be made between pensions paid to an individual for his services to the government, and those paid to him as subsidies for his newspaper. The recipients had an interest in maintaining that pensions were being paid to them for services distinct from journalism; it lessened the risk of the payments being discontinued if their newspapers ceased to give satisfaction. Often they had some justification, in that they had acted as government agents, in addition to their work as journalists. In practice, the distinction had little meaning. Knowing that his pension might vanish if he ceased to support the government, a pensioner rarely put it in jeopardy by any show of independence. George Grace of the *Clonmel Herald*, however, lost his pension as well as the proclamations by his support of the opposition in 1812; Gregory had investigated the services for which it had been granted, and decided that they did not justify its continuance. But when the government relented and allowed him the proclamations once more, the pension, too, was once more granted to him, retrospectively from the time it had been taken away.[1]

The assumption must be that other pensioned journalists would have suffered in the same way, if any of them had dared to thwart the government. They rarely did. Giffard managed to keep his pension, when the government finally removed him from the *Dublin Journal*; but his fault had been over-zealous advocacy of the government cause, for which they could hardly penalize him by taking away an income that he had enjoyed for over a quarter of a century.

[1] B.M., Add. MS (Peel) 40202 f. 297: Aspinall, *Politics and the press*, p. 123.

The secret service account books recording payments to newspapers and newspaper proprietors show that payments were irregular, possibly because the government had not always the means to hand. The *Correspondent* and its owners, Stephen Webb and Henry Townsend, received about £600–£700 a year. Comerford and Corbet were paid a similar amount for the *Patriot*. It was from this source that Giffard of the *Dublin Journal*, Grace of the *Clonmel Herald*, and Harvey of the *Freeman* received their allowances, and that the payment was made to Watty Cox, when he came to terms with the government. Altogether, between £2,000–£3,000 a year was disbursed to journalists in this way.[1]

(d) PLACES

Whether government 'places' that were given to newspaper owners who supported the administration were, like pensions, the reward for their journalistic work, or were obtained for other service, is difficult to decide. But again, the precedent of Giffard, who had lost his job in the customs owing to his dispute with Lord Hardwicke, was a warning that they were to be forfeited if the holder incurred the government's displeasure—inducement for any placeman who was connected with a newspaper, to keep that paper behind the government.

Both the Fitzsimons' of the *Hibernian Journal*, had places'. Placemen were rarely satisfied until their family and friends were also looked after. Giffard's son was given a judgeship in Ceylon, eventually becoming chief justice there; and Peel gave another kinsman a place in the customs, on Giffard's request, in 1816.[2]

*   *   *

The *Chronicle's* estimate therefore of £30,000 may have been exaggerated, but certainly the amount spent by the government annually on the press must have been close on £20,000. Almost all of it went to the newspapers that supported the government, the remainder being doled out among the neutrals. The opposition press received nothing. The money was disbursed with the object of securing support for the government—an inducement to serve, or as a reward for services rendered.

The ways in which Peel sought to obtain a press that would serve the government did not differ from those of his predecessors. He simply

[1] Aspinall, *Politics and the press*, pp. 114–24.
[2] B.M., Add. MS (Peel) 40252 f. 163.

carried them to their logical conclusion. The cost of publishing news-papers was made so high that only two types of paper could survive. The neutral advertising journals, *Saunders'* and the *Morning Post*, could largely be ignored. Newspapers which had a circulation large enough to be financially independent, like the *Evening Post*, had to be dealt with forcibly. The remainder were offered the alternative of accepting government subsidies—on government conditions—or losing money. The continued expenditure of thousands of pounds annually on the press was made necessary by the weight of taxation: the heavy taxation was needed to keep potential opposition papers off the market. If proprietors had seen any prospect of making money out of independence, they would certainly have renounced the government connection, which, as they well knew, reduced circulation. The government therefore had to keep the cost of publishing independent journals prohibitive (unless they were so filled with advertisements that they had little space for news, and less for comment) and to sustain the government press by subsidies.

By 1816, this policy had been successful, to the point that the opposi-tion press had all but disappeared. The *Dublin Chronicle* still survived, but its circulation was slender, and it must have been running at a loss. The commercial value of newspapers was conditional on the prospects of continued government support. It had become hardly possible for individuals to start a new paper, or convert an old one to an inde-pendent line, as a commercial proposition. Under Peel's guidance the freedom of the press in Ireland had disappeared, even more completely than it had in the rebellion years.

(iii) *The results of Peel's policy*

Peel, at first, was well satisfied with the results of his press policy. His letter to Croker on the subject a few weeks after his appointment as chief secretary was full of confidence. He had arrived to find the *Dublin Journal*, the *Patriot*, and the *Hibernian Journal* securely welded to the administration, and none of them showed any disposition to change their allegiance. The *Patriot* remained the leading Castle paper, Peel making special arrangements so that it might obtain exclusive 'inside information' from the government, and himself contributing para-graphs on occasion.[1] Corbet, the proprietor, and Comerford, the editor, continued to act as informers and government agents when required, as did Edward Fitzsimons of the *Hibernian Journal*; on one occasion, when O'Connell had pleaded indisposition in order to postpone appear-

[1] Ibid., 40214 f. 69: Parker, *Peel*, i. 105.

ing at proceedings against him in London, Fitzsimons wrote to Peel to tell him that O'Connell had been seen in apparent good health in Dublin;[1] and he frequently passed on information about the Catholics and their plans.

A new ally was found in the *Correspondent* which, although it continued for some weeks after Peel's arrival to denounce the Castle papers, and the 'monstrous system of corruption' associated with the expresses, soon began to make a distinction between Peel's 'enlightened and upright' courses and the system he had found on arrival. Peel promptly grasped the hand held out to him, and in a few weeks the *Correspondent* was restored to favour, accepting its share of the expresses whose misuse it had so vigorously condemned. A few months later Gregory referred to a conversation with the editor, who had departed 'highly satisfied'; and Peel replied: 'the *Correspondent* had made a very good fight for us recently; Saxton says he had no idea it would have come forward so gallantly as it has done on some occasions against the *Dublin Evening Post*'.[2]

The *Freeman* remained aloof for some months after Peel's appointment: but by the summer of 1813 it was being rebuked by the opposition as a waverer, and its proprietor, Harvey, named as suspect on account of his pension. Peel, that autumn, commented favourably upon its increasing moderation, and the following year Gregory opened negotiations with its owner.[3] He feared, however, that the paper was too rich to be brought to terms. The *Freeman*, *Carrick's Morning Post* and *Saunders'*, all morning dailies, carried more advertising than the evening papers, and consequently were in a better position to resist government blandishments. Nevertheless, Watty Cox accused Harvey in 1815 of publishing verses adulatory of Peel to insure himself against the risks of transportation; and although the *Freeman* retained sufficient spirit to make a mild protest about Peel's denunciation of the Irish press in the commons the following year, its tone remained moderate, and Peel had little reason to be dissatisfied.

Peel's satisfaction, however, was shortlived. He quickly found that government newspapers, even when they professed loyalty to the administration and anxiety to be of service to him, could prove an intolerable nuisance.

The *Dublin Journal* was unlikely to keep out of mischief for long with John Giffard as its owner: and as early as May 1813, Gregory was com-

[1] B.M., Add. MS (Peel) 40260 f. 205.
[2] Ibid., 40201 f. 293: 40195 f. 232: 40281 f. 129: Parker, *Peel*, i. 114.
[3] *Freeman*, 3–4 May 1816: Aspinall, *Politics and the press*, p. 116.

plaining of Giffard's most reprehensible conduct, in printing an obvious and malicious forgery—'a most dangerous friend', Gregory described him, 'who has always injured the cause he espoused'. Peel agreed, suggesting that the proclamations should be withdrawn from his paper.[1] Giffard's effusive loyalty made it difficult for the administration to take this step, in spite of further misdeeds—'I hate writing anything to John Giffard', Peel told Gregory in 1815: 'I know, too, your great horror of a controversy with John. . . . Say to him that I am much obliged to him for sending me the address, and that I have no doubt it is well-intended, but that I think decidedly that these proclamations from self-constituted authorities in Dublin are highly objectionable'. A year later, Peel had lost all patience with him. Giffard, he said, had put words into his mouth that he had not spoken; and accounts sent in for the *Dublin Journal* showed that its outgoings were £2,432, and its income £2,491. 'The amount', Peel wrote, 'would be more fairly stated thus—gain to himself £60, loss to government £1,400, and in point of injury and discredit as much more.' He gave orders that the *Dublin Journal* be stopped. An arrangement was reached, however, with the proprietor (one of the original Faulkner family, from whom Giffard leased the paper) whereby it was allowed to continue, but without a direct subsidy, and without Giffard, who was induced to retire from journalism by the addition of an extra £100 on to his pension.[2]

Even before Giffard had made himself a nuisance, Edward Fitzsimons, of the *Hibernian Journal*, had attracted the unfavourable attention of the government he was anxious to serve. By January 1813 Fitzsimons was apologizing to Peel for some unnamed offence, and regretting that his paper had not made so good an impression upon Peel as it had on his predecessor Wellesley-Pole. Fitzsimons promised to mend his ways, which he did so strenuously that Gregory shortly afterwards wrote to Peel, in disconcerted amusement, that 'the editor of the *Hibernian Journal* has been pleased to let off a flaming puff at us, for which he shall get a jobation. The duke says it is my writing; but as you are absent, I shall of course attribute it to you.'[3]

Gregory was shortly to feel less good-humoured about the *Hibernian Journal*. Fitzsimons had resented the return to the government fold of the prodigal *Correspondent* in 1813, welcomed as it was with the fatted calf of the expresses; and he was unable to restrain himself from voicing

[1] B.M., Add. MS (Peel) 40196 f. 196: Aspinall, in *E.H.R.* lvi. 272.
[2] Parker, *Peel*, i. 218: B.M. Add. MSS (Peel) 40286 f. 240: 40288 f. 187: 40290 f. 177: 40202 f. 297.
[3] Parker, *Peel*, i. 114: B.M. Add. MS (Peel) 40224 f. 32.

his rage. Peel, after one outburst, thought that a hint to the proprietors, if they offended again, would be enough: but almost immediately Gregory complained of another attack, promising punishment for the offenders and calling their paper 'the most impudent and most useless tributary scribbler that was ever employed'. Thereafter the *Hibernian Journal* is referred to in the government correspondence only with irritation. In 1817, Peel declared that it was 'always offensive', and always ready to inflame instead of to allay animosities.[1]

In the summer of 1814 the *Patriot* accused the respectable Sir John Newport of corrupt practices. Peel was annoyed and alarmed; if there was a libel action the *Patriot's* connection with government would certainly be emphasized. By the following year Peel's disillusionment with the paper was complete. 'I consider the *Patriot* newspaper,' he wrote, 'if it cost us nothing, to be worse than useless: and as it costs us £1,500 I am most anxious to abolish so expensive an evil'. A few weeks later he wrote again:

> I wish you would try to bring to a final and favourable issue the project we had of putting an end to the *Patriot* newspaper. I estimate the value of its services so low, the amount being certainly a minus quantity, that whatever we can save from the present expenses of the establishment will be more than clear gain.

He gave Gregory full authority to act, saying that he would be 'most pleased when my eye is no longer offended even by the title, beyond which I do not venture, of this execrable paper'. That the *Patriot* continued publication cannot have been owing to any reformation, because when in 1818 the editor, Comerford, was drowned, Gregory suggested that the paper might be allowed to sink with him, and Peel agreed.[2] It nevertheless survived.

The *Correspondent*, alone of the government press, was seldom the subject of complaint in Peel's correspondence. But on more than one occasion it was involved in disputes with the Castle, one apparently leading to the temporary withdrawal of proclamations, which suggests that their relationship was not entirely happy.[3]

(a) INEFFICIENCY

A commentary upon the incompetence of the government press is to

[1] B.M., Add. MS (Peel) 40281 f. 129: Aspinall, in *E.H.R.*, lvi. 273: *Politics and the press*, p. 141.

[2] B.M., Add. MSS (Peel) 40205 f. 167: 40288 f. 52: 40295 f. 25: Aspinall, in *E.H.R.*, lvi. 273: Parker, *Peel*. i. 116.

[3] B.M., Add. MSS (Peel) 40242 f. 267: 40261 f. 47: Aspinall, *Politics and the press* p. 190.

be found in the *Evening Post* for 21 August 1813, in the form of an article purporting to be extracts from its rival newspapers discussing the state of Ireland, being in fact a parody of their various styles. In the extracts the *Hibernian Journal* lashes out at the rest of the newspapers, the *Dublin Journal* is scurrilous, the *Patriot* affectedly highbrow (its editor Comerford prided himself on his learning), the *Correspondent* insufferably long-winded, and the *Freeman* self-consciously impartial. The *Morning Post* and *Saunders' News-Letter* have no comments of their own to make on the state of Ireland; they copy out opinions from the English newspapers. Judged by the journalistic standards of the times, the article was cleverly written, hitting off the newspapers' more obvious characteristics. The *Correspondent*, for example, had been extremely verbose from its foundation. One of its editorials included the sentence: 'The emolliency of our abominable antipathies, nor even their positive cessation, could not at once work a miracle, and brush away the inveteracies which the habits of long ages had been producing'—an appeal for conciliation that gives a fair sample of the paper's readability.

The government papers were bad because they were government papers—not by chance, or coincidence. The government represented a negligible fraction of the community; its support was secured by patronage and, outside placeholders, it could command only that negative approval that comes from a fear of something still less palatable. Its newspapers were produced by men of elastic principles, who were prepared to prostitute their abilities to hold their jobs. Many of them—Giffard, for example—were able to convince themselves that the cause they upheld was just. But Giffard was so detested, and the views he held so obnoxious, that his newspaper, even if less turgid, was not more read than the straightforward 'Castle prints', none of which attracted many readers.

Although there is little direct evidence about the size of their circulations, what there is shows that it was extremely limited. Writing to the Castle in 1813, Corbet boasted that the *Patriot* had 750 subscribers, 'big for a paper that does not trim'. Two years later he was complaining that the *Correspondent* had gained circulation at the *Patriot's* expense, by avoiding controversies liable to make it unpopular. 'An experience of 30 years during which I have been connected with government newspapers enables me to say that nothing can be more difficult in Ireland, than obtaining circulation for a government paper'.[1] By February 1815 the advertisements in the *Patriot* had dwindled to a single column, and half of them were proclamations.

[1] B.M. Add. MS (Peel) 40214 f. 69, 40201 f. 293.

The *Dublin Journal's* circulation was even smaller: in 1813 it was less than 500. To judge by a memorial[1] sent by its proprietor in October 1816, after Giffard's retirement, it later diminished still further: again, this is borne out by the evidence of the advertisements, which by the time of his departure had been reduced to half a column, excluding proclamations. The paper began to revive and was soon boasting that it had increased its circulation threefold under the new management. The memorial states that its circulation was equal to the *Patriot's*, and five times as large as the *Hibernian Journal's*, which would suggest that the *Hibernian Journal's* was very small indeed. Watty Cox, in his *Irish Magazine*, often jeered at the *Hibernian Journal's* negligible sales.

The extent to which a newspaper could suffer by advocacy of government measures is shown in a letter to Peel from George Grace, who confessed that his *Clonmel Herald* lost half of its 370 subscribers by showing favour to the Peace Preservation Bill.[2] Conversely, the only Dublin newspaper that offered serious opposition to Peel, the *Evening Post*, had much the largest circulation of any paper in the country. Even after its conversion it still held the lead, presumably because there was so little choice. The *Chronicle* was too aggressively Catholic in flavour to take its place among a newspaper-reading population that was still predominantly Protestant.

A list of the amounts of advertisement duty paid by each newspaper in 1819, the year after Peel's departure, is illuminating:[3]

	£ 1819	£ 1820
Saunders' Newsletter	2,512	2,393
Carrick's Morning Post	1,560	1,308
D.E. Post	1,475	1,238
Freeman	1,377	1,185
Correspondent	1,146	921
Patriot	339	260
Hibernian Journal	187	162

Saunders', smugly quoting the accounts, said that 'advertisers will necessarily crowd to journals which they know as sure to give the most extensive opportunities of laying their wants and wishes before the public'. The figures, however, were misleading. Of the evening papers the *Evening Post, Patriot, Hibernian Journal* and *Dublin Journal* were published thrice weekly, whereas the morning papers came out every

[1] Ibid., 40259 f. 156.
[2] Ibid., 40248 f. 71.
[3] Off. papers, 579/527/20.

day.[1] The morning papers, too, circulated mainly in the city, and were better patronized by advertisers; the evening papers sent out through the country carried less advertising in proportion to their circulation. The figures for the evening papers, however, give a fair indication of relative popularity; they bear out the confession later to be made by the *Hibernian Journal* that 'in Ireland the papers in opposition to government are those most sought after to put advertisements in'. The *Dublin Evening Post* still kept its advantage, presumably because its rivals were still more sycophantic: the *Patriot* and the *Hibernian Journal* had no appeal to advertisers, and although the *Dublin Journal's* figures were unaccountably omitted, a glance at its columns during the period shows that it was doing no better. The slump in newspaper advertising was the product of a decaying economic order: but it was equally a reflection of the general debility of the press.

(b) IMPORTUNITIES

If Peel had hoped that the government newspapers would exercise a salutary effect upon the public, to justify the expenditure on them, his hopes remained unfulfilled. In addition, his tutelage of the newspapers had further unpleasant consequences, not the least being that he and Gregory were incessantly plagued with a crowd of journalists, writing querulous letters and making themselves a thorough nuisance to the Castle.

At a time when every supporter of the ascendancy thought his services well qualified him for office, the journalists stood out as the most importunate, sycophantic, and annoying mendicants in the country. Most of their letters follow the pattern of those written to Cooke by Francis Higgins during the rebellion period. Some of them give information: a few deal with matters relevant to the conduct of the newspaper: but the vast majority concern themselves mainly, if not exclusively, with requests for more assistance, the writer whimpering, threatening, cringing, whining or beguiling, according to circumstances.

Giffard remained incorrigible. On one occasion the Castle thought that something had at last been found in which Giffard could be really useful—to supply information about the Orange Order, of which Giffard was a deputy grand master. But as Gregory complained to Peel,[2]

---

[1] The *Correspondent*, although an evening paper, was a daily: the *Patriot* changed from daily to thrice-weekly publication in 1816.

[2] B.M., Add. MS (Peel) 40199 f. 27.

all Giffard supplied was 'a long panegyric of his civil and military exploits'. He was a constant source of irritation to the two secretaries.

As a correspondent Giffard was out-written by Edward Fitzsimons of the *Hibernian Journal*. Fitzsimons was not above recommending himself direct to the prince regent, but usually he wrote to Peel, mixing protestations of devotion with requests for places.[1] He already held the job of inspector of taxes at £300 a year. In May 1814 he pointed out that one of the commissioners of revenue appeals was old and infirm and infrequent in attendance, suggesting himself as successor. 'Were I a commissioner of appeals', he wrote, 'I should be stationary in Dublin, and consequently more capable of energetically continuing my services to the government through the medium of the *Hibernian Journal*, and my own exertions—without being in any danger of undergoing a removal to any distant part of Ireland, which I am liable to at the present moment, far from my paper and the requisite communications with the Castle'. The following year he reminded Peel of his claims to the post, and, when the ailing commissioner died that winter, wrote hurriedly to press his claim. Peel replied regretting his inability to act, whereupon Fitzsimons wrote back, 'had I succeeded through your kind intervention I could not be more thankful than I feel myself at this proof of kindness to one whom you have bound to your service ever'. Peel jotted nervously on the back, 'I hope I said nothing that could justify all this gratitude'.

The following April Fitzsimons was asking for the post of advocate general to the court of admiralty, which would 'when granted me, bind me more than ever to your service. It would bring my income only to £600'. In October he twice asked for a police magistracy, following the deaths of the magistrates. And in July 1817 he took advantage of a friendly gesture from Peel to say that he was going to the continent to improve his writing—that in travelling, rank would be a help—and 'that I should be thankful if you would have the kindness to recommend me to his excellency the lord lieutenant, for the honour of knighthood'. The tone of Peel's answer to this request can be judged from Fitzsimons's profuse apologies a few days later, for the 'ignorance of forms' that had led him to make such a gaffe. A year later, he was again asking for a place. Even after Peel had left Ireland Fitzsimons continued to plague him, in spite of rebuffs, until Peel told his secretary to write: 'I am directed by Mr. Peel to acquaint you, with reference to your letter to him of the 21st inst., that he will not trouble you to write to him, as he receives informa-

[1] *George IV correspondence*, letter no. 558: and see under E. Fitzsimons in index to the Peel MSS, B.M., and in Aspinall, *Politics and the press*.

tion from Ireland upon all points on which he requires it from other quarters'.

The most persistent nuisance was George Grace, the proprietor of the *Clonmel Herald*.[1] The paper had been set up during Hardwicke's vice-royalty, Grace obtaining proclamations in return for a promise of his support for the government. When the value of the proclamations fell off, he managed to secure a £100 a year allowance in their place.[2] Peel ordered that this should be discontinued, along with the proclamations, in 1812, giving as an excuse that Grace had fallen into arrears with the stamp commissioners. Grace believed that it was because he had supported the opposition candidate in the elections; and from that time on he was constantly writing to the lord lieutenant, to Peel, and to Gregory, complaining about the treatment he had received, and beseeching them to restore his allowance, and the proclamations. His initial appeals failed, but the arrival of the new lord lieutenant, Whitworth, set him going again; Grace wrote to him saying that as a landowner, a lawyer, a magistrate, and a married man with a large family, he deserved justice. A year later he wrote to Peel to say that the loss of the proclamations and the annuity had so preyed upon the mind of his wife, the mother of twelve children, that she had gone mad. In April 1815 he spoke of 'the pressure under which I am struggling'; in October, he feared that the *Herald* was going on the rocks; and the following January wrote: 'I do most solemnly declare, as I hope for God's mercy, that nothing should make me again trespass on you in this way but unspeakable pressures of embarrassment.' This letter appears finally to have moved Peel to action; he gave instructions for the proclamations to be restored, and Grace's next letter is full of thanks for his return to favour. But no sooner did Grace detect any trace of encouragement, than he demanded further favours. When Peel wrote a friendly letter to him in 1814 Grace sent his acknowledgment by hand—the hand of his son, for whom he asked Peel to find some place; later, Peel complained to Gregory that Grace 'under pretence of apologizing for the persecution of his son, renews his own'.

Grace, in fact, had no sooner recovered the proclamations when he was asking for government advertisements. When the £100 a year allowance was restored, Grace found to his delight that it was paid retrospectively back to the date of its cessation. This suggested to him that the same might apply to the proclamations, and he wrote to Peel point-

[1] See under G. Grace in index to the Peel MSS, B.M. and in Aspinall, *Politics and the press*.
[2] Off. papers, 556/413/29.

ing out that he was owed 3¼ years at £240 a year; however, since he realized the government was short of money, they might instead put him 'into some situation in which the requital of its duties might afford a comfortable, though tedious compensation'. In spite of the government's help, just before Peel's departure, Grace wrote to tell him that the *Clonmel Herald* was at its last gasp. The value of the paper was 'dreadfully diminished': many of its subscribers had withdrawn because of his loyalty as a magistrate and newspaper proprietor; and if Peel could not help, he could at least intercede with his successor. Like Fitzsimons, Grace continued to badger Peel long after he had ceased to be chief secretary, writing to him in 1822 to say that support of his measures had been the cause of the *Clonmel Herald's* decline, and asking him on that account to intercede with his successor, 'affording me, in my old age, some of those comforts that age requires'. Peel answered curtly that he made it a rule never to interfere with Irish appointments.

Most of the Irish newspaper owners pestered the government in similar fashion, at one time or another. Henry Townshend, of the *Correspondent*, went behind Gregory's back to Peel in 1815, complaining that Gregory was unco-operative.[1] William Corbet, when he had reason to fear in 1815 that the government was about to abandon the *Patriot*, reminded them that only while the *Patriot* lived was the *Correspondent* manageable.[2] Comerford, the editor of the *Patriot*, had earlier insisted upon compensation with some permanent appointment, should the paper disappear, on the terms of the original agreement made when it was founded. He used to write fulsome letters to Peel; in one, he boasted about a threatening anonymous letter he had received which showed how effective his articles were; in another, he touted for a subscription to a book of verse he was about to publish. Peel ordered four copies. The book came out so long afterwards that Peel, forgetting, almost subscribed twice.[3] Fitzsimons was another verse writer; he told Peel in 1815 that he was publishing an edition of Irish melodies in order to counteract the seditious effect of Tom Moore's. Peel unguardedly replied that the intention was most praiseworthy: Fitzsimons promptly asked permission to dedicate the next edition to him, and Peel reluctantly had to give his consent, which entailed ordering four copies.[4]

The acquisitiveness of the Castle journalists was at times ghoulish. On 29 March 1818 Comerford, the editor of the *Patriot*, who had been

---

[1] B.M., Add. MS (Peel) 40242 f. 267.
[2] Ibid., 40201 f. 293.
[3] Ibid., 40243 f. 259: 40247 f. 125: 40288 f. 52.
[4] Ibid., 40247 f. 130.

spending a convivial evening with the manager of the Theatre Royal, missed his way home in the dark, walked into the Royal Canal, and was drowned. This was on a Saturday; on the Sunday, Gregory wrote to Peel that three Dublin newspaper owners had offered to conduct the paper in Comerford's place: Townsend, Fitzsimons, and Walter Thom, who had taken on the *Dublin Journal* after Giffard's retirement.

Fitzsimons wrote:

> As the *Hibernian Journal* is a morning paper, and the *Patriot* an evening one, it strikes me that I could easily conduct the latter so as to make it and the former jointly serviceable to the same cause.

Thom wrote:

> The *Patriot* being published on alternate days from my journal, the editing of the one could not interfere with that of the other . . . therefore I feel justified in proposing to conduct the *Patriot*.

A clerical candidate for the post, the Rev. Edward Groves, allowed Sunday to elapse before putting in his application for the vacant editorial chair.[1]

Only a fraction of the correspondence between the newspaper owners and the Castle can have been preserved, because much of it must have gone to Gregory, whose correspondence appears to have been destroyed. And there is no computing the number of interviews that newspapermen sought, and occasionally obtained. Their importunities would have been less unwelcome if they had confined themselves to matters relevant to their work, or if they had any results to show for the favours bestowed upon them. As it was, their correspondence must have been a constant source of irritation to the Castle.

(c) EXPENSE

Another source of worry to Peel in connection with the Irish press, was the need to justify the government's expenditure in the house of commons.

The subject came up in his first year of office in connection with the annual vote for the insertion of proclamations in the press. Henry Parnell opposed the usual grant of £10,500, on the grounds that it was used to corrupt the press, some of the papers owing their very existence to the proclamation fund. This could hardly be denied, and Peel was able to

[1] Aspinall, *Politics and the press*, pp. 488–9.

escape from an awkward position only by making the old point that the ministry of 'All the Talents', in which Parnell had served, had spent on them a still larger sum.[1]

The following day Sir John Newport took up Peel's challenge, saying that as chancellor of the exchequer for Ireland in 1806 he had been compelled to adopt the estimates of the previous government. Then— presumably in case somebody should ask him why he had not revised them in 1807—he went on to contend that a minister who has adopted a policy should not thereby be disqualified from arguing against it subsequently, in the light of 'ulterior information'. He now believed that the proclamations exercised a pernicious influence on the Irish press. In this he was supported by General Matthew, rising to accuse the government of depriving the *Clonmel Herald* of proclamations for its support of the opposition in the elections. The chancellor of the exchequer, whose contribution to the discussion had hitherto been negligible, seized his opportunity to steer away the debate into a discussion of the particular incident. From this, it was a short step to an exchange of personalities, the Speaker finally having to bind both general and chancellor to keep the peace, by which time the original subject of the debate had been forgotten.

Peel, however, took fright, writing off anxiously to Gregory asking for information to sustain him in argument, should the subject be broached again. Gregory replied: 'I will return answers to your queries to-morrow, but you have a bad parliamentary cause to defend, and the less you say the better'.[2] The information despatched consisted of an account of how the proclamations were distributed, what papers received them, and how much they were paid for the insertions. But 'what can you say', Gregory concluded in the letter which enclosed them, 'in defence of the system, except that your adversaries expended larger sums in the same way?'

When the vote became due the following year Peel was once more alarmed. Somebody had shown him a copy of the *Correspondent* for April 20 in which the public were belatedly notified that a levee to be held on April 14 was 'to be postponed'. 'Calm my fears', Peel asked Gregory;[3] but Gregory could only confirm them. On many occasions government papers printed proclamations after they were out of date— the *Chronicle* unkindly pointed out that the *Patriot* continued to print

---

[1] 12 Apr. 1813 (*Parl. deb.*, xxv. 791 ff.).
[2] Aspinall, article in *E.H.R.*, lvi. 271.
[3] B.M., Add. MSS (Peel) 40198 f. 153: 40286 f. 135.

certain temporary government regulations for the export of pig-iron months after they had ceased to operate.

In 1816, and again the following year, Peel wrote uneasily for comfort as the date of the vote on the estimates approached. 'Ministers have recommended the appointment of a committee to examine every item of our expenditure', he told Gregory in 1817, 'I tremble for the proclamations'.[1] Possibly the opposition were restrained from a more vigorous assault on the proclamations by the knowledge of their own acceptance of them when in office: or possibly they tired of reverting to a subject in which the same arguments, year after year, produced the same negative results. Whatever the reason, they did not assail the government on the proclamations with the force that Peel evidently expected, and feared. Nevertheless, the threat was always there: and it must have been particularly galling to Peel to realize that this expenditure, which was so difficult to defend, was so barren of advantage for the government.

*   *   *

Peel had proved that it was possible, given the resolution, for the government to rid itself of an opposition press, at a cost; but also that without the stimulus of opposition newspapers, the press as a whole became stagnant, unreadable, and offensive even to the government it professed to support.

As late as 1816, when the opposition press had all but disappeared, he told the house of commons that[2]

> among the other causes which had unquestionably contributed to produce the present disturbances and outrages, in Ireland might be reckoned the press of that country. . . . He was far from meaning to say that the benefits which resulted from a free press did not greatly, if not wholly, overbalance the evils of its abuse. He would even venture to assert that what might be called the extreme licentiousness of the press, in a former period of our history, mainly assisted in securing to us invaluable privileges. But what could be said in favour of a press which never sought to enlighten the public mind—which never aimed at the dissemination of truth—which never endeavoured to correct the morals or improve the happiness of the people? On the contrary, the most studious efforts were made to keep alive and foment discord, and the malignant influence of the worst passions of our nature.

Considering that the only opposition newspaper that had been published in Dublin for nearly two years previously had been the *Chronicle*,

[1] Parker, *Peel*, i. 211: Off. papers, 563/457/3.
[2] 26 Apr. 1816 (*Parl. deb.*, xxxiv. 35).

with its negligible circulation, this petulant outburst could only reflect on the government-controlled press. Peel had to take Cox's *Irish Magazine* as his example: 'until the present year it had had a wide circulation amongst the lower orders in Ireland . . . it was generally distributed gratis, or at least at a price so very much below what the mere cost of printing must be that it was evident profit was not considered, but only the accomplishment of the most pernicious and villainous purposes'. This was nonsense. The lower orders in Ireland could not read; nor could Cox have afforded to circulate his magazine below cost, unless he was in receipt of a subsidy from some undisclosed source, which is highly improbable. Besides, to ground any case against the Irish newspapers on what the *Freeman* called an 'example dug out of the entombed rubbish of Watty Cox's cabinet',[1] was absurd. Obviously Peel was angered not by the sins of the opposition, but by the incapacity of the government press.

That he realized his policy had been a failure, even though his mind was of that cast which refuses to admit such things to itself, is clear enough from his later correspondence,[2] in which he was to advise his successors against the methods he had himself used. Before he left, he wrote to Croker, 'A fortnight hence, I shall be as free as air . . . free from the acknowledgment of that gratitude which consists in a lively sense of future favours'.[3] Free from Giffard, and Grace, and Fitzsimons. His enemies had been vanquished; he was escaping from his friends.

[1] *Freeman*, 3 May 1816.
[2] Cf. p. 186.
[3] Parker, *Peel*, i. 116.

Chapter V. 1818–30

1. INTERLUDE, 1818–21

The structure Peel had built up did not immediately collapse on his departure. For the next three years the Irish press was to remain very much as he had left it, cowed and unenterprising. This stagnation was the reflection as much of inertia as of government supervision, because the chief secretary, Charles Grant, had the reputation of being liberal. He lived up to it sufficiently for Gregory, who stayed on as under secretary, to speculate mournfully on the possibility, if Grant gave any more encouragement to the Papists, of the spectacle of the Elevation of the Host in the streets before a year was out.[1] But Grant's conciliatory ideas were spoiled by a constitutional indolence, and he left dealings with the press in the hands of Gregory, under whom they were carried on as before. In 1820, a literary magazine which had made its appearance in Dublin could lament that few newspapers were published in the capital: 'Our opinions like our presses have been proscribed, and we must import them like other foreign luxuries, or be content to remain in ignorance and apathy.'[2]

Nevertheless, there were soon to be signs that a policy such as Peel's could only be maintained while a Peel was there to enforce it. One was the appearance in 1821 of a Catholic newspaper, the *Dublin Evening Herald*. It was brought out by Michael Staunton, who during the Peel administration had been editor of the *Freeman*. Soon after Peel left he had founded a weekly which had attained a substantial circulation; and its popularity persuaded him that there must be an opening for a Catholic evening paper. There were slight signs, too, of a revival in the spirit of the existing newspapers. The three confessedly government papers began to squabble among themselves, which gave the *Evening Post* the chance to justify its rather faded boast of independence by disparaging

[1] *Mr. Gregory's letter-box*, p. 118.
[2] The *Dublin Magazine*, quoted in the *Irish Monthly Magazine*, 1832, i. 124.

all three of them. The *Patriot*, it appeared, had spoken of the 'disgusting scurrility' of the *Hibernian Journal*, and the 'stupid balderdash' of the *Correspondent*; and the *Post* promised to keep its readers informed of the course of the contest 'as it is very likely that he never sees any of these papers'.[1] Thereafter the *Post* concentrated its attacks upon the *Hibernian Journal* until, to the *Post's* malicious delight, the Fitzsimons' ceased publication the following summer.

That one of the government newspapers should have been allowed to disappear was in itself significant. Peel had often threatened to withdraw support from them, and he had been profoundly irritated by the Fitzsimons': but he had never put his threats into effect, and the *Hibernian Journal* had not changed its ways. When Giffard retired Edward Fitzsimons, himself a prominent Orange functionary, made his paper the champion of the Orange cause, and filled it with such abuse of the Catholics, that Grant had to complain to Gregory: 'I really think such words coming from a paper notoriously paid by government, when one of the members of that government is known to be of the opinions thus attacked are likely, if allowed to continue, to lower in the public view, not only the respectability of that individual, but also the character of the government itself'. Gregory replied that he had told the editor to avoid personalities in future; but the tone of his letter suggests that he had more sympathy with Fitzsimons than with Grant.[2]

His instructions had little effect upon the *Hibernian Journal*, which continued in its Orange ways, to the extent of opposing the king's visit in 1821. It warned that if the projected Catholic Relief Bill went through and received the king's signature, the Irish Protestants could not be held answerable for their actions. This was too much for the Castle to stomach. In June 1821 the *Hibernian Journal* was denounced in the house of commons, and Grant took the opportunity offered by the adverse publicity to tell the proprietor that the government could not continue to subsidize his paper.[3] Fulfilling the *Evening Post's* prophecy that it could not survive without the government's financial support, the *Hibernian Journal* ceased publication within a week. Its editor continued to plague the Castle with letters until he extracted a pension of £100 a year.[4]

Although the total withdrawal of the *Hibernian Journal's* subsidy was an exceptional measure, the government had, in fact, embarked upon a general reduction of expenditure upon the press. When, in

[1] *D.E. Post*, 27 July 1820.
[2] *Mr. Gregory's letter-box*, pp. 121, 129.
[3] Aspinall, *Politics and the press*, p. 419: *Parl. deb.*, N.S., v. 1446.
[4] Off. papers, 582/444/925.

1821, opposition speakers in the house of commons began once more to pursue this line of inquiry, which had so worried Peel, Grant was able to reply that the amount spent on publishing the proclamations had been reduced to £9,000 by 1820, and to £7,000 the following year. The information did not prevent the radical, Joseph Hume, from denouncing the whole system of proclamations as government bribery. Grant could only reply that he was not well acquainted with the methods by which the government's advertising was distributed.[1] Further consideration of the problem was deferred until the following financial year. By that time the administration in Ireland had changed, and the subject was for a while forgotten.

2. THE REVIVAL OF THE INDEPENDENT NEWSPAPERS

(i) *Catholic newspapers*

The growing independence of the neutral press, the collapse of the *Hibernian Journal*, and the reduction of the proclamation fund, reflected the growth of a more conciliatory government attitude. The trend away from Peel's policy was accelerated by the king's visit in the summer of 1821. The king could not have failed to notice that his most ardent acclaimers were the Catholics and O'Connell—the Orangemen, by contrast, were inclined to be suspicious. A few weeks later, the liberal element at the Castle was reinforced by a far stronger acquisition than the ineffectual Grant, when Talbot was replaced as lord lieutenant by the marquis of Wellesley, the duke of Wellington's elder brother, whose distinguished career as governor-general of India, coupled with his brother's reputation would, it was hoped, be enough to overawe the extremists on both sides. He immediately disclaimed any intention of making radical changes; his aim, he said, was to administer, and not to alter the laws. His views, however—reflected in such changes as the appointment of Plunket, who had introduced a bill into parliament to remove Catholic disabilities, as attorney general in place of Saurin—were enough to make the ascendancy hostile.

No startling change took place for some months. Catholic newspapers could appear without fear of a prosecution awaiting their first false step; but they found it hard to attract enough readers to make

[1] 28 June 1821 (Parl. deb., N.S., v. 1446).

them viable commercially. Heavy taxation still retarded the growth of the Irish press, by keeping the cost of newspapers so high that only the well-to-do bought them. Coffee-houses existed where less affluent citizens could read their papers—Spadacini's in Dublin was advertising that the *Evening Post*, the *Morning Post*, the *Freeman*, *Saunders'*, the *Weekly Register*, *Correspondent*, *Patriot*, and *Evening Herald* were all obtainable;[1] but a coffee-house circulation was not sufficient to ensure solvency.

Staunton's *Evening Herald* did not thrive. Lord Cloncurry was a subscriber and occasionally wrote letters to the editor; but he found it 'too full of long, drawling, priest-ridden stuff to do any real good'.[2] About 300 copies of each issue were sold in the early stages of the paper's career; the number dwindled to less than 200 in 1822,[3] and the following year it ceased publication. Staunton's *Weekly Register* was, however, still obtaining support; and this encouraged him to try his luck with a morning paper of the same name. It lasted three weeks. The following year Staunton tried again. This time the *Morning Register* caught on. The number of subscribers was small, around 500 in 1825;[4] but Staunton managed to attract more advertisements than the circulation would appear to have warranted; and the *Morning Register* gradually took its place as the equal, in influence if not in circulation, of any of the old-established dailies.

Accusations were immediately made that the paper was run by O'Connell, owned by the Catholic Association, and subsidized by the 'Catholic rent'. 'A large portion of the Catholic rent, being allocated to the support of the liberal press', one newspaper correspondent wrote, 'it becomes a matter of some interest, to those who have subscribed to that fund, to ascertain the nature of the publications which are to be printed and circulated at our expense'.[5] There was some ground for this belief. Conway, the editor of the *Dublin Evening Post*, was prominent in the association; for a time he was its secretary. The association had adopted in principle a resolution that the rent should be used, among other things, 'to encourage and support a liberal and enlightened press, as well in Dublin as in London'; and O'Connell urged that £15,000 a year should be spent on the press. The rent, however, was only sparingly

---

[1] Ad. in *D.E. Post*, 7 Aug. 1821.
[2] *Lady Morgan, memoirs*, ii. 197.
[3] *Parl. papers*, 1826 (235) xxiii. 383.
[4] Ibid.
[5] *Proceedings of the Catholic Association*, p. 446: *Dublin Evening Express*, 28 Apr. 1824.

used for this purpose in Ireland. The association numbered in its ranks members who viewed any attempt to influence the press with suspicion. For example, a motion to discontinue the subscription to the hostile *Dublin Evening Mail* was opposed by one speaker who praised the paper's readability, while disapproving of its principles. O'Connell's proposed expenditure was whittled down to no more than a routine payment for insertions and advertisements; no subsidy was given. The association's accounts show an outlay of only £75 for the first few months of the association's existence, divided between seven Dublin newspapers, and the accusations heard that the association owed upwards of £1,000 to certain newspapers were explained away by O'Connell as debts contracted years before by the Catholic Board.[1] Otherwise, the only direct advantage accruing to any of the Catholic newspapers was the purchase of copies for the association rooms. Even this practice was opposed, a member urging the discontinuance of the subscription to the *Freeman* and the *Evening Post*, on the grounds that their purchase caused jealousy among other friendly newspapers, and that the fund might more profitably be spent on other purposes. The rent accounts of the period were open to inspection, and it seems clear that the Catholic rent was not, in fact, used to subsidize the Catholic press.[2]

The *Morning Register*, as a newspaper which was at once respectable, spirited, and commercially sound, was a distinct asset to the Catholic cause. Before its appearance a liberal periodical, in an article on the power of the press, had been compelled sadly to admit that, although the Orange press was full of vigour, 'a sort of indefinable apathy pervades, at the present juncture, all the liberal papers'.[3] That this apathy was dispelled and the Catholics given a daily tonic to sustain them in their quest for Emancipation, was the work of Staunton. And in his insistence upon the substitution of reports of events at home instead of the old unedited despatches from abroad, he was soon to diffuse his influences till further, helping to alter the face of Irish newspapers. This was achieved by the employment of a corps of reporters, after the London model. Up to that time reporting staffs had been virtually non-existent in Ireland; but all the Dublin newspapers had to follow Staunton's lead, or risk losing their customers. He also strove to give the press a consciousness of its dignity. On the royal visit to Dublin in 1821, when the

---

[1] Aspinall, *Politics and the press*, pp. 320–2: *Proceedings of the Catholic Association*, p. 432.

[2] *Proceedings of the Catholic Association*, p. 419: Cf. *Lady Morgan, memoirs*, ii. 197: Off. papers 588/444/925: *M. Register*, 17 June 1825.

[3] *New Monthly Magazine*, October 1822.

king was being shown over the premises of the Dublin Society, tickets were sent to the newspapers which only gave their representatives access to the street outside. Staunton immediately complained that no gentleman of the press could be expected to subject himself 'to this inconvenience and, indeed, indignity'. The omission was hastily rectified, but the *Herald* refused to report the occasion.[1] An 'illuminated address' is rarely a trustworthy source of information: but the one presented to Staunton on his election as lord mayor of Dublin, many years later, probably gives him no more than his due, as 'the man who, if he be not the father by right of years, does yet, so far as its efficiency is concerned, deserve the title of CREATOR OF THE IRISH PRESS'.[2]

(ii) *Protestant newspapers*

The limited number of Catholics who could afford to become subscribers to Catholic newspapers deprived them of the chance to exercise much influence: if the Irish press was to reassert its independence, a Protestant paper would have to be the medium. For a while it had looked as if it might be the *Patriot*. That it was able to win a substantial circulation without antagonizing the Castle must be attributed to the personality of Joseph Timothy Haydn, who had stepped into the editorial chair when Comerford was drowned. From a negligible circulation in 1818, the *Patriot* under his control had four years later obtained the largest number of subscribers of any paper in the land. He managed to extract the official figures from the stamp office as proof, provoking a rebuke from the *Evening Post* for publishing them: 'while they answer as puffs to the papers in great circulation . . . they are calculated to disclose the condition of the struggling but, perhaps, more meritorious prints'.[3] The *Evening Post* further expressed its sorrow that the *Patriot* should have chosen a time to boast when the whole Dublin press was at last in harmony (except for the Orangemen) in supporting Wellesley. The *Patriot* had, in fact, no serious opposition rival with which to contend. Nevertheless, Haydn must have worked hard for his paper's success. It was better printed and more attractively presented than the *Evening Post*, and it contained such features as Elia's dissertation upon roast pig, reprinted from a London magazine. For a government paper this was unusually enterprising; and Haydn made no secret of its govern-

---

[1] 28 July 1821.
[2] The address is preserved in the Dublin City Hall.
[3] Aspinall, *Politics and the press*, p. 120.

ment connection. When Hume criticized the subsidized Irish press in the commons, the *Patriot* inquired why the government should not be allowed a newspaper, if whigs and radicals could have them.[1]

Haydn, however, appears to have realized that the *Patriot's* good fortune could not last. Sooner or later it would have to decide whether to accept the lord lieutenant's liberal ideas, or to cater for the nervous Protestantism of the bulk of its subscribers. During 1822 the paper's policy grew more Orange in hue. Possibly Haydn resigned because he realized the Castle would not tolerate this attitude; possibly he was removed for expressing his opinions too freely. That winter he and the *Patriot* parted company.

Wellesley's conciliatory views hardly extended beyond the desire to curb the more extreme Orangemen, and to distribute government patronage more fairly, instead of continuing the old Protestant monopoly. The effect on the ascendancy was described a few years later:[2]

> Moderate, however, as these views were, they could not be acted upon without indirectly limiting the influence of a party in Ireland who were jealous of a monopoly they had long enjoyed, not only of a principal part of the patronage, but also of the *ear* of the Irish government. Their long possession of the exclusive confidence of government had enabled them to keep all other parties aloof from the Castle, and to represent themselves and their friends as the only persons who could safely be employed in places of trust and emolument, or who could safely be relied upon for correct information regarding the state of the country. . . . The underlings in office, who were all indebted to this party for their situations, were devoted to its interests and were constantly on the alert to watch and impede any change of system, and Lord Wellesley has uniformly experienced their secret and unremitting opposition and counteraction in every department. It was chiefly by their means that the press was turned against him. Of two newspapers in the pay of government, one espoused Lord Wellesley's policy upon his arrival in Ireland, and it was immediately rejected by every individual connected with that party. The advertisements of all the departments under government were withdrawn from it, and the consequence has been ruinous to the proprietor. A new paper called the *Dublin Evening Mail* was established by this party for the professed object of defending the Protestant ascendancy, but really for the purpose of writing down Lord Wellesley's government, and not a single number of that paper has been published without a personal attack upon his private or public conduct.

The *Dublin Evening Mail*, which appeared for the first time in February 1823, was edited by Haydn. The first number was innocuous. Its editor was compelled for a few days to have his paper printed by

---

[1] *Patriot*, 11 May, 10 Aug. 1822.
[2] Col. M. Shawe to Sir W. Knighton, 18 Sept. 1827 (*George IV correspondence*, letter 1407).

Richard Lonergan.[1] the owner of *Carrick's Morning Post*, whose neutrality was being cast off in exchange for a more Catholic and liberal policy. At first, therefore, Haydn may not have felt sure of his ground; but within a few weeks the *Mail* had unmasked itself as scurrilously anti-Wellesley and anti-Catholic.

Haydn was erratic and unscrupulous, but he knew how to attract attention. Nothing had been seen in Dublin like his newspaper since the days of the *Volunteer's Journal*. It was filled with cartoons, scandalous squibs, and contentious editorials, which kept Haydn continually in trouble. At one time he boasted of having four affairs of honour on his hands in ten days, one of them with Henry Grattan, Jr.; at another, he was horsewhipped by the lord lieutenant's A.D.C.[2] The publicity had the desired effect. Within a year of its foundation the *Evening Mail* had a circulation nearly three times as large as any other Dublin newspaper.[3]

The peculiarity of the *Evening Mail* was that it was anti-Catholic, whereas the most successful newspapers in the past, the *Northern Star*, the *Press*, and the *Dublin Evening Post*, had been well-disposed to Catholic claims. The reason for the change was that the Protestants had become aware of the precariousness of their position, should the huge and growing Catholic majority attain any power. While the Catholics remained helots, it was easy enough for a Protestant to feel sorry for them, and to join an organization pledged to assist them, in the same charitable spirit as he contributed to the society for sick and indigent roomkeepers. But he wanted to help the Catholics on his own terms. As soon as O'Connell and his followers began to make claims of their own —or when the British government sent over a Fitzwilliam or a Wellesley —he could be stampeded by the cry of 'Popery!'

Offensive though Haydn's methods were, they had the beneficial effect of awakening the Irish press. Haydn, as a former editor of the *Patriot*, knew the inner story of the Castle press. He took a particular pleasure in denouncing his former benefactors, 'Old Corbet' of the *Patriot*, and Lonergan of the *Morning Post*. Watty Cox, who had returned once more to Ireland, published extracts[4] from the slanging match which arose between Haydn and Lonergan; they might have been the source from which Dickens took his editorials for the *Eatanswill Gazette* and *Independent*. 'We have, as far as we have gone, shown this

---

[1] W. Cox, *Bella, horrida bella* (P) 1823, p. 23.
[2] *D.E. Mail*, 14 July 1823.
[3] *Parl. papers*, 1826 (235) xxiii. 383.
[4] W. Cox, *Bella, horrida bella*; the war began with an article in the *Mail* on 28 July 1823, and continued for a fortnight.

imbecile, yet obnoxious reptile, to be a calumniator and a coward,' wrote Haydn, 'we must now prove him to be a LIAR.' Lonergan replied by calling Haydn a 'desperate madman', and 'a hangman-headed dog'. Lonergan was easily able to prove that Haydn's calumnies were false; but the *Mail's* readers probably never saw his vindication, as the *Morning Post's* circulation was small.

The owners of the *Mail* soon became aware that the substantial profits they were making were in danger of being dissipated by Haydn's impetuosity. If their account is to be believed, his indiscretions cost the paper thousands of pounds in settling actions out of court, and they could never be certain when the paper would contain a libel that could not be thus settled—the following year £300 damages were to be awarded against them, long after Haydn had been removed from his post.[1] Haydn was bought out, apparently for a substantial sum, and the *Mail* settled down into prosperous respectability. Not that its basic policy was changed—a typical *Mail* jibe was the parody of the viceregal levee announcement:[2]

Private Chaplain's Office, Phoenix Park: Feb. 17, 1826. There will be a Rosary at the Lodge on the evening of Monday the 20th inst. The ladies and gentlemen who attend are requested to bring their own beads.

—but the proprietors boasted that they had stopped personalities, and began to pride themselves on the *Mail's* credit, consequence, and character.

Haydn had promised the owners of the *Mail* that he would not edit any other Dublin paper in the *Mail's* lifetime. Accordingly, he set up the *Dublin Morning Star* in February 1824 with an employee as nominal editor. In the *Star* he carried on his early *Mail* methods, with still greater irresponsibility. The first number contained what purported to be an historical account of Lord Wharton, who had been viceroy over a century before. It was obviously directed against Wellesley, the passages meant to be particularly applicable to him being put in capitals:

HE TREATED THE CLERGY OF THE ESTABLISHED RELIGION WITH CONTEMPT!

and

HE VIOLATED PUBLIC DECENCY BY HIS LOW AMOURS!

The attorney general had no option but to begin proceedings. Confident

[1] *D.E. Mail*, 29 July, 23 Nov. 1825.
[2] Quoted in *O'Connell correspondence*, i. 88.

of securing a well-disposed jury, Haydn retaliated with further libels, including a cartoon of Wellesley receiving a present of some headgear from a donkey:

> Excuse me, friend, I fear I cannot bear it
> Pshaw! If the cap don't fit, you need not wear it!

One day the *Star* would boast that the attorney general had been compelled to abandon all outstanding prosecutions against the paper: the next, that he had initiated new ones.[1] Probably the attorney general's hesitancy came from a desire to catch Haydn, rather than the nominal owner, Johnston. In the end both were brought up, charged with the 'Wharton' libel in the paper's first number. Haydn had since become sole proprietor of the *Star*: but the attorney general sought to prove that he had been the real editor from the start. He went to great pains to demonstrate the libellous nature of the article. O'Connell, who defended Haydn, took the chance to put forward the ingenious plea that if the prosecution had to spend so long in proving an article libellous, it was obviously not *very* libellous. The jury disagreed amongst themselves and had to be discharged.[2]

The government's inability to secure the conviction of the *Star* was only one of a number of instances where juries drawn from the ascendancy refused to give a verdict for the crown. The appointment of Plunket as attorney general, more than any other action that Wellesley had taken had frightened the ascendancy, who avenged themselves, in their capacity as jurymen, by refusing to admit the guilt even of such palpable libels as those in the *Star*. Ugly as was this reflection of the ascendancy's control of the courts, it was not without usefulness to the press; by the creation of a dividing line between executive and judiciary it broke for a time the government's hold. The ascendancy had no respect for the doctrine of the freedom of the press, but their hatred of Wellesley and Plunket helped indirectly to restore it.

At first, the *Star* appears to have made the same impact as the *Mail* had a year before. Advertisements flowed in, filling nearly half the paper in some issues, and a prospectus was soon issued announcing an associated *Evening Star*—which was to be the only daily evening paper in Dublin. A *Sunday Star* was contemplated. Haydn made no secret of his connection with the new papers, and it was his lack of balance that was to be their undoing. Where he published libels on individuals rather than on the government, he could not be certain of the jury's sympathy.

[1] *Star*, 9–28 Feb. 1824.
[2] *D.M. Post*, 26 Jan. 1825.

A reference to a citizen as 'a branded spy, a hideous informer, and a foul and blackened reprobate' cost Haydn £300 in the summer of 1824. The verdict was subsequently set aside on a technicality, but this was only one of sixteen actions that had been taken against the *Star* by the end of November,[1] some of which, it may be presumed, had to be settled out of court. Others were still pending. In one of them a verdict was found against Haydn for £50. The same plaintiff was awarded £300 in an action against the other proprietor, Johnston, who became a bankrupt and, when he applied for his discharge, received instead a sentence of a year's imprisonment and a reprimand for going into partnership with Haydn, in view of Haydn's known self-denying compact with the *Mail*.[2]

The *Star's* book-keeper in this trial said that his duty was to enter profits, but there were none. The inference was omnious; and the *Morning Register*, a few days later, reported the 'threatened conversion of the *Star*', quoting paragraphs from it about friends' ingratitude and supporters' desertion.[3] Whines of this nature were the common symptom of a newspaper's impending dissolution. A fresh attempt was made to set up a daily *Evening Star* in the place of the morning paper, but the project failed, and the *Star* disappeared. Actions against its proprietors continued to be heard in the courts: £600 damages were awarded against Haydn soon afterwards in a civil suit at Kilkenny.[4]

(iii) *Expansion*

By the time of the *Star's* disappearance, however, the revival in the independent press had spread. At one period in 1824, twelve metropolitan newspapers were in being—excluding weeklies, which also established themselves in public favour at this time. Staunton's *Register* was joined in 1821 by an Orange weekly, the *Warder*, the name of H. B. Code appearing once again in journalism as its proprietor. Code for many years had continued indirectly to serve for the government; one of his stage works was filled with jingo clap-trap which irritated Tom Moore into rejoicing over the brief run of so 'pestilently bad' a play.[5] While the ascendancy thought itself secure, the *Warder* was not a success; Code had to suspend publication and when he tried again the fol-

[1] *Star*, 19 Aug., Nov.–Dec. 1824.
[2] *D.M. Post*, 23 May 1825.
[3] *Star*, 10 June 1825.
[4] *D.M. Post*, 13 Aug. 1825.
[5] *Moore memoirs*, i. 305.

lowing year, the response was still unenthusiastic. He wrote to Peel for assistance, giving as his reasons that the *Warder* was the only paper of its kind which the government did not support, and that Peel's 'exalted purity and consistency' would not allow him to fail a man with a family of eight children.[1] Fortunately, as it happened, for the *Warder*, Peel refused help. The newspaper was left free to take up the Orange cause, which in a few months' time was to bring it a settled circulation of nearly 1,000 readers, in spite of the competition of a rival Orange weekly the *Antidote*, which appeared in the winter of 1822. By emancipation year the *Warder* had acquired over 2,000 subscribers and although the *Antidote* had disappeared, its place had been taken by another weekly, the *Star of Brunswick*. These papers were bigoted—the *Warder* on at least one occasion was besieged by an angry Catholic mob, as a result[2] —but, like the *Dublin Evening Mail*, whose popularity continued to rise until its circulation in 1829 reached almost 3,000,[3] their liveliness was at least in contrast to the dullness of their predecessors.

On the other wing, Staunton's *Weekly Register* continued to thrive; and although the *Morning Register's* circulation grew painfully slowly, it nevertheless grew, each year. *Argus*, a weekly whose prospectus promised support to Catholic claims, ran for a while in the middle 'twenties; so did an *Irishman*. And after the *Patriot* had for a second time turned its coat in 1828, its place in the Catholic ranks was promptly taken by another evening paper which was soon to make a reputation for itself— the *Pilot*.

The old-established commercial morning papers suffered from the growing competition. *Saunders' News-Letter* managed to increase its circulation by maintaining its traditional practice of avoiding controversy about—and if possible, reference to—Irish affairs, and concentrating upon advertisements. But the *Freeman* and the *Morning Post*, both of which tried to advocate Catholic claims without committing themselves to unqualified support for the Catholic Association, found that this policy only resulted in condemnation by both sides. The *Morning Register* and the *Evening Mail* joined in disparaging them. The *Morning Post's* circulation had been about 750 in 1821; by 1828 it had been halved. The *Freeman's* circulation fell away even more disastrously, but it had more subscribers to lose. The *Evening Post* unkindly drew attention to its difficulties by referring to it as a paper 'of which the public has for some time lost sight'. An evening paper which Lonergan ven-

[1] B.M., Add. MS (Peel) 40348 f. 10.
[2] *Warder*, 8 Nov. 1828.
[3] *Parl. papers*, 1826 (235) xxiii. 383: 1829 (164) xxii. 273: 1830 (408) xxv. 306.

tured to bring out in 1824, fared no better; the *Dublin Evening Express's* moderate advocacy of Catholic claims attracted so little support that the paper was discontinued after a few weeks.

The *Evening Post* managed to maintain its circulation. F. W. Conway, its editor, drew a state pension, and co-operated with the government;[1] and he came into conflict with the Catholic Association, of which he had been for a time secretary. He nevertheless retained some independence, serving the growing class of Castle Catholics who, though anxious to obtain the benefits of emancipation, had no liking for O'Connell and his ways. Conway often criticized O'Connell; but when the Wellington government urged him to range the *Post* against emancipation, his reply was: 'I do not think the *Evening Post* could sustain the great popularity it has attained if I could bring myself to act the ungrateful and dishonest part of endeavouring to thwart the progress of a measure for which I have all my life been contending.'[2]

In general, however, the Irish press bore out the common view that a neutral paper was impossible to maintain; the public appetite was for controversy. Even when contention drifted towards scurrility, the heat engendered had its uses. Lonergan, complaining of 'the elaborate villainy marked by the woodcuts'[3] in Haydn's *Evening Mail,* had to admit that they were 'a new feature in newspaper warfare'—new, that is to the generation that had grown up since the Union. The general improvement in the appearance of the newspapers in the 'twenties, their print, and their layout, was most marked. Newspapers began to take a pride in their appearance and achievements: the *Morning Register,* on one occasion, proudly claimed that two 'slight young men' had printed an average of 530 sheets in an hour one afternoon, exceptionally quick work for the time.[4] The employment of reporters after the London model gave new life to the papers, which became much more readable. The *Register* set a new standard of reporting home news of interest—particularly the debates of the Catholic Association—which the other papers were compelled to follow. The extent to which the improvement in the standards of the newspapers resulted in any increase in their influence is, unfortunately, difficult to judge. The lack of enthusiasm of the newspapers for O'Connell, a feeling which he reciprocated, meant that they had little decisive effect on the emancipation campaign; but

[1] B.M., Add. MSS (Peel) 40334 ff. 237, 246.
[2] Conway to Gregory, 29 Mar. 1829 (B.M., Add. MS (Peel) 40399 f. 110).
For further details of Conway's career, see Madden (I.P.L.) MS 269.
[3] *D.M. Post,* 30 July 1823.
[4] 7 Dec. 1824.

Wyse, the historian of the Catholic Association, considered that they were of importance in the movement's early days.

Haydn and Staunton, pursuing their very different paths, had contrived to alter irrevocably the character of the Dublin press. Staunton's work was the more durable; Haydn's the more spectacular. Haydn, later to attain distinction as the compiler of the dictionary of dates, was at that stage of his career a gutter journalist; but this was largely the irresponsibility of the adolescent who has extorted his independence from nervous guardians, whose half-hearted attempts to impose their restrictions only excite to wilder excesses. For all the hysterical bigotry, the Eatanswill invective, and the slimy personalities, Haydn's newspapers had an enviable vitality which, by goading rivals into retaliation, went a long way towards reanimating the moribund metropolitan press. A writer in a contemporary magazine could justifiably assert that the chain of silence which had bound Ireland body and soul had at last been burst asunder, and 'the affairs of that country may now be said to occupy exclusively the public mind'.[1]

3. THE DECLINE OF THE CASTLE PRESS

(i) *Symptoms*

Evidence of the changes brought about by the new journalism can be obtained from the circulation figures of the newspapers, which were published by order of the house of commons in 1826.[2]

The figures actually produced represented the number of government stamps sold to each paper each year, totals which were misleading without reference to the number of issues a week. Converted into approximately the average number of copies sold in each issue, they show that in 1821 the *Dublin Evening Post* had the largest circulation; but this had sunk to little more than 1,500. Of the confessedly Castle papers, the *Patriot* had 1,400 readers, the *Correspondent*, 600: the *Dublin Journal*, 300, and the *Hibernian Journal*, barely 100.

The following year, the first of Wellesley's viceroyalty, saw little change. The *Patriot* gained some readers, but the *Correspondent* lost more: the *Dublin Journal* was declining, and the *Hibernian Journal* had disappeared. In 1823 the appearance of the *Dublin Evening Mail* altered the situation. Its circulation promptly rose to the 2,500 mark, at the expense of the Castle press. The *Dublin Journal's* circulation sank to

[1] *Dublin and London Magazine*, March 1825.
[2] *Parl. papers*, 1826 (235), xxiii. 383.

about 160, and the *Patriot* lost a third of its subscribers. Thereafter, the government papers continued to decline. By 1826 the *Dublin Journal* had ceased publication, and the *Correspondent* and the *Patriot* could barely muster a four-figure circulation between them; the *Mail* had a higher circulation than ever.

At the same time, the Castle newspapers were finding it more difficult to obtain the subsidies upon which they relied for their survival. The commons' request for the circulation figures in 1826 had been made in order that they could be compared with the amounts paid to the individual newspapers for the insertion of proclamations; these, too, were printed for each year back to 1821. At that time the *Patriot* was in receipt of £975; the *Correspondent*, £511; the *Hibernian Journal*, £388; and the *Dublin Journal*, £280. *Saunders'* had £314; the other newspapers —apart from the *Morning Post*, which received £24—nothing. The total expenditure on the Castle press in Dublin was about £2,500, the rest of the proclamation money, which totalled £7,000 that year, going to the provincial papers. By 1826 the proclamation fund had been reduced to £6,000, largely at the expense of the Dublin press, which received only £1,750. Quarterly accounts furnished to the Castle by their official in charge of the of proclamations had already shown that the government were perturbed about the amount they were spending. He took pains to draw the Castle's attention to economies; clearly he was under pressure from the government to justify his expenditure. An enclosure with one account endeavours to prove that proclamations were not inserted too often, or to no purpose.[1] The proclamation fund was at last being effectively reduced.

The amount of money that was being paid out to journalists and newspaper owners from the secret service funds was also dwindling.[2] In 1817, the *Correspondent's* proprietors received over £800, and the *Patriot's*, £700. In 1821 the corresponding figures were £600 and £380. Giffard's death and the disappearance of the *Hibernian Journal* further reduced the secret service expenditure. The return of sums paid to newspapers for the insertion of government advertisements had also shown a reduction, from £1,873 in 1816, to £1077 in 1821.[3] As the bulk of this departmental advertising went to the government newspapers they were the losers by its diminution.

The publication in 1826 of the circulation figures for all the Irish

[1] Off. papers, 579/527/20, 588a/560/4
[2] I.S.P.O., Secret service account books: Aspinall, *Politics and the press*, pp. 119–20.
[3] *Parl. papers*, 1822 (588) xviii. 465.

newspapers, immediately followed by publication of the amounts those newspapers received from the proclamation fund, accelerated the disintegration of the subsidy system. Opposition speakers had been condemning it for forty years, reiterating the complaint that the proclamations went to newspapers that hardly anybody read: but they had always lacked conclusive proof. The proof was now there for all to see that in Dublin in—say—1821 the *Evening Post* and the *Freeman*, which between them had about 3,000 regular subscribers, had no proclamations, while the *Athlone Journal*, which only contrived to sell a total of 2,000 copies in a whole year, had over £150 worth.[1]

The publication of the statistics was the work of Joseph Hume. In the commons that April[2] he stated the case against them once again, basing it on the statistics, and demonstrating with their assistance that the proclamations could not possibly be published with the design that they should reach the public: they existed simply as a means by which the government could control the press. Goulburn, who had succeeded Grant as chief secretary, made the best defence he could. The proclamation fund, he was able to show, had been substantially reduced; as for the way in which it was distributed, he claimed to have better things to do than waste time over such details. He pleaded ignorance of Dublin newspapers' politics, pretending not to know which were friendly and which were unfriendly to the government—a plea that his correspondence disproves. A better point he made was that the press attacks on him showed that considerable freedom of opinion must now exist. Other government speakers were less subtle. One of them—ignorant, apparently, of the published figures—claimed a big circulation for the *Correspondent*, and ingeniously argued that the proclamations ought always to be printed in the same newspapers, regardless of circulation, so that the public would know where to find them. But no amount of sophistry could be effective against the bleak evidence Hume had provided.

No doubt, if the Castle newspapers had been giving good service, their masters would have been more careful to see that these secrets were preserved. But the government were, as always, dissatisfied with their press.

The number of Castle newspapers had by 1826 been reduced to two, the *Patriot* and the *Correspondent*. The *Dublin Journal* had at last disappeared, another victim of the fate that overtook subsidized papers for which the government ceased to accept full responsibility. Giffard's

[1] Aspinall, in *E.H.R.*, Oct. 1841.
[2] *Parl. deb.*, N.S., xv. 539 ff.

lease had been terminated ten years before, at a time when the *Dublin Journal's* circulation had sunk almost to nothing.[1] Under its new owners it showed for a while signs of revival. They were boasting of a substantial acquisition of new subscribers a year after Giffard's departure; and in 1818, they claimed the highest circulation of any Irish newspaper, except the *Evening Post*. Increased advertisements suggest that the paper did, in fact, begin to enjoy a more extensive circulation. But the revival was caused less by any real improvement in the *Dublin Journal* than by the feebleness of its rivals. 'The only difference', the *Freeman's Journal* noted,[2] 'we can discover between the lucubrations of its present manager and those of Mr Giffard is that in the latter, in spite of their bad taste, their folly, and their virulence, there were occasionally discoverable glimpses of intellect'. The *Freeman* was not an impartial critic: nor was the *Evening Post*, which later followed its example and lampooned the new *Dublin Journal* as 'Sergeant Eitherside'; but their instinct was sound. The *Dublin Journal* was trying to have it both ways, to show a patriotic face to the public and a loyal face to the Castle. Although this might succeed for a while, it was a policy requiring greater talent than was purchaseable by newspaper owners of the day, if it was to be kept up indefinitely. As the *Post* had warned, the Castle would not long tolerate wavering, and the *Dublin Journal* soon lost its patriotic veneer, and its circulation. From about 650 copies a day in 1821, its circulation fell away to less than half that number in 1824,[3] and the following year it ceased to exist.

The *Dublin Journal* had been the oldest established newspaper in Ireland, and for all the ugly reputation that it had picked up for intemperance and bigotry, enough goodwill was expected to remain attached to the name for the owners of the *Irish Times*, which had been started a few months before, to announce that they had bought the interest of the paper from the Faulkners. For some weeks their paper appeared as '*The Irish Times*, to which will shortly be added the title of *Dublin Journal*'. Finding that this combination did not produce the desired results, the owners switched again, in July, to a new title—the *Morning Courier and Dublin Journal*. If the *Evening Mail* could do so well, there obviously should have been an opening for a well-conducted Protestant morning daily. Its circulation, however, to judge by the few advertisements carried, remained small: and the owners, trying to cut their losses by

---

[1] B.M., Add. MS (Peel) 40259 f. 156.
[2] *Freeman*, 3 July 1817.
[3] *Parl. papers*, 1826 (235) xxiii. 383.

internal economies, only succeeded in provoking a strike,[1] which the paper did not long survive.

In the last number the owners expressed regret that their hope that *one* Protestant daily paper might be sustained by the public had not been fulfilled. 'We cannot any longer conceal the fact that ever since the resuscitation of this journal we have been carrying it on at a ruinous loss'. Without the promise of immediate and effective support, they said, the *Courier* would have to be given up.[2] The support was not forthcoming.

The two surviving government newspapers had found it convenient, by 1826, each to reflect one side of the dual personality from which the administration suffered during Wellesley's viceroyalty. The *Correspondent* remained Protestant; the *Patriot*, after Haydn's departure for the *Mail*, was converted to a pro-Catholic policy.

The Catholics welcomed the new recruit, to the extent of sending him a few pounds worth of association advertising; otherwise the *Patriot's* conversion met with little favour. Haydn bitterly assailed his old paper, giving what purported to be accurate accounts of the sums expended on it annually by government,[3] and unearthing the embarrassing information that his successor as editor, Thomas Burke, was also the publisher of some squibs against the administration—which Burke could not deny. By this time the chief secretary, Goulburn, had himself lost patience with the *Patriot*; he actually wrote to the *Mail* to deny that the *Patriot* was a Castle paper.[4] A month later, he confessed to Peel that the conduct of the *Patriot* was something about which he was ashamed of himself; he was going to keep an eye on it, in future.[5]

The *Patriot* mended its ways for a time, and retained its subsidies: but in 1826 it was in trouble again. The administration in England was no less split than its representatives in Ireland on the Catholic question; and the *Patriot's* Catholic sympathies, though they might not worry Wellesley, profoundly irritated Peel, to whom somebody had sent copies of the paper. After a panegyric had appeared on one of the members of the Catholic Association, Peel, who at this time was home secretary, wrote to Goulburn to tell him that if one of the consequences of voting for the proclamation fund was direct or indirect support of the *Patriot*, he would not concur in the vote. Goulburn's reply was that he agreed, and had expressed his opinion to the lord lieutenant; but Wel-

[1] *M. Courier*, 10 Oct. 1825.
[2] *M. Courier*, 23 Nov. 1825.
[3] *D.E. Mail*, 29 Oct. 1823.
[4] Ibid., 12 Nov. 1823.
[5] Parker, *Peel*, i. 383.

lesley had argued that the Protestant government paper—the *Correspondent*—was just as ill conducted. Goulburn had to admit that the *Correspondent* abused Canning and the pro-Catholic section of the administration as liberally as the *Patriot* criticized the Protestant section: but in his opinion—though the lord lieutenant and the attorney general would not agree—the *Correspondent's* abuse was less mischievous, 'because support of Catholic politics in this country is necessarily connected with hostility to government'.[1]

At the same time the *Patriot* was not forthright enough for Catholics. A newspaper which gave as an argument for Catholic emancipation the likelihood that it would increase conversions to the established Church, was hardly likely to satisfy them. Until 1826 it had retained an air of prosperity, with a steady flow of advertisements: but after its circulation figures were published[2] the number rapidly diminished. In November 1828 it resorted to a common expedient of a newspaper in difficulties, changing its name and its opinions. The *Statesman and Patriot* professed affection for the benign administration of Lord Anglesey, the new lord lieutenant, but it added a rider in favour of the established Church. The writer of the editorial claimed to have founded three out of the four Dublin evening papers; evidently, as a last resort, Haydn had again been called upon. If so, it was too late. After a spasmodic attempt at brightness—the first number included parodies on the other newspapers' styles—the *Statesman and Patriot* relapsed into a respectable advocacy of Protestantism. It was too moderate to satisfy Protestants at a time when emancipation was threatening: and, in emancipation year, it ceased publication.

Meanwhile the *Correspondent* had continued to follow substantially the same policy that had made it, in Peel's term of office, at once the least offensive and one of the least effective of government newspapers. As best as it could, it tried to combine support for both the government and the established Church, justifying its antagonism to the *Dublin Evening Mail*, which otherwise might have appeared an inconsistency, by accusing the *Mail* of hiding sinister motives behind its support of the establishment. Its circulation was small; less than 500 copies of each issue were being sold, until after 1826, when it showed a small increase, at the expense of the wavering *Patriot*.

The position of a Castle paper in a time when the Castle spoke with a divided mind was trying. Just as the *Patriot's* advocacy of Catholic claims satisfied the Canningites and irritated the Wellington-Peel section

[1] Aspinall, *Politics and the press*, p. 143.
[2] *Parl. papers*, 1826 (235) xxiii. 383.

of the Cabinet, so the *Correspondent* pleased the tories and annoyed the Canningites. Goulburn admitted to Peel that he had toyed with the idea of getting rid of both papers; and Peel agreed that if the *Correspondent* abused Canning that would be reason enough to withdraw support from the paper; but the owners continued to get their £600 a year from the secret service money, as well as the proclamations and department advertisements.[1]

The owners were sufficiently humiliated in 1826 by the publication of the newspaper circulations, to complain that such figures should not be made public. The *Morning Register* was able to remind them that the *Correspondent* had been the first to boast about its circulation, in its early days. The formation of the Wellington–Peel ministry in January 1828, however, gave them renewed confidence; and—like the *Patriot*, but with better results—they put the past behind them by altering the name of the paper to the *Evening Packet and Correspondent*, renewing the quest for ascendancy subscribers with more vigorous opposition to emancipation. In this they were so successful that Francis Leveson-Gower, when he succeeded to the chief secretaryship, expressed himself anxious to withdraw government support from them.[2]

The *Correspondent's* revival dated from the time it struck out upon an independent line; although it continued to receive a small Castle subsidy it was not in the strict sense a Castle paper. Castle papers, in fact, for a time virtually ceased to exist. After Wellesley's successor, Anglesey, had been lord lieutenant for a few months, he could say that he had not a single newspaper in his pay or in his confidence;[3] and in 1830 Leveson-Gower, replying to criticisms in the house of commons of the way in which the proclamation fund was administered, said that whatever the amount of influence formerly exercised by the government, he could safely say that it now exercised no influence whatsoever.[4] This was not yet quite true: although the proclamation fund had dwindled to £3,750 in 1829, it was still inequitably distributed. The *Patriot* up to its disappearance had been given over £350: whereas the *Evening Mail* had only £15, and the *Morning Register* nothing. But in the first three-quarters of the year 1831, no metropolitan newspaper received more than £50, and all were given something, even if, in the case of the Catholic *Pilot*, it was only £1.[5]

[1] Aspinall, *Politics and the press*, pp. 119, 143–4.
[2] Ibid. p. 146.
[3] Ibid., p. 124.
[4] *Parl. deb.*, N.S. xxv. 923.
[5] *Parl. papers*, 1830 (120) xxv. 371: 1833 (238) xxxii. 631.

The sums paid to newspapers from the secret service money also dwindled. In 1830 the *Correspondent* still received its small subsidy, and Corbet and Grace, their pensions; but that appears to have been all.[1] The only source of income from the state which may not have diminished was departmental advertising. Spring-Rice had earlier drawn attention to the advertisements 'inserted by the revenue board, excise, customs, post office, stamps, and the military and civil offices', urging that they, as well as the proclamations, should be published by the newspapers, if at all, without charge.[2] They do not appear to have been distributed on any fixed principle. A contemporary commentator hinted that the *Evening Packet* did well out of chancery advertisements, owing to the favour of the master in chancery:[3] other newspapers may have obtained their share for no better reasons. Direct Castle manipulation of the press by subsidies had, in fact, virtually ceased by 1829. The system adopted by pre-Union Irish governments, and perfected by Peel, had disintegrated.

(ii) *Causes*

It is always difficult to determine whether the conscious realization of a system's faults has led to its revision, or whether the politicians have discovered reasons why the system should be changed only when the decay can no longer be ignored. The main reason for the collapse of Peel's structure is obvious. A government press without unanimity was absurd: to pay big sums to support newspapers opposing each other only made the government look foolish. While the Castle had pursued a consistent policy, its newspapers could be kept in some semblance of order. When the lord lieutenant thought one way, and his chief secretary another, chaos followed. The split in the tory cabinets of the 1820s, on the subject of emancipation, made the continuance of Peel's control impossible.

The same incompetence, malice, bigotry and irresponsibility that had irritated Peel continued to disfigure the government press after he left Ireland. In 1822 one proprietor even thought up a new way to give offence to his masters, by claiming, and receiving, proclamation money for insertions in a newspaper that had ceased to exist.[4] But Peel's successors might not have bestirred themselves to put an end to the system

[1] I.S.P.O., Secret service account books, 1830.
[2] Aspinall, *Politics and the press*, p. 420.
[3] *Westminister Review*, 1830, xii. 92.
[4] Off. papers, 580/529/3.

if circumstances had not made it unworkable. Goulburn, telling Peel in 1827 that he had often thought that it would be better to have no government papers at all, was careful to add the qualification 'as the government is now constituted'. He would have had less scruples about making considerable reductions in the proclamation fund, and getting rid of both *Patriot* and *Correspondent*, if he did not fear that at some later date it might be desirable for the government to resume some control over the press.[2] He recognized the absurdity of the two government papers opposing one another; but a neutral paper, he confessed, would not be saleable.

Goulburn's successor Lamb, the future Lord Melbourne, took a more positively liberal line. He thought it wrong that any means should be taken to influence the press in Dublin which were not taken in London or Edinburgh; and although there might be difficulty in abolishing all payments, because some of them might be for past services rendered, he was determined that the services should be investigated.[1] Lamb had been prompted to this course by advice from Spring-Rice, under-secretary for home affairs, who had just sent him a long letter describing the general state of the Irish press. After describing how the proclamation fund had been used to influence the press, by enabling newspapers to exist independently of advertisements or circulation, Spring-Rice asked:

Is this mode of influencing the press worthy or honourable? Does a good government require this aid? Can it support a weak one? And above all, does it not contain within it mischiefs infinitely greater than any it seeks to avert? The best answer to these questions will be found in the present state and influence of the Irish periodical press. The influence of these proclamations is so well known and admitted, that the papers writing under this retaining fee have but little weight with the public.

The editors, in place of thinking of the public, only worship the Castle: and they generally pay for the favours they receive in adulation, base, unprincipled, and tasteless.

On the other hand, the papers excluded from a participation in these profits, are driven into furious discontent. In this they are more sincere than their opponents; and they acquire new power over the public mind by being considered ill-used, and political martyrs, as well as party advocaters. Frequently by extravagant violence they endeavour to make it the interest of the government to purchase their neutrality or their support. Again, the favoured few being monopolists, they consider they have a right to do what they choose, and charge what they like; and the result has been a general system of jobbery and corruption. . . .

[1] Aspinall, *Politics and the press*, p. 143.
[2] 17 Sept. 1827 (ibid., p. 124).

The whole has produced the degradation of the Irish press, without in any degree contributing to the power of the government; and the accomplishment of both these mischievous consequences is produced at a very considerable expense to the country.

Spring-Rice suggested that Lamb should investigate the accounts; he would then see that those who were profiting most from the system were often the very men whose views he most detested. It was a letter of considerable perception, and Lamb was at once convinced. His colleagues were not. Replying to Spring-Rice, he wrote:[1]

> Plunket, when he heard of our scheme about the press, laughed loudly and said, 'Oh, this is Utopian!' I only mention this to show you what strong possession the idea has of minds here. I am not apt to be very positive about future measures, but if I feel confident of anything, it is that taking away all the payments would not in the least diminish the strength of the government.

Lamb was to resign from his post and leave Ireland within a few months, when Wellington formed his administration. But Leveson-Gower carried on the project, by reducing the proclamation fund, and distributing what was left more fairly amongst the newspapers. Even Peel at the home office was so far disillusioned that he wrote to Leveson-Gower, in 1828:[2]

> My experience of the Irish press would rather lead me to dissuade you from having what is called a government newspaper. If it was moderate and judicious it would have no circulation, and if it was high-seasoned enough for the Irish palate, it would be mischievous. You would have the greatest difficulty in finding a person of sufficient ability to conduct it, *whom you could trust*. I have witnessed two or three experiments of this kind, and just as many signal and expensive failures. If you could have an impartial and moderate paper, and could also persuade people to read it, it might do good, but I am very much afraid that there is no appetite for the truth in Ireland.

The advice—which Leveson-Gower took—was prompted by a letter Peel had received a few weeks before, which might have given him some sardonic amusement. It was from Wellington, containing an enclosure setting out in some detail a plan to secure the Irish press to the government, by giving them proclamations in proportion to their support.[3]

[1] Torrens, *Melbourne*, i. 250.
[2] Aspinall, *Politics and the press*, p. 145.
[3] 26 March 1829 (P.R.O.I. Leveson-Gower letter books, 1.10): B.M., Add. MS (Peel) 40307 f. 165.

4. THE RESUMPTION OF PROSECUTIONS

Assailed as Wellesley's administration were from two sides—the *Evening Mail* denouncing them for truckling to the Catholics, and the Catholic press criticizing their dilatoriness in securing promised concessions—they would often have liked to retaliate, if they could. But so long as Plunket remained attorney general, the courts were in effect closed to them. The ascendancy jurymen might distrust O'Connell, but they hated the government; and verdicts proved unobtainable. Not until 1828, the year in which Wellesley was recalled and Plunket vacated the post of attorney general, was a state prosecution for libel, initiated by private individuals but taken over by the crown, brought to a conclusion satisfactory to the government.

The victim was the same Æneas MacDonnell who had been proprietor of the *Dublin Chronicle*, and imprisoned as such under Peel. Some violent speeches he had made which had been reported in the *Morning Register* attracted the government's attention. He elected to take the responsibility for his words himself, rather than allow Staunton to stand trial. The court found him guilty and sentenced him to eighteen months in jail.[1]

MacDonnell had been appointed to the post of London agent to the Catholic Association, in which post he had shown energy and ability. Some Catholics, however, mistrusted him, and with reason; he had already entered into a correspondence with Peel that was to culminate in his emergence as a tory.[2] Whether his prosecutors realized it or not, their choice of a victim was discerning; the Catholics were unlikely to raise any serious fuss about the imprisonment of a man they did not trust. A fund was raised to sustain him; but soon afterwards the *Morning Register* acquired and printed a letter that he had written to the Castle, promising to hand over the entire proceeds of the trust if he was freed—a disclosure which was the more damaging because it was followed by his release, several months before his sentence was due to expire, on the score of ill health. The *Evening Mail* alleged that there was nothing the matter with him; and the circumstances of his release were made the subject of a discussion in the lords, where Wellington could do no more than remind the house that the exercise of the king's prerogative of mercy was not subject to investigation.[3]

[1] *M. Register*, 13 Feb. 1828.
[2] B.M., Add. MS (Peel) 40559 f. 250.
[3] *D.E. Mail*, 16 June, 8 Sept. 1828: 17 Apr. 1829.

A second advocate of Catholic claims marked down for prosecution was Jack Lawless, sometime owner-editor of a number of short-lived liberal papers, who was engaged on a campaign to rouse the north of Ireland in favour of emancipation. In October 1828, Wellington wrote to Peel that he was anxious to have Lawless prosecuted: and the following June he was indicted. Again, the choice of victim was significant. Lawless, although an ardent supporter of emancipation, was distrusted by O'Connell. Had a çonviction been secured, the government would have saved its face without the risk of provoking the wrath of the Catholic Association. This was the view expressed by the *Evening Mail*, which jeered at the proceedings as a sham: but they were not, in fact, pressed. The cabinet agreed to their abandonment after Leveson-Gower had informed them that all parties in Ireland would approve if they were dropped.[1]

To Leveson-Gower's appointment, in fact, the Irish newspapers probably owed their comparative immunity in the months immediately before and after the passage of Catholic emancipation. Leveson-Gower disliked extremists, whether Protestant or Catholic: and both sides gave him opportunities to deal out retribution. When prosecutions were initiated, however, in 1829, it was not the O'Connellite or the Orange papers that found themselves before the courts, but the *Evening Post* and the *Freeman*, relatively moderate in tone. Leveson-Gower explained in his correspondence:[2]

> It was always my intention to take the first case of serious libel which I could light on for prosecution. These in question appeared to me to constitute an aggravated offence against not any individual government, or member of government, but against society in general, and as such, if my own brother had been the author, I should equally have put the case, as I did these, into the hands of the attorney-general.

Leveson-Gower agreed that it was particularly unfortunate that the *Evening Post* had got into trouble; although a staunch advocate of emancipation, it had been kept friendly to the government. Undoubtedly, Leveson-Gower admitted, the liberal press would protest without the Orange press being silenced: but he was determined to stick to his principle.

A few days later he sent a further self-exculpatory letter to Peel, saying that even if the prosecutions inflamed public opinion, he was determined to press them home. He would have preferred to assail the Orange news-

[1] Ibid., 29 June 1829: Parker, *Peel*, ii. 70: Leveson-Gower letter books, ii. 241: iii. 30.
[2] Leveson-Gower letter books, ii. 110 (4 Sept. 1829).

papers: but he would never be able to reach them if these prosecutions of liberal papers were not carried through first. By this time he had received expressions of abject contrition from the newspaper proprietors concerned, with 'lamentation for the past and promises for the future'. The *Evening Post*, in particular, reiterated promises of repentance, which he had ignored. In spite of the risk of driving the paper into the arms of the repealers, he still felt it best that the government should steer a straight course, prosecuting libel whenever it occurred. But he was sufficiently swayed by the newspapers' appeals to express the hope to the attorney general, in a letter inquiring the nature and extent of the proceedings to be taken against the two papers, that the most lenient measures would be adopted consistent with the government's determination to stamp out sedition.[1] In both cases a compromise was reached.

Henry Grattan, Jr, the proprietor of the *Freeman*, had at first protested his innocence; later he changed his mind and pleaded guilty. This, as the attorney general remarked, was a prevarication, because Grattan at the same time was trying to pretend that he had severed his connection with *Freeman* some time before the libels were printed. His counsel explained that he had retained the property, while ceasing to exercise any control over the newspaper. He was convicted, but never called up for judgment.[2] James Magee, the owner of the *Evening Post*, also pleaded guilty; he even tried to speed up the normal dilatory court procedure, asking to be sentenced in that law term, as he would prefer to be imprisoned in winter than in summer. The court refused—fortunately for Magee, because the attorney general subsequently announced that proceedings against him had been abandoned on account of his health, and other circumstances[3]—possibly the fact that political tension was relaxed, and sentence could be foregone. The revival of political agitation in 1830 led to renewed discussion by the government about the advisability of press prosecutions, Peel, from London, expressing himself strongly in favour:[4] but the tories went out of office before the matter was settled. Newspaper owners and journalists, with the single exception of MacDonnell, could congratulate themselves that by good fortune they had come unscathed through what might even have been a period of great risk, so strong were the feelings that the emancipation campaign had aroused.

[1] Ibid., ii. 113, 218.
[2] *D.E. Mail*, 21–4 May 1830.
[3] Ibid., 12 Feb. 1830: 5 May 1830.
[4] P.R.O., H.O., 122/15, p. 75.

5. THE PRESS IN 1830

The years between Peel's departure from Ireland and the end of tory rule in Britain had seen a striking change in the Dublin newspapers. Up to 1820 they had not fundamentally altered in appearance or content since the days of the Volunteers. Printing had improved, but they held to the old ways; their columns were still mainly occupied with foreign news copied directly out of the English papers, and the amount of space given to home news had not substantially increased since before the Union. By 1830, however, they had begun to give home news extensive coverage; they were more business-like in their internal organization; and they wore an indefinable but unmistakably more confident, authoritative air.

There were signs, however, that in spite of the marked improvement in the Dublin press it was still in a very vulnerable condition. Few newspapers were on a sound commercial footing. The general improvement in standards in Ireland during the 1820s had not been reflected in any comparable extension of circulation. The total number of newspapers sold gradually increased after 1817, the first year in which returns were kept: but 1817 was the year in which the Irish press reached the nadir of its fortunes, and fewer people, probably, were reading newspapers in 1830 than in 1800. The revenue from the advertisement tax had actually declined from £21,000 in 1813 to below £15,000 in 1829[1]—a reflection both of the country's declining commercial prosperity, and of the advertisers lack of confidence in the power of the press.

While taxation weighed heavily upon the newspapers they could not expand. The twopenny stamp on every copy sold, the 2s 6d tax on every advertisement published, the duty on newsprint, and other charges, still kept the price of newspapers so high that only a small section of the community could afford them; and the owners began to recall the arguments of Grattan and Sheridan that any curtailment of the circulation cf newspapers was by extension a curtailment of the freedom of the press. They were able to put their case to a commission set up by the commons in 1828 to examine ways in which the stamp revenue might be more cheaply and efficiently collected. The commissioners' report[2] revealed gross corruption and incompetence prevailing in the Dublin stamp office. The registry which dealt with newspapers was run by an

---

[1] *Parl. papers*, 1830 (406) xxv. 306.
[2] Ibid., 1828 (7) xiv. 19.

official who supplemented his wretched salary by blackmail: 'This officer had been in the habit of having his bills discounted by persons whose interests were committed to him, namely newspaper proprietors.' From the tenor of the commission's questions they clearly wished to abolish the Dublin stamp office, and they called a number of editors before them to discover how the transference of the stamp office to London would affect the Dublin newspapers. The editors were less hostile to the idea than might have been expected. Most of them bought their newsprint in London, because the quality was better, and the cost—owing, they said, to workers 'combinations' in Dublin—no greater than the Irish product. They feared, however, that with the transfer of the office to London they might lose certain facilities—for example, the right to buy their own paper and send it in to be stamped, rather than buy newsprint from the stamp office, which cost anything up to 50% more. They must have realized, too, from the questions put to them by the commissioners, that an assimilation of the offices might be followed by an assimilation of the duties, which would double the Irish stamp duty and increase the tax on advertisements. In general, the editors' replies were pessimistic. Thomas Sheehan of the *Evening Mail* explained that the newspapers' source of subscribers had suffered a contraction:

> There was a class of people who used to support newspapers in Ireland, who have since the Peace ceased to exist. I refer to that class called middlemen; during the war these people had properties of from two to three hundred a year, arising out of profit rents of farms, and they all subscribed to newspapers. They have within the last few years become paupers, and there is now in their places only the occupying tenant.

Conway of the *Evening Post* echoed Sheehan's sentiments, instancing the decline in the revenue from the advertisement tax to support his arguments: 'It is scarcely the custom to advertise here—we are very poor in Dublin and the people are frightened at the expense'. Staunton of the *Register* produced statistical evidence to show that he only received an average return of 3s 7d from each advertisement inserted in his paper. The expense of buying a newspaper, he told the commissioners, operated particularly harshly against owners of morning papers, which were published daily, and whose readers were mostly in the city. Newsvendors were able to take advantage of the accessibility of customers to hire out morning papers several times in the day, before eventually disposing of them at half price, a practice which severely curtailed the owners' profits. So badly off were many of the papers that they had been compelled to reduce their advertisement rates, or even to print advertisements free, in order to keep up an appearance of prosperity. He doubted whether any newspaper owner had a gross income of more than £3,000 a year.

The commission's report recommended that the stamp office should be moved to London, but that the greatest care should be taken not to let the move in any way increase the burdens already shouldered by the Irish press; the change must be accompanied by special provisions to secure the Irish newspaper owners equal facilities to those that they had enjoyed when the office was in Ireland. The commissioners had realized how narrow was the margin upon which Irish newspapers survived. Spring-Rice had already come independently to the same conclusion, blaming the advertisement duties which 'operate as a tax upon the transfer of commodities, and as such are objectionable on every principle by which taxation ought to be regulated'.[1] Accounts laid before the commons in 1830[2] showed that the position was in reality worse than the returns to 1829 had indicated. Comparing the first four months of 1829 and 1830 the revenue from the advertisement tax and the stamp duty had fallen off. Interest in the emancipation campaign had created a demand for newspapers that was not to be maintained when the campaign had come to a successful conclusion. Even the *Mail* suffered a reduction in sales at this period.

All the evidence pointed to the need for a reduction of the duties, if the Irish newspapers were to thrive. By 1830, however, Goulburn had been appointed chancellor of the exchequer in the tory ministry; and he was to show as little understanding of the problems of the Irish press as he had when he had been chief secretary. His budget included the proposal rejected by the 1828 commission that the English and Irish duties should be assimilated at the English level. In future, he suggested, Irish papers should pay 4d. a copy for stamps and an increased rate for advertisements. The proposal brought the newspapers together in a harmony they had not known since 1784.[3] The *Morning Register* was the first to draw attention to the danger, saying that the project could only have for its object the extinction of the press in Ireland. The *Evening Post* joined in, setting out the details of the taxes a newspaper already had to pay. On April 22 all the newspaper owners of Dublin, and two from Cork, held a meeting, with James Magee in the chair, to discuss the position. They adjourned for a few days in order to give other provincial owners an opportunity to be present. At a second meeting they asked Magee, Staunton, and Thomas Sheehan of the *Evening Mail*

[1] Aspinall, *Politics and the press*, p. 420.
[2] *Parl. papers*, 1830 (528) xxv. 369.
[3] Dublin newspapers, 20–30 Apr. 1830.

to form a standing committee to fight the new tax. Sheehan pledged himself the following day 'to oppose politically, aye, and personally, and that regardless of party espousing, every individual who is not in his place in parliament during the discussion of the exchequer's proposed measure, and who does not divide against him on it'. He urged every newspaper in the country to make the same resolve. The *Mail* also published the text of the owners' petition to parliament; and another from the newspaper reporters of Dublin, protesting that the increase would cost them their livelihood. Figures were produced showing that the average circulation of Irish newspapers was 547, compared with 732 in Scotland, and 3,260 in England. This meant little; but a comparison of the advertisements per issue was more revealing—Ireland, 16; Scotland, 57; England, 80. The *Mail* attributed what increase there had been in the number of newspapers printed in Ireland to the artificial stimulus of the political agitation of the 'twenties. The *Register* on the same day noted, too, that the amount of stamp duty paid in Scotland had doubled in recent years, and the revenue from advertisements had risen while Ireland's had declined—the inference being that Ireland was in no position to pay more.

The *Mail* continued to threaten any member who might not oppose Goulburn's bill: 'We will drive such men not only from the hustings but from the kingdom, and there is not a quality, vituperative, satirical, or annoying, that shall not be put in requisition . . . we have found from experience that this species of warfare has succeeded where legitimate argument and astute reasoning have failed'. Alarmed, possibly, by these warnings, the Irish members met, and condemned the proposed additional duties. In June, Sir John Newport secured an interview with Goulburn and Wellington, to argue the newspapers' case.[1] He was not able to claim that he had convinced them: but a few weeks later, O'Connell wrote to Barrett of the *Pilot* to tell him that the proposal had been abandoned.[2] Shortly afterwards the tories, who had been in power uninterruptedly for over twenty years, went out of office.

[1] *D.E. Mail*, 7 May, 2 June 1830.
[2] *O'Connell correspondence* i. 207.

Chapter VI. 1830-41

1. THE REFORM ADMINISTRATION, 1830-4

The formation of a whig cabinet gave promise to the Irish press of the removal, or at least the lightening, of the burden of taxation, which the whigs had condemned while they were in opposition. The whigs, too, had condemned state prosecutions of newspapers as inimical to the freedom of the press. Government subsidies had gone and, with them, the Castle press. The prospect of a reduction of duties to enable them to sell at a price which would widen their circle of readers, and of freedom to express themselves as they liked on the questions of the day, encouraged the newspapers to look forward to a period of unusual prosperity. They were soon disillusioned. During the next three years a new wave of prosecutions broke over them; the Castle press was revived: and, in general, they were to be so harshly treated that they came to look back almost nostalgically to the days of tory rule.

O'Connell was indirectly responsible. The success of the emancipation campaign prompted him to try his luck with 'repeal': and to a campaign against the Union, the whig was no better disposed than the tory. The whigs might have had more sympathy with the peasants' tithe grievance, the other great problem of the time; but they were alienated by the way in which the campaign against tithes was conducted, with its frequent breaches of the peace. The change of government, in fact, made little appreciable difference to Ireland. The tone of the letters passing between the Castle and Whitehall scarcely varied before and after the change took place.[1] Both governments thought that any association pledged to repeal of the Union was *ipso facto* seditious: both thought that incitement to the peasantry to withhold tithes was criminal. Newspapers which reported speeches made in either campaign, therefore, laid themselves open to prosecution. Had the tories remained in office a few weeks longer, they would certainly have taken the action the whigs felt themselves compelled to take, less than a month after coming into power.

[1] Cf. P.R.O., H.O. 79/9.

(i) *Prosecutions*

This haste was probably the result of their choice of lord lieutenant.
Anglesey, the friend of emancipation, had been more popular during his
brief previous administration than any viceroy since Fitzwilliam: he returned to find himself regarded with antagonism and mistrust. The contrast convinced him that Ireland was in an extremely dangerous condition, and that he ought to show O'Connell immediately that the government was going to tolerate no mischief. On 19 January 1831, O'Connell
was arrested; and with him, Richard Barrett, Lawless, and others of the
Repeal Association. Barrett, a former editor of the *Patriot*, had by
this time established his *Pilot* as the chief O'Connellite paper, echoing
his chief's denunciations of 'Algerine Anglesey' and the administration.
The *Pilot*, an evening paper, was published at the *Morning Register*
office, and Staunton hurried around as soon as he heard of the arrest to
stand bail for his colleague.[1] A few days later, Staunton himself was
facing a prosecution; so, too, was Patrick Lavelle, Henry Grattan Jr's
successor as owner-editor of the *Freeman's Journal*.

These writs would have been served some days before had not Anglesey taken the precaution of sending copies of the newspapers to Whitehall for a legal opinion on the advisability of prosecutions. In their
reply, the British law officers agreed that the publications were libellous,
but suggested that they were scurrilous about individuals, rather than
dangerous to the community.[2] Whether prosecution was expedient
would depend on circumstances in Ireland; but, for their part, the law
officers thought that to proceed against editors for printing speeches
made at the Repeal Association would be thought extremely severe, if
not unjust—if the reports were faithful. 'As long as the association
meets and debates, what is said there becomes an article of intelligence,
which the government and the public are interested in knowing correctly'. They also deprecated the idea of prosecuting the editors in the
hope that this would force O'Connell to come forward and avow his
responsibility. It might not. Finally, they objected to the proposed procedure by information *ex officio*, instead of through the normal channel
of indictment. 'In the former case the public is made a party to the
prosecution, and a verdict of acquittal is not a triumph over the government. But if there is a danger of a bill of indictment being thrown out by

[1] *Pilot*, 19 Jan. 1931.
[2] 6, 15 Jan., 1831 (P.R.O., H.O., 100/236).

195

a grand jury, it can hardly be less probable that the petty jury would feel extremely unwilling to convict.'

These admirably balanced opinions arrived too late. Melbourne, now secretary of state at Whitehall, had written earlier to Dublin to say that he had passed the papers on to the law officers, but that if the Irish executive felt that it was necessary or highly expedient to act without delay, they should do so. Stanley, the new chief secretary for Ireland, welcomed the excuse. He was as convinced as Anglesey that action was necessary, partly to put down O'Connell, partly to curb the press. He informed Whitehall that the arrests had been made. Melbourne asked nervously for further details: Stanley replied with the news of the prosecutions of Staunton and Lavelle, undertaken with the intention of enfilading O'Connell. The *Freeman*, which Stanley considered the most violent of the Dublin papers, was the first to be charged for publishing a letter of O'Connell's on his case while it was still *sub judice*.[1] As it happened, the *Register* had published the letter the same day, a fact which was 'by some strange means conveyed to the Castle';[2] proceedings were thereupon initiated against the *Register*, too. Both owners were 'attached' for contempt of court, a method which had the merit to the government that it dispensed with trial by jury. Stanley's confessed object was to frighten them into giving up the MSS of the O'Connell letters. In this, he was unsuccessful. Lavelle remained obdurate; Staunton decided to go into hiding, so that the writ of attachment could not be served. The attorney general, however, thought that he detected signs of revolt in the newspapers from O'Connell's domination, and he felt that sooner or later O'Connell would either have to avow responsibility, or incur the odium of letting men be sentenced on his account.[3] O'Connell did not have to make that difficult decision, because the court decided against the state on a minor point of law which, though it did no more than delay the prosecution, was a setback to the Castle. The fact was that the ascendancy had not yet reconciled itself to a whig administration. The court of king's bench was still inclined to show its independence; and the Castle, rather than risk further rebuffs, was prepared to accept the opportunity for a settlement presented to them by O'Connell's desire to reach London in time for the opening of parliament.

O'Connell and Stanley denied that they had come to terms, but to outward appearances an agreement had been reached. O'Connell asked

[1] 10–26 Jan. 1831 (ibid., 79/9: 100/236: 122/15).
[2] *Pilot*, 28 Jan. 1831.
[3] 29–30 Jan. 1831 (P.R.O., H.O., 100/236).

the attorney general for a postponement of the trial;[1] Blackburne replied by offering to enter a *nolle prosequi*, provided that O'Connell
pleaded guilty, which O'Connell did, the following day. It would have
been difficult, under the circumstances, to proceed against the newspapers, and Staunton, who had been in hiding in England, felt safe to
return immediately. Tom Moore, who encountered him on the Holy-
head Mail, reported that Staunton thought it was 'very much of a
giving-in on the part of his brother agitators, and was evidently not a
little pleased at it'.[2] Barrett, emboldened rather than chastened by his
arrest, became more outspoken in the *Pilot*, which shortly was again
threatened with prosecution: that, too, fell through, to the *Pilot's*
amusement.[3]

The prosecutions were, nevertheless, an indication that the new administration would constitute a serious threat to the newspapers as soon
as it could win the confidence of the ascendancy. For this purpose, it was
patricularly well served in its choice of Stanley as chief secretary, and
Blackburne as attorney general. Both were soon to become tories.
Blackburne had actually voted against emancipation: O'Connell said
of him that the whigs could not have better proclaimed their hostility to
Ireland, than by his appointment. His first efforts had been too precipitate; he had underestimated the strength of the ascendancy's prejudices.
But by the time that his administration had been a year in office, he had
given proofs that he was not a dangerous liberal, whom the ascendancy
might have reason to fear; and he could resume proceedings against the
press, confident in his ability to secure the co-operation of the courts.

The first newspaper to suffer was the *Comet*, a weekly founded in
1831, which had quickly obtained a substantial circulation and notoriety
by its laceration of the established church, notably in the 'Parson's horn
book', published in its early numbers.[4] Blackburne waited until the
paper's initial popularity had begun to wane before prosecuting John
Sheehan and Thomas Browne, the owners, for a violent article on tithes.
Secure, as they thought, in ascendancy's hatred of the whigs, they contented themselves with a reminder to the jury to be careful of public
opinion. They miscalculated: the court of king's bench promptly
brought them up for contempt, and fined them £50 apiece.[5] For the

---

[1] Melbourne to Anglesey, 18 Feb. 1831 (ibid., 79/9): *O'Connell correspondence*, i.
247.
[2] *Moore memoirs*, vi. 168.
[3] *Pilot*, 7 Mar., 29 June 1831.
[4] See Fitzpatrick, *Life of Cloncurry*, p. 423.
[5] *M. Register*, 11-15 Aug. 1832.

tithe article they escaped less lightly, each receiving a sentence of a year's imprisonment, and a £100 fine. In reply to Sheehan's plea that he was in bad health, the chief justice, Jebb, said he could go to Wicklow Jail, 'a healthful place'; and it was with some difficulty that Sheehan managed to persuade the court to rescind this decision on the grounds that it would have ruined his business.[1]

Commenting upon the prosecutions the *Comet* remarked: 'The *Free Press* is to get a squeeze—the *Waterford Chronicle* has got a squeeze with a vengeance—the *Mail* got a twitch—the *Comet* is in for it—the *Pilot* is in for it—the *Freeman* is doubly in for it'. The government had begun to initiate actions against newspapers all over the country.

In the 1820s, the provincial newspapers had shown little of the spirit of the metropolitan press. They had received a disproportionately large share of the proclamation fund, a share that grew still larger as the number of government newspapers in Dublin diminished. As late as 1829 a close enough watch was being kept upon them for the chief secretary to order the discontinuance of the proclamations to a Wexford newspaper.[2] The bulk of the country press had remained under government control. The *Waterford Chronicle* had been an exception. The opposition of its proprietor, Pierce Barron to the government, had got him into legal trouble in 1826;[3] and in February 1832 he found himself charged with inciting the peasantry not to pay tithes. The government were taking no chances; they ordered that he should be tried in Dublin, rather than down the country, the *Morning Register* deploring the fact that such an odious power should be used by a reforming government against the press. Barron and his printer were sentenced to a year's imprisonment. Meanwhile, the proprietors of the *Newry Examiner*, a Catholic paper, had been sentenced to four months in jail and a £50 fine for criticizing the Orange magistracy; and the owner of the *Tipperary Free Press* was also awaiting trial.[4]

At the same time, as the *Comet* had said, prosecutions were pending against the *Pilot* and the *Freeman* and—what was more surprising—the *Evening Mail*. The owner of the *Mail*, Thomas Sheehan, had already been in trouble that year, for publishing a report of the committee of the house of commons before the report had been officially released for publication; an offence for which Sheehan, who refused to purchase his freedom by divulging the source of his publication, was committed for

---

[1] *Pilot*, 30 Jan. 1833.
[2] Leveson-Gower letter books, i. 10.
[3] Madden, *I.P.L.*, ii. 192.
[4] *M. Register*, 28 Apr., 19 July, 15 Nov. 1832.

two days to the custody of the sergeant-at-arms.[1] But this was in London, where the reputation of the *Mail* meant little. That it should be prosecuted in Dublin was remarkable; that the prosecution should succeed, more remarkable still. Blackburne chose his ground cleverly, charging Sheehan and his partner with a libel on the provost of Trinity, so that the trial could not develop into a test of strength between the whig government and the tory ascendancy. Sheehan's brother Remigius, who edited the paper, offered to take full responsibility for the insertion, which the owners claimed not to have seen. Jebb replied that this was immaterial, because they had not published a retraction. They were sentenced to six months' imprisonment and fines of £100, the printer also be sent to jail.[2]

In all probability the success of the prosecution surprised the Castle as much as it surprised the *Mail*. It may have been begun less with the hope of silencing the ascendancy press—much as the Castle would wish to do so—than to demonstrate that the administration was impartial; that it was prepared to retaliate against libels from whatever quarter they came. The success gave Blackburne renewed confidence, with which he turned to deal with his real enemies, the *Freeman* and the *Pilot*.

The *Freeman* had been served with a writ for an article in which it asserted that, in Ireland, the only law was the will of the executive;[3] but this charge was dropped in favour of one more promising; the publication of a letter from O'Connell on the subject of the tithe affray which came to be known as 'the Wallstown massacre'. The letter was originally printed by a radical paper in England, the *True Sun*, in which O'Connell felt sufficiently sure of his ground to charge the authorities with murder. He had the sense, however, to warn Barrett not to reprint the letter in Ireland.[4] The *Morning Register*, apologizing for its omission, blamed the precious effects of the British connection, which meant that London could do things with impunity which in Dublin would lead to the suspension of *habeas corpus*. The *Evening Mail*, however, saw the opportunity to wipe the eye of its rivals by printing the letter, with a covering note to the Castle: 'With what face, Mr Attorney General, can you ask a jury to convict the *Comet*, the *Pilot*, the *Freeman's Journal*, and the *Tipperary Free Press* for comments or remarks innocent and innocuous compared to that which this night appears in the *Mail*?'[5] Patrick Lavelle

[1] *Parl. deb.*, 3rd S. xiii. 193, 230–9, 310.
[2] *D.E. Mail*, 23 Nov. 1832.
[3] *M. Register*, 13 Aug. 1832.
[4] *O'Connell correspondence*, i. 304.
[5] *D.E. Mail*, 24 Sept. 1832.

of the *Freeman* decided to publish the letter, and Barrett had no alternative but to disobey O'Connell's instructions, and follow suit in the *Pilot*. The attorney general, after some hesitation, decided to take the *Mail's* hint, and began proceedings against both papers.

The case was not, however, as strong as Blackburne could have wished, owing to the refusal of his colleagues in England to proceed against the *True Sun*. In reply to his promptings, the English law officers pronounced that in English common law, at least, O'Connell would have a very fair chance of proving his contention that the Wallstown affray *was* murder;[1] and Blackburne, fearing perhaps that O'Connell would obtain these opinions to use against him, allowed the charge to lapse on a technicality, biding his time until a fresh opportunity offered —which, with the *Pilot* making references to the Coercion Act as 'this atrocious bill, this monster spawn of the adulterous connection of the whigs with office'[2] was not likely to be long. On 1 May 1833, Barrett informed his readers that another prosecution of the *Pilot* was pending, for a letter of O'Connell's. He added the hope that he would be tried by tories: 'if we are to be domineered over let it be by gentlemen'.

Prosecutions of provincial newspapers also continued: the owner of the *Carlow Morning Post* was imprisoned and fined for his opinions on tithes, and almost immediately afterwards given a stiffer sentence for criticism of a member of parliament; and the Hon. Frederick Cavendish, the eccentric owner of the *Castlebar Telegraph*, was imprisoned and fined for a seditious libel.[3] The Castle's main concern, however, was the prosecution of Barrett. The *Pilot* had a small circulation, but it was the paper which the Castle was most anxious to humble, as the platform from which O'Connell's opinions were most assiduously promulgated. And by choosing one of O'Connell's letters as the excuse for a prosecution, Blackburne was able to leave O'Connell once again with the difficult choice—whether to come forward, avow responsibility, and risk sentence; or to leave the responsibility to Barrett and risk public contempt if Barrett was convicted.

The case came up in June 1833. O'Connell was in London, disputing with the whigs over coercion. An acquittal, he hoped, would help in his efforts to bring about their downfall, even if this meant alliance with his old enemies of the tory press. A letter he wrote at the time hinted at their possible subornation:[4]

[1] 15 Dec. 1832 (P.R.O., H.O., 100/243).
[2] *Pilot*, 1 Mar. 1833.
[3] Ibid., 29 May: 3, 12 June 1833.
[4] *O'Connell correspondence*, i. 352.

Barrett's jury is high tory. If Sheehan or Dr. Boyton wish to lay me under an everlasting obligation, NOW IS THE TIME. . . . Look to this discreetly. You can, I believe, vouch for my not being ungrateful. If we could but get a fair and impartial jury, Barrett would certainly be acquitted.

But within a few days O'Connell had come to terms with the whigs, and Littleton became the new chief secretary for Ireland. O'Connell had sufficiently high hopes of him to say, 'a little bird whispers me, no prosecution'.[1] The prosecution did, in fact, receive a setback, but it was not through Littleton's intervention. The trial was to be held out of term, 'at bar', a procedure adopted usually only in extremely serious charges—on this occasion, the *Pilot* alleged, to overawe the jurymen. They were alarmed, but in a different way from that which Blackburne had intended. His apology[2] for the temporary breakdown, which the lord lieutenant transmitted to England, showed that the care with which the jurors had been selected had only succeeded in making them nervous of appearing, in case they should be marked out for vengeance by the O'Connell party. A few of them preferred to incur the £50 fine for failure to put in an appearance; as the law term had ended, no more could be sworn in, and the case had to be held over. Blackburne expressed the opinion that it would do no harm to have the prosecution hanging over Barrett, but this was rationalizing; he was clearly mortified by the course events had taken.

The case was resumed in November, in spite of the fact, which the *Pilot* noted, that the whigs were once again on dining terms with O'Connell. Sheil had been briefed to defend Barrett; at the last moment, O'Connell appeared to lead in person. He took the same line as he had in the trial of John Magee, treating the jury, which was exclusively tory and Protestant, to a flow of vituperation worse than that for which the newspaper had been indicted. Presumably he wished to win the jury's sympathy by abusing the government, but the jurymen must have known of his recently friendly relations with the whigs. They found Barrett guilty. He was sentenced to a fine of £100 and a jail sentence of six months, the jury's recommendation to mercy moving the bench only to allow him to serve the sentence in Kilmainham rather than Newgate.[3]

A month later,[4] subscribers to the *Pilot* found themselves reading a newspaper entitled:

The *Morning Register*
THE PILOT is suppressed.

[1] Ibid., i. 356.
[2] 14 June 1833 (P.R.O., H.O., 100/224).
[3] *Pilot*, 20 Jan. 1834.
[4] 19 Feb. 1834.

201

The stamp commissioners had taken advantage of the old statute which laid down that stamps must not be issued to a newspaper owner convicted of seditious libel; the paper could only continue by appearing ostensibly as a second edition of the *Morning Register*.

This action at once recoiled upon the government. The English press, led by *The Times*, took up the *Pilot's* cause. O'Connell wrote to Barrett that all England was up in arms, promising him that the statute would at once be repealed, and he would get a free pardon. In the meantime, he devised ways in which Barrett could get around the statute. Lawyers were consulted whether he could not continue to publish the *Pilot* on the stamps he had in stock, or whether he might legally become proprietor of another newspaper. If not, somebody else must be engaged as proprietor. O'Connell would indemnify him, and pay Barrett's salary as editor of the *Pilot*, or the *Patriot*, or whatever name the paper might be called.[1]

The stamp commissioners' action was debated in the commons on February 25, when O'Connell and other Irish members were able to make a formidable indictment of the whigs' treatment of the press in Ireland. The government, it was disclosed, had initiated thirteen prosecutions for libel in three years: and detailed evidence was given of the way in which juries had been packed in order to obtain convictions. Only a handful of Catholics were on the Dublin grand jury; the method of selecting jurymen from the panel was highly suspect; and the crown lawyers had no trouble in striking off any Catholic names that remained on it before a trial. The same Protestant jurors appeared in cases year after year; some of the jury that convicted Barrett had acquitted Haydn of the *Star*, nearly ten years before.

The commons were persuaded to order the publication of the correspondence between the government and the stamp commissioners prior to the withdrawal of stamps. This revealed, as O'Connell had guessed,[2] that Littleton was responsible; the Dublin commissioners had never heard of the statute. Expecting trouble, Littleton had ordered a search for precedents. The Dublin commissioners were only able to discover two cases where convictions had been secured for seditious libel. In one, the owner had resigned from or retired from the paper, and in the other, it had been the printer, and not the owner who had been

[1] *O'Connell correspondence*, i. 309, 408.
[2] *Parl. deb.*, 3rd S. xxi. 791 ff. *O'Connell correspondence*, i. 412.

prosecuted.[1] But the voluntary retirement of the proprietors in several border-line cases—John Magee of the *Evening Post*, Barron of Waterford, and Grattan of the *Freeman*—was at least negative evidence that the statute's validity had not been questioned; and Littleton had ordered the stamp commissioners to enforce it.[2] The *Pilot* was, however, able to resume an independent existence for a while on its stock in hand; and thereafter for some months it borrowed—an illegal procedure. According to the first half-yearly return for 1834, it received no stamps[3] from the stamp office.

From time to time the *Pilot* continued to report further revelations made to the commons of the conduct of the trial. Five lawyers, it was disclosed, had been briefed for the crown. Of these, three were out of town at the time of the trial. Three substitutes had been called in, making fees for eight barristers in all—though only two had appeared at the trial. Later, it published the accounts of the prosecution's expense, which had amounted to over £700.[4] The Castle remained unembarrassed, secure in the knowledge that O'Connell had abandoned the repeal campaign and was working with the whigs—even if not yet very amicably—for remedial legislation. It could claim that its object had been achieved. The newspapers had been subdued.

The four years of whig rule had repeated the lesson taught to the Irish press by 'All the Talents'. Out of office, the whigs believed in the freedom of the press; but the line that they drew between liberty and licence was not appreciably different from the line drawn by the tories. The whigs had shown themselves just as ingenious in the use of legal twists to expedite prosecutions; they had even thought up new ones of their own, such as the attempt to try Barrett 'at bar'. As soon as Blackburne had won the confidence of the ascendancy, he had been able to secure the support of the judiciary. Jebb was a judge in the Clonmell-Norbury tradition; if he lacked his predecessors' personality, he shared their ability to identify justice with the interest of his class. Leveson-Gower had frequently complained of Jebb's partiality to the Orange order and of still less amiable traits. On one occasion, Jebb not only defied traditional judicial practice by choosing his own part of the country-side for his circuit but, 'not content with this outrage, he has chosen, out of that respectable district, three most questionable names

---

[1] Æneas MacDonnell of the *Dublin Chronicle* and Harding Tracey of the *Cork Commercial Chronicle*.

[2] *Parl. papers*, 1834 (85) xlviii. 557.

[3] *Pilot*, 28 Feb. 1834: 11 Aug. 1834.

[4] Ibid., 17 Mar. 1834: *Parl. papers*, 1834 (54) xlviii. 267.

for sheriffs, the two first being the proposer and seconder of his son's election'. 'Is not this', Leveson-Gower asked, 'a sufficiently scandalous addition to his extravagances on the bench?'[1] But Jebb remained. While he remained, newspapers could not hope for fair trial.

During this period of whig rule, too, the press was faced with a threat more dangerous than any the executive had yet devised. In a letter to Whitehall written in January 1833,[2] the lord lieutenant, complaining of the difficulty of prosecuting for seditious speeches, suggested an alternative procedure; 'it deserves to be considered whether the tribunals of courts martial should not have jurisdiction over seditious libels'. Although Anglesey seems only to have envisaged such action in proclaimed districts, a metropolitan newspaper might be circulating in the district in which the sedition appeared, so that the whole press would in practice have been subject to martial law. But nothing came of the proposal.

(ii) *Taxation and the radical newspapers*

The social and political ferment created during the passage of the Reform Bill was reflected in Ireland by the appearance of a number of new polemical newspapers, mainly designed to promote the causes of reform and repeal. The two campaigns could be combined because O'Connell, in his desire to keep behind him the mass support he had won during the emancipation campaign, was interesting himself in workers' aims in general, and in the new Dublin Trades Political Union in particular. Considerable enthusiasm was aroused for the two causes, and half a dozen new papers sprang up in Dublin as a result of their impetus. But as soon as the initial impulse had spent itself, the papers disappeared. The weight of taxation was too heavy for them.

The first of the new papers to be published was the *Repealer, and Tradesmen's Journal*. The *Repealer* represented something new in Irish history: a paper designed to circulate among the working classes. A new Castle paper, the *Dublin Times*, commented sarcastically on the methods used to push the paper's circulation: two members of the Trades Political Union had boasted at a meeting that they had been the round of fourteen public-houses on the previous Saturday night, refusing to drink in any of them that did not stock the *Repealer*.[3] The class which it was sought to interest could not afford newspapers, ex-

---

[1] Leveson-Gower letter books, ii. 218, 437.
[2] P.R.O., H.O., 100/244 (19 Jan. 1833).
[3] *D. Times*, 15 June 1832.

cept, perhaps, a weekly (the *Repealer* came out twice a week); and a public-house circulation would not have been sufficient to keep a newspaper alive. In this case, however, advertisers were interested—perhaps by the novelty of the paper—and for a time, the *Repealer* prospered. Its prosperity attracted rivals. In the summer it was joined by the *Plain Dealer*, and in the autumn, by the *Express*, a daily evening paper of mildly O'Connellite views. The Trades Political Union, too, became dissatisfied with papers which, although brought out in their interest, remained under independent ownership. They decided to set up a weekly of their own, the *People*, whose prospectus promised that it would 'mirror the views of the humbler orders of society'. To the delight of the *Dublin Times*,[1] a section of the T.P.U., still remained dissatisfied, circulating the members with a warning not to support the new venture because it was to be published at the office of a non-repeal paper, and—more dangerous—was to be printed by machinery. These allegations led to a proposal of no confidence in the *People*. Its proprietor announced the severance of the connection between the paper and the T.P.U. in spite of the withdrawal of the proposal, following a remarkable speech by the editor-designate, who forecast the immense advantages machine-printing would bring to the press.

A full account of these discussions[2] appeared in the first number of the *Press*, yet another new radical paper, pledged to work for repeal, church reform, the ballot, shorter parliaments, and an extended franchise. The *People* itself came out a few days later. But by the end of the year all these new arrivals had ceased publication. They must have helped in one another's downfall, by flooding a restricted market. To some extent, their failure was the result of their inadequacy—not by contrast with the established newspapers, with whom they compared favourably, but rather by their inability to break away from the conventional pattern of the newspapers of the time. The tradesmen for whom they were designed were not prepared to pay fivepence for a paper which did not differ appreciably from the *Register* or the *Freeman*; and taxation still made it impossible to sell a newspaper for less. The *Tribune*, a radical weekly founded in 1834, actually cost 7d., which must materially have limited the number of people who listened to its call to the masses to rise, like the Romans, 'against the intolerable burdens of aristocratic oppression and usurious exactions'.[3]

---

[1] Ibid., 23 Jan. 1833.

[2] *Press*, 25 Jan. 1833.

[3] *Tribune*, 21 June 1834: Madden (I.P.L.) MS 278, has some details concerning this newspaper.

Evidently the stamp and advertisement duties were still operating as a formidable obstacle to any extension of the influence of the press. The advertisement duty was lowered by 1s 6d in 1833 to 1s for ten lines: but to the weaker newspapers this proved of little assistance. Their public was still too limited; they needed more readers to attract the advertisers' attention. The cost of newspapers was too high for any but the wealthiest members of the community to take them; and the profits from their sale were too low for owners to embark upon features which might attract a larger audience. Illustrations, for example, were uncommon. Circulations remained very small:[1] the *Dublin Evening Mail*, alone of Dublin newspapers, attracted more than 2,000 subscribers, and only one of the morning papers, the advertisement-filled *Saunders' News-Letter*, reached four figures. For the Catholic papers the struggle was particularly hard. The Protestant *Mail* and the *Packet* could count upon wealthy ascendancy support, and the *Evening Post*, catering for the well-to-do Castle Catholics contrived to remain relatively prosperous. But the independent Catholic newspapers, the *Freeman* and the *Register*, were unable to attain real commercial prosperity; and the *Pilot*, with its unqualified support for O'Connell, had only a few hundred readers.

(iii) *Castle newspapers*

Hope deferred must have discouraged the independent newspaper owners; but the reform administration was not entirely devoid of encouragement for them. An active attorney general, with ascendancy help, could make the press cautious: he could not, unaided, make it sycophantic. If the whigs failed to make as much impression as Peel, it was because their efforts to supplement the negative control through the courts and the exchequer with positive propaganda through their own press were half-hearted, and consequently ineffective.

Peel, in 1830, had in desperation revived the project of a Castle newspaper,[2] urging that a periodical—not a newspaper—should be founded with the title of the *Union*, on the lines of the *Anti-Union* of 1799. The whigs rejected the idea, and reverted to 'tied' newspapers. The *Dublin Times*, a morning daily, appeared in 1831. After a few months in existence it had made its presence felt sufficiently for the *Pilot* to complain that 'the beloved Anglesey has the inestimable satisfaction of having, amongst his other gifts to Ireland, bestowed upon us a newspaper to

[1] *Parl. papers*, 1831-2 (242) xxxiv. 123: 1833 (505) xxxii. 628: 1834 (412) xlix. 407.
[2] Parker, *Peel*, ii. 161.

which the slanderous, pasquinading, ribald, and obscene *Mail* is dignity, decency, and patriotism itself'.[1] The *Pilot* often referred to Anglesey as the 'editor' of the *Dublin Times*: and, although the lord lieutenant may have had little to do with it, Littleton was later to confirm that it had been set up by the Castle, and heavily subsidized from the secret service money.[2] In 1832, the *Dublin Times* bought out the interest of the *Morning Post*, whose circulation had dwindled away almost to nothing; and a few weeks later it printed the prospectus of a new government evening paper, the *Empire*. But neither paper could make headway, commercially. The *Empire* lasted only a few months; and in October 1833 the *Dublin Times* announced that, as the whigs were firmly established in power, its labours could be terminated. Littleton later claimed that he had stopped the paper 'because it was doing more harm than good'. He had no objection in principle, he admitted, to the government running papers of their own—he could think of few ways in which money could be better employed than in enlightening the public—but he felt that the *Dublin Times* was valueless.[3]

Apart from these two, the Castle were not certain of the support of any Dublin newspaper, though after the passing of Catholic emancipation, the *Dublin Evening Post* could usually be found taking the whigs' part. F. W. Conway had broken with O'Connell over repeal, and the *Pilot* abused him vigorously thereafter, attributing his support of the government to venality. He was on visiting terms with the Castle in 1831, and the *Evening Post* was later to be used by Littleton to disseminate news favourable to the government,[4] so that there was some justification for Gavan Duffy's assertion that after the whigs came into power Conway 'openly occupied the position he had so long secretly held, of a stipendiary writer for the Castle'. But the *Evening Post's* remuneration must have been small, relative to the amounts the Castle press had received in the past; one of the commons' periodical investigations into the proclamation fund showed that the amounts being paid out of it to newspapers in the early 'thirties were negligible.[5] Perhaps because the reward was insufficient, the *Evening Post* never became wholeheartedly a Castle paper, and on occasion could take an independent line.

In one other respect, the press could congratulate itself on a small but

---

[1] *Pilot*, 2 Dec. 1831.
[2] Aspinall, *Politics and the press*, p. 125.
[3] *Irish Monthly Magazine*, November 1832: Aspinall, op. cit., p. 125.
[4] P.R.O., H.O., 100/236 (19 Jan. 1833): Aspinall, op. cit., p. 265.
[5] *Parl. papers*, 1833 (633) xxxii. 629.

perceptible advance during the period of the reform administration. Solidarity between independent newspapers of different political colours had previously been lacking, except when they were roused by some single event which affected all of them, such as the Foster's Press Act of 1784, or the threat of increased stamp duties in 1830. The unity of 1830 had been short lived: as soon as the project was abandoned, they had resumed their mutual distrust. When the *Mail* found itself proceeded against in 1831, it reminded the other papers how it had always sustained them in similar circumstances in the past; to which the *Pilot* replied[1] that, so far from the *Mail* having ever sustained anything but itself, it had teemed with instigations to the government to prosecute the *Register* and the *Pilot*, actually provoking such action on one occasion. The *Pilot* continued to wage intermittent warfare with the *Freeman* and the *Evening Post*,[2] as well as the *Mail*; and the *Comet* in the early issues flayed the tory papers, concluding that 'in vulgar presumption, unblushing peculation from its contemporaries, and crawling sycophancy to hypocrisy and humbug, all give place to the *Warder*'.[3] The *Comet* referred also to the *Packet* as 'worthlessly spongey', which may have accounted for the *Packet's* verdict upon the sentences passed on the *Comet's* owners later in the year—that they were too light. But, in spite of innumerable instances of rivalry and mutual distrust, the Dublin newspapers tended to come together in face of prosecutions, particularly as Blackburne did not concentrate his attacks on one section of the press. At first, symptoms of unity were confined to newspapers sharing similar views: the *Morning Register* started a collection to pay the costs of the *Waterford Chronicle's* prosecution, and commented favourably on other funds of the same nature.[4] Similarly, the *Pilot* backed an appeal for funds to help Cavendish of the *Castlebar Telegraph*. By the time of the Barrett prosecution, press unity had reached a further stage. For some time the *Pilot* was suspicious of the *Mail's* tentative overtures. Sheehan, however, persisted in its original attitude to the prosecution: if it took on the appearance of being against the press, the *Mail* would oppose it. When the trial came on the *Mail* took the *Pilot's* part, so unreservedly that Blackburne asked the judges to sentence Sheehan for contempt of court. The *Mail* promptly assailed the government for withholding stamps from the *Pilot*.[5] Barrett gratefully

[1] *Pilot*, 9 Nov. 1831.
[2] *Pilot*, Jan. 1933.
[3] *Comet*, 8 Jan 1832.
[4] *M. Register*, 15, 20 Aug., 6 Dec. 1832.
[5] *D.E. Mail, Pilot*, Nov. 1833–Feb. 1834.

backed the *Mail* when it faced an action, a few weeks later, saying that with the exception of the enslaved *Evening Post*, all the papers in Ireland stood together, whatever their politics, when prosecutions threatened.

* * *

When the whig administration fell in November 1834, O'Connell privately expressed the opinion, 'it is well we are rid of the humbuggers';[1] and the Irish newspapers might corporatively have echoed him. A whig administration had shown that they feared an independent press just as Peel had done, and lacked only his ability to suppress it. 'Hereafter', an anonymous writer prophesied in a Dublin periodical[2] issued at the height of the Castle's campaign against the press:

> the historian will signalise the present administration of the marquis of Anglesey as the most tyrannical yet feeble government England ever forced on us. As regards the press, it is remarkable for the unblushing practice of all that was despotic and disgraceful in the conduct of its most profligate predecessors. . . . How did he act towards the press? He first used all those insidious private arts, for which power never wants dexterous agents, to detach the ablest advocates of the people from their cause, or at least to silence them: he failed in this, and then he held out threats of his resentment, to deter them from the due discharge of their duty. . . . and at length he resorted to open hostility. The most distinguished conductors of the press were arrested; their properties threatened with confiscation; and their liberties, if not their lives, endangered.

2. THE MELBOURNE ADMINISTRATION, 1835–41

The brief interlude of tory government in 1835 had little direct influence on the Irish press, except through the passage of an act designed to check blackmail legal actions against newspapers by informers, who were taking advantage of obsolete but unrepealed statutes to institute proceedings in the hope of obtaining either hush-money from the papers or a reward from the state.[3] Indirectly, however, Peel's short term in office was to have important results: it forced the whigs and O'Connell into the close alliance that was to provide the Melbourne administration with much of its dynamic, during the next few years. In

[1] *O'Connell correspondence*, i. 502.
[2] *Irish Monthly Magazine*, Nov. 1832.
[3] *Public General Statutes*, 1835 (5 Will. IV, c. 2): *Pilot*, 13 Mar. 1835.

April 1835, when Melbourne took office, the Irish newspaper proprietors found their positions suddenly and decisively altered. The owners of the *Pilot* and the *Morning Register*, for example, began to give whole-hearted support to the new government, to the amusement of the *Evening Mail*, which was able to jeer at them as 'Castle prints'. For the first and, as it happened, the last time, there was to be a period of years during which the liberal press ranged itself behind the Castle.

The condition of the press in these years reflected the condition of the country. For Ireland, it was to be the most tranquil period of the century. Earlier administrations had been sympathetic to liberal ideas, but none had combined sympathy with competence until Thomas Drummond arrived as under secretary in 1835, to provide the country with government more capable than any it had known. For as long as he could count upon O'Connell's support, Drummond felt safe from any serious attack from the repeal flank; and with this security he was able to ignore ascendancy hysterics from the other side—a policy which worked better than had Wellesley's attempts at retaliation. The system, too, worked particularly well with the press, because the Castle was able to enjoy a wide measure of support from newspapers without having to pay for it.

Only on rare occasions, during the next few years, could the ascendancy press charge the government with rendering improper assistance. In 1839 the *Mail* complained that the *Pilot* had been furnished with an advance copy of the royal speech at the opening of parliament, through O'Connell's influence; but the *Pilot* insisted that it had obtained the speech by rail, instead of the usual express riders.[1] In April 1838 the *Dublin University Magazine*, a prosperous tory periodical whose literary merits even its political opponents admitted, accused the government of refusing the *Achill Missionary Herald* the usual press postage facilities (on the grounds that it was not a *news*paper) for political reasons. But this was the first attempt, the writer admitted, 'to carry out the despotic principles of whiggery to the extent of a censorship of the press'. Any benefits the papers favourable to the government may have received were probably more than balanced by the fact that the distribution of departmental advertisements remained in ascendancy —tory—hands. The tory newspapers, the *Mail* and the *Packet*, obtained the bulk of them.

During this period, too, the first step was taken towards reducing the weight of taxation on the press—a reduction in the stamp duty. Agita-

---

[1] Ibid., 13 Feb. 1839.

tion against this tax had been conducted for some years, particularly in England where the duty was 4*d*. a copy (it was 2*d*. in Ireland). In 1836 Spring-Rice, the chancellor of the exchequer, announced that he proposed to consolidate the duties in the two countries at a new level of 1*d*. a copy. The announcement was received in Ireland without enthusiasm. The attitude of the Irish owners was that the reduction ought to be proportionate: if the English owners were to pay 1d. the Irish should only have to pay a halfpenny. All the Irish newspapers joined in denouncing Spring-Rice's proposal.[1] At a meeting of Dublin newspaper owners a unanimous condemnatory vote was passed, and the decision was made to draft a petition to parliament, urging the reduction of the Irish duty. William Smith O'Brien acted as the owners' spokesman in the bill's second reading in the commons; but he could make no impression on Spring-Rice, who replied that the penny was not a duty, but a payment for free state services to the press—in postage, for example. If the radicals' proposal that the duty in England should be removed altogether had been carried, he argued, would O'Brien have suggested on the same principle, that the Irish owners should receive a bounty?[2] No account remains of the debate on the subject in the debate on the estimates. It was hopelessly confused by an opposition amendment calling for a reduction, instead, of the duty on soap. The opportunity for witticisms about the relative advantages of mental and physical cleanliness proved irresistible. The house was convulsed; after the debate had degenerated into what the *Evening Mail's* reporter called 'a scene which it is next to impossible for language to describe', the galleries were cleared by order of the Speaker, and the reporters were excluded.

Later, the chancellor of the exchequer relented to the extent of allowing the Irish newspapers a 25% discount for prompt payment; but he held to his determination to assimilate the duties. The compromise was decided upon after he had received a deputation from the Irish newspaper proprietors, whose case—that Irish newspapers were not capable of bearing so much taxation as English, because of their proportionately smaller circulations—he put to the opposition, when they objected to the idea of the Irish receiving any concessions. Irish members showed little interest, only five appearing to record their votes.[3] The consolidation bill was carried.

The reduction of one penny in the price of newspapers did not produce any startling rise in circulations: at fourpence, they were still out of

---

[1] 20–30 Mar. 1836.
[2] *Parl. deb.*, 3rd s. xxxii. 872.
[3] *D.E. Mail*, 22 July 1836.

the reach of all but a small minority of Irishmen. The newspapers that might have been expected to reap the benefit, the *Morning Register* and the *Pilot*, chose instead to share in and suffer from O'Connell's declining popularity; it was the Protestant *Packet* and the Castle Catholic *Evening Post* who were the beneficiaries. The Dublin press in general obtained little immediate benefit from the change. Official figures published in 1840,[1] showed that Scotland, with less than half Ireland's population, had paid almost as much in stamp duties—the figures were £16,600 to £17,000— and very much more in advertisement duty—£13,700 to £9,500—in the previous year. The number of copies of newspapers sold in Ireland rose in the months following the reduction in the duty, but it remained small in proportion to the population.

The reduction was not even sufficient to stimulate fresh journalistic enterprises of any importance. Of the few new Dublin papers published in this period, none made any mark. For a time a weekly *Dublin Record*, later the *Statesman and Record*, enjoyed fair prosperity through its endeavours to 'make it as clear as the noon-day out of scripture to every individual, Roman Catholic and Protestant, who shall read it, that Popery is the Babylon of God's wrath—*ipsissima abominatio*—the veriest abomination'. In 1836 it was joined by the twice weekly *Dublin Standard*, whose Protestantism was hardly less forthright; they survived long enough to show that there was a market for bigotry, provided that it was of an Orange flavour. Contemporaneously with them appeared what was probably the first sporting paper in Ireland, a weekly which lived down its title, *Paddy Kelly's Life in Dublin*. But no reputable addition to the Dublin press appeared until the *Dublin Monitor*, of radical leanings, late in 1839; and the *Monitor* failed to maintain its early promise.

The history of the press under the Melbourne administration, therefore, seems featureless, by contrast with the years that had passed—and, still more, by contrast with the period of activity that was to follow in the 'forties. But the Melbourne period is significant, because it gives an unusual opportunity to judge the general structure and status of the press at the time. From 1784 the press had been sporadically at war with the government, in campaigns that tend to divert attention from the study of the press as an institution. But during the Melbourne period, when there was virtually a five years' truce, it is possible to give more attention to the newspapers' handling of other problems that were beginning to face them, now that the grip of the state was being gradually relaxed.

[1] *Parl. papers*, H. C. 1840 (266) xxix. 503.

For example, there was the problem of the relationship between owners and workers. It was in this period that the trade union movement, which had been operating illegally for many years, can be said to have formally established itself. The printers' union showed that it was a force that could no longer be ignored; and the journalists also made a first tentative effort to form themselves into a united body. At this time, too, the controversy over 'the right to report' came to a head. With the increase of state boards, committees, and commissions, the question had to be decided how far the public had a right to read accounts of their proceedings: and the first efforts were made to define these rights, by ensuring that press representatives would be admitted to meetings of public representatives. And in this period the problem of the relations between the press and the nationalist movement clearly revealed itself, in the course of a dispute between O'Connell and the liberal newspapers. Where previously the press had seen only a single serious threat to its liberties—the power of the Castle—it was now forced to recognize the extent to which nationalism, too, might demand sacrifices of independence in the country's cause.

(i) *The influence of trade unions*

(*a*) PRINTERS

The first official recognition of the importance of the union in the printing trade was in 1838, when its representatives were invited to give evidence before a select committee of the house of commons on combinations of workmen.[1] The length of time these combinations had existed was attested by the long list of acts and regulations against them; and the evidence given before the 1838 committee, both by the workers' representative and by newspaper owners, showed that the newspapers had recognized the existence of a printers' trade union *de facto* for as far back as they could recall. Although a few isolated disputes were remembered from the early years of the century, the first seriously to affect a newspaper had taken place in 1825; it had, in fact, been discussed at a similar parliamentary committee of inquiry.[2] In the spring of that year Richard Lonergan, of *Carrick's Morning Post*, provoked a dispute with his staff because—if his own account is to be trusted—he had taken on an apprentice against their wishes. The *Carrick's* printers remonstrated unsuccessfully; finding him determined, they left in a

---

[1] Ibid., 1837-8, viii. (2nd report).
[2] Ibid., 1825 (437) iv. 499.

body. He managed to secure the services of some non-union men, and engaged more apprentices. On the night of February 27, as he and some of his men were crossing Carlisle bridge on their way home, they were waylaid by the strikers armed with bludgeons, who injured two men before they were driven off. After a police investigation, seven of the printers were charged and bound to keep the peace. The light sentence was probably the result of the difficulty of obtaining evidence, as the police complained that prospective witnesses were terrorized into silence by the threats of the combinators. Speakers at a meeting of the Dublin manufacturers alleged that the newspapers, too, had allowed themselves to be intimidated. Lonergan and other journalists denied the charge, the brevity of newspapers' reports was caused by their shortage of staff.[1]

In the same year a strike suspended publication of the Dublin *Courier*. An advertisement which the owners put in other newspapers while the strike was on hinted that the compositors' dissatisfaction with the *Courier's* politics had been the reason for the strike. In a counter-advertisement, the compositors ridiculed the idea:[2]

> In the name of Heaven! Who ever heard of a master printer refusing to give, or a journeyman to accept employment on the score of political feeling! Alike it is to the journeyman, as regards his mere political operations, whether publicity is given to the speech of the Duke of York, or the effusions of Mr. O'Connell, provided he is paid for his labour.

The compositors asserted that so far from their strike being a dark conspiracy, it followed days and weeks of trying to extract from 'the bungling and imbecile management of this concern' not an increase, but any wages at all. Possibly the owners, whose paper was not proving profitable, were hoping to cut their losses by enlisting public sympathy against the combinators. The *Courier* reappeared after a few days, but references in it to 'slovenly and inefficient compositors', whose threats had kept away other labour, led to another week's gap in publication, and its final disappearance, doubtless hastened by the stoppages, took place a few weeks later.[3]

These strikes were symptomatic of labour's growing solidarity, and during the year 1825 a union of journeymen-printers was founded,[4] whose secretary, Thomas Daly, appeared before the 1838 parliamentary committee of inquiry.

---

[1] *S.N.L.*, 22 Apr. 1835.
[2] *M. Register*, 8 Oct. 1825. And see p. 180 above.
[3] *Courier*, Oct.–Nov. 1825.
[4] Clarkson, *Labour and nationalism in Ireland*, gives a general account of the growth of the trade union movement in Ireland.

Daly told the committee that the union's objects were 'the formation of a permanent fund for affording relief to those who may be out of employment from time to time, to settle the price of labour between employers and employed, and other matters affecting the general welfare of the printers' community'. Daly was the union's only paid officer, receiving twenty guineas a year. Delegates, one from each office, met in a public-house every Saturday night, representing some 260 members and 180 apprentices. The union paid unemployment money, 7s. 6d. for the first six weeks, and then 5s. a week, up to a maximum of £4 a year. Unemployed journeymen who wished to emigrate were assisted with grants, £4 if going to England, and £8, if to America. 'Tramps'—printers wandering round the country in search of work—were given 5s. on production of their union card: and there was a burial allowance of £3 for the family of a deceased member.

Daly's evidence suggested that the union was primarily a friendly society: P. D. Hardy, an employer, maintained that it existed to limit the number of apprentices employed in printing offices, to ensure that only union men were employed, and to enforce a minimum wage. As a result, he said, he felt that he no longer had any authority in his own office. He had been forbidden to employ more than four apprentices, irrespective of the number of printers in his establishment; and he had come up against so many union restrictions that, in common with other master printers, he had become disheartened and had reduced his commitments. He was followed by Michael Staunton, who referred to a number of strikes that had taken place as a result of disputes—one as far back as the war years, at a time when he had been editor of the *Freeman*, for a minimum wage; another on the *Evening Post* against the employment of non-union labour; and another on his *Register*, for shorter hours (the printers at that time worked a twelve-hour day, seven in the morning to seven at night, with two hours off for meals). He had given way to the union on this occasion, and also when they had demanded that he should limit the number of apprentices to four. At the best of times, he said, a morning newspaper was a poor commercial proposition: these concessions had only served to make the *Register's* position more precarious.

The Dublin master printers admitted that relations between them and their staffs had on the whole been harmonious; at least, no violence had been recorded since the assault upon Lonergan in 1825. Relations in some of the provincial newspapers had been less happy. The owner of the *Newry Commercial Chronicle* had prosecuted his journeymen when they had threatened to strike; seven of them had spent a month in jail.

When the printers of the rival *Newry Examiner* had left work to escort the convicted men to the prison, their employer had initiated prosecutions against them, which had only fallen through because his foreman, on whom he relied for corroborative evidence, turned out to be in the union himself. Francis Dalzell Finlay, owner of the *Northern Whig*, described his disputes with his staff in some detail. On receiving an ultimatum from them in 1836, he had sacked the lot and brought in men in their place from Scotland and Dublin. He and the new men had been threatened with violence, for which he was able to obtain the conviction of two of his former printers. Then the new men joined the union, and his troubles began again. It was illegal at that date for the men to strike, but they could give notice in a body; and they did, when he tried to use one of his editorial staff as a printer. This time, he proudly told the committee:

> I adopted rather a novel plan and a plan which I think, if acted upon by other employers would free them from the miseries of combination upon many occasions. I fitted up privately in the rear of my own premises a printing office, unknown to my men, and known only to one or two confidential persons. I got a fount of types put into it; I went to the country free schools, I brought in children from them, put them into the secret printing office, I slept them upon the premises, I fed them upon the premises, and privately at night I took them out to give them exercise and air, and sent them into the country on a Sunday, to take gymnastic exercises in my garden, at my own cottage. I attended to the business in the printing offices, and attended to the teaching of these boys myself; and by the time this strike came, I had these little boys taught, some not more than ten years of age, whom I perched upon stools, and thus set at defiance the threats of these mighty combinators.

Finlay was an exception; in general, masters and journeymen showed a disposition to understand each other's arguments and to reach some settlement advantageous to both. Hardy said that he had realized he should not be judge in his own case, and had asked for the formation of a joint committee, a suggestion which had been turned down by the journeymen on the grounds that they could only negotiate through their union. Staunton agreed; he would prefer to see matters settled by employer-employee discussions, rather than by statute. Both denied that there had been any employers' organization set up to oppose the union. Staunton admitted that he sometimes consulted with the owner of the other Dublin morning paper (the *Freeman*), but he asserted that they never made any compact. Finlay, however, boasted of coming to terms with other Belfast owners. The chairman gently reminded him that this was illegal. Finlay replied that he never had entered into any *written* contract with them; to comply with the law he made the agreements verbally. The chairman then asked whether he did not think that workers ought to have a right to form unions? Certainly, said Finlay; he was entirely in sympathy with the printers forming an association—provided that it did not conflict at any time with the wishes of employers.

The evidence obtained by the committee was of little value, except to show that the trouble, lying as it did in the post-union economic depression in Ireland, could not be cured simply by promoting better relations between master and man. Staunton in his evidence admitted that the *Freeman* printers had successfully demanded a minimum wage of £2 a week in 1815. Twenty years later the minimum wage was dropped to 32/6. The workers' agitation had not been for increased wages; they had been striving to prevent their livelihood from dwindling down to the subsistence level. Unemployment had increased: over 300 printers had been forced to emigrate from Dublin between 1834 and 1837. The limitation of the number of apprentices was a natural enough demand, when so many printers were out of work; they could point to the *Evening Mail* office, where only one apprentice was employed in a staff of twenty.

The employers' arguments were no less reasonable. Newspapers had such small circulations that profits were insignificant; any additional expenses and the owners might be forced out of business. Printing firms owed much of their general work, besides newspapers, to the ability to undersell their English rivals; if increased costs put the two countries on a level, the Irish firms would lose orders. The effect of the taxes on the press had been to leave so narrow a margin between survival and extinction of a newspaper, that even the most modest claims of his workers might tip the balance against the owner, driving him out of business, and leaving his workers worse off than before. Such arguments, admittedly, are frequently used by employers in answer to workers' claims. But it is probable that they were substantially just at this time, particularly in the case of the *Morning Register* whose circulation was only a few hundred copies.

The importance of the investigation lay less in its findings than in its revelation that the workers were already well organized in a trade union that was to attain considerable power. That its representatives should be consulted by the committee on equal terms with the employers marked a decisive stage in its development.

(b) JOURNALISTS

At the time that this investigation was proceeding an effort was being made to establish another press association, of a different character.

On 26 May 1838 a meeting of editors, sub-editors, and reporters of the Dublin newspaper press was held to consider the propriety of forming a 'press association', with John Stevenson, editor of the *Freeman*, in the chair. No newspaper proprietor was present, but most of them had sent messages of goodwill. Lynar, the editor of the *Morning Register*, presented the report of a committee which had earlier been appointed to examine the position. 'By being members of a united body', the committee had decided, 'each should be individually bound to watch over the honour of all'. The meeting passed a series of resolutions: that the interest and respectability of the Dublin press would be advanced by such a body; that it would secure co-operation amongst the newspapers; and that it would help to bridge the disparity between the standing of the literary profession and its influence. Finally, Charles Gavan Duffy, at that time a reporter on the *Morning Register*, proposed that the association be formed. A committee was elected, two members from each daily paper, one from each evening and weekly paper. Proprietors could become *ex-officio* members if they wished; and, on another suggestion by Gavan Duffy, members of the staffs of periodicals were admitted, including Clarence Mangan, whom he introduced as 'one of the most successful and popular members of the *University Magazine*'.

The press, particularly the *Register* and the *Pilot*, welcomed the association, the *Register* admitting that 'a want of cordial intercommunication and co-operation has left the individual members of the press a place in the social scale far below that to which their collective influence upon society and the importance of their profession justly gives them claim'.[1]

The association does not seem to have made much impact on the journalistic life of the time. Gavan Duffy makes no mention of it in his recollections: his account of the Dublin press[2] in the late eighteen-thirties does, however, help to explain why it failed. The staff of the journals who supported O'Connell, he recalled, had slight sympathy with O'Connell's policy, and few settled opinions or purpose of any sort. 'The editors of the three particularly Catholic papers were all Protestants, and the co-editors of a pre-eminently Protestant organ had been born and bred Catholics. Most of them had lived through the first repeal movement; and whatever public spirit they possessed probably evaporated with its collapse'. The attempt to form a journalistic association was made at a time when the public and national spirit was weak: and in the circumstances its failure was to be expected.

[1] *M. Register*, 1 June 1838.
[2] C. Gavan Duffy, *My life in two hemispheres*, i. 27.

(ii) *The right to report*

That the association should have been formed at all was an indication of the reporters' growing realization of their responsibilities; and it came in time to give the press confidence in one of its periodic contests with authority over the limits of the public's right to read accounts of the administrative deliberations of public boards.

The question arose in 1839 whether the reporters should be admitted to the meetings of the boards of guardians appointed to administer the new Poor Laws. At first, reporters were occasionally admitted, but when boards of guardians decided in their favour, there would sometimes be dissentients.[1] The decisive step was taken in December 1840, when the guardians of north and south Dublin decided to allow reports of their meetings. The *Pilot*, however, foresaw trouble ahead:[2]

> Publicity has forced itself on every institution in the country, even on the legislature: and is it to be endured that foreign commissioners should come here, and enormous patronage and almost unlimited powers of taxation, who want to put a gag on that publicity which has been found the best safeguard against abuse, and the only guarantee for justice?

A few weeks later, Nicholls, on whose report the Poor Law system was based, declared that reporting of the guardians' meeting was inadvisable, a view that was also taken by the crown law officers. The Poor Law commissioners forthwith ordered the guardians to stop reporters attending their meetings, and the guardians accepted this ruling under protest.[3] Faced with growing opposition, the commissioners then shifted their ground; they ruled that reporters should be allowed in, but that they could be excluded at the wish of any one guardian, on the principle operated in the house of commons. They defended their action in a circular:[4] while acts of the guardians must be recorded and made public, 'the deliberations precedent to the act—the opinions of individual guardians—the information adduced on particular points perhaps confidentially obtained—ought, in the commissioners' judgment, to be confined to the board itself, and left strictly private'. If reporters were admitted, the commissioners thought, guardians might be swayed by popular clamour, and the publication of hasty or ill-considered expressions might inflame or mislead the public.

[1] *Pilot*, 27 Nov. 1839.
[2] Ibid., 4 Dec. 1840.
[3] Ibid., 18 Dec. 1840.
[4] Ibid., 28 Dec. 1840.

The commissioners fear, too, that such publicity may tend to indispose the fittest person to undertake the duty of a guardian, and may eventually drive from the board men of quiet, business-like habits whose presence there is most important for the interest of the ratepayers, but whose labour and well-considered judgments could be liable to be borne down by the fluency of members more practised in public debate, and speaking under the existing influence of having what they say reported in the newspapers.

The commissioners' arguments were plausible and not without insight into the national character. But they were lost on the guardians, who may have been moved less by a desire for publicity than by annoyance at being considered unable to run their own affairs. 'The commissioners', one of them complained,[1] 'will not give us knives lest we should cut ourselves.' Long reports of guardians' meetings, which continued to be published, indicated that the commissioners' advice was not always accepted by the boards. The *Pilot* drew attention to the exclusion of reporters on the few occasions when it occurred. The newspapers were given a useful handle when the chairman of the North Dublin Union, complaining of misrepresentation in the *Freeman*, had to admit that reporters had not been present at the time.[2] The information, he said, must have been passed to the paper by some member of the board. Such misrepresentation could not have occurred if reporters had been present.

The Dublin press did not establish a general right to report the deliberations of any public body. Contests of a similar nature were to occur many times in later years, and the press was not always the winner. The value of the 1840 precedent lay less in the admission of a principle than in the extension of the field of newspaper reporting. Citizens unconsciously grew accustomed to seeing accounts of the meetings of official and semi-official bodies, even if they never read them; and they could be stirred to indignation when their newspaper announced that its reporter had been excluded. Thereafter, the press less often had to fight on its own behalf. The decision to admit reporters ceased to be challenged when men in public life grew accustomed to the presence of reporters at their meetings.

(iii) *O'Connell and the press*

When O'Connell founded the Precursor Society in 1839,[3] with a view

[1] Ibid.
[2] Ibid., 22 Oct. 1841.
[3] I have dealt with this incident in greater detail in an article 'O'Connell and the Irish press' in *I.H.S.*, no. xxix. (Mar. 1952), which can be consulted for references.

to reviving the dormant campaign for the repeal of the union, he expressed anger that his change of policy created little enthusiasm in the liberal press. The newspapers were probably reflecting the public's apathy, but O'Connell chose to blame them for it in the course of an after-dinner speech. The liberal press, he complained, had failed to recognize the new spirit that was abroad, and if they did not wake up, he would feel bound to chastise them. Staunton, who was at the dinner, attempted to reply to the charge, but he was howled down. The reporters present decided to leave in a body, and they were shown out with hoots, hisses, and volleys of left-over food: Staunton was actually assaulted. The reporters decided that they were justified in suppressing O'Connell's speech, and they were backed by Staunton, and even by the *Pilot*, which put the blame for the scene on O'Connell's sycophants.

O'Connell retaliated in a speech in which he openly threatened the liberal newspapers: and at the same time, he took direct action against the three most important of them, the *Pilot*, the *Freeman*, and the *Register*. The *Pilot's* next issue contained an abject retraction of its criticisms, and a claim that O'Connell's speech had been omitted from its previous issue 'by mistake'. Mrs Lavelle, who had taken over the *Freeman* on the death of her husband, was informed that the Precursor Society's favour—including its advertisements—would be cut off if O'Connell's speech was not printed; the reporter who had withheld the speech was thereupon sacked. Staunton held out a little longer, but the financial position of the liberal press at the time was so weak that he, too, felt unable to face the loss of such influential backing and within a week the affair was settled, with O'Connell boasting that the peace had been dictated on his terms.

The incident only confirms the impression that is created by the study of O'Connell's relations with the liberal press. He wanted the newspapers to be his instruments in the national cause: they must follow his course, wherever it might lead them, on the assumption that only he had the authority to drive the country forwards to fuller nationhood. The liberal newspaper owners were anxious to support him: but they also felt another loyalty—to the principle of an independent press of the 'fourth estate' conception. The newspapers' case had been put in 1828 by Jack Lawless, whom O'Connell had accused of playing ascendancy's game because he had criticized the liberal administration:

> Though I may acknowledge Mr O'Connell's claims to gratitude, yet am I to surrender up my judgement when that judgement tells me that he is wrong? Am I to lower myself in the public estimation by following him on all occasions, perfectly indifferent to the voice of conscience, reason and

221

truth? I should be unworthy of a place in your councils if I could stoop to be the automaton of any man. When men speak of unanimity, and wish for that desirable result, they should take care to avoid the evil of being unanimously wrong. How are men to come to a correct and honest conclusion? How, but by discussion! Let discussion, free and unembarrassed, take place, and then let us be unanimous, in the support of truth!

Staunton was to argue along similar lines at the time of the Precursor row; he justified the *Register's* attitude on the grounds that in the long run, an independent press would be of more value to O'Connell's cause than servile newspapers, and that in any case the freedom of the press was of more value to the nation than the dominance of any single individual. O'Connell would not accept this argument. He did not worry overmuch about the attacks, some of them vicious, on his policy and person by the ascendancy newspapers: that was part of the game. But he could not stomach criticism of any kind from the newspapers which professed to be on his side.

Not only did O'Connell expect obedience from the liberal press: throughout his career, he assumed that any newspaper owner friendly to his cause ought to be prepared to shelter him from the possible consequences of his speeches and letters, where they provoked Castle wrath. The imprisonment of Magee and Tracey during the Peel administration, and of Barrett in 1834, were only the most notorious of many cases in which journalists were prosecuted and sentenced for the publication of libels that O'Connell had written or spoken, and which he refused to avow, on the ground that the national cause had too great a need of his services to permit him to languish in jail.

The position of the newspaper owners would have been less difficult if O'Connell had been more consistent. If throughout his life he had remained a consistent repealer, for example, it would have been a comparatively simple matter for supporting newspapers to nail their colours to his repeal mast. But O'Connell was constantly changing his tactics even on so important a matter, at short notice—and colours which have been nailed up can only be hauled down with embarrassment. The *Pilot* did its best to follow the leader without qualifications, but it was not always successful. In 1840, for example, the *Pilot* was busily assailing the *Freeman* for its indolence in refusing to press the new repeal campaign. O'Connell suddenly decided that the *Freeman* might be a useful ally, publicly praised it, and criticized liberals who squabbled among themselves: and the *Pilot* had to do a right-about-turn, as it had done in the case of the Precursor speech, to its obvious discomfiture.

This was a small matter: but there were many occasions in which

O'Connell changed his course on more important subjects with a facility that men of the type of Staunton felt unwilling to accept. On repeal of the Union, on the retention of the forty-shilling freehold franchise, and on the Poor Laws O'Connell changed his mind with bewildering frequency; and it was a further cause for worry to his followers that—as he himself once put it—he was apt to support 'with all the fervour of the renegade' the very policies he had recently been denouncing.

A further cause for friction between O'Connell and the liberal newspapers was the ferocity with which he attacked them when they did not obey him. When, for example, he launched a tirade in 1825 against the 'base' and 'vile' Dublin press with its 'envious rancour' and 'impotent malignity', he was referring not to the *Star* or the *Mail* or the *Warder* or any of the ascendancy newspapers, but to the *Freeman* and the *Register*, with whom he happened to be quarrelling at the time.

That O'Connell did his own cause a disservice by such methods seems clear from the evidence of the newspapers' circulation figures. The existence of a great potential demand for a liberal newspaper in the national interest was to be shown by the extraordinary success of the *Nation* when it was first published in the 'forties. But the liberal papers before that time, torn as they were between the desire to retain their reputations for consistency, and yet to support O'Connell, found great difficulty in collecting readers: and the avowedly O'Connellite newspapers never thrived. The *Pilot* failed to reach a circulation of four figures at any time in its career; the *Dublin Evening Post*, published on alternate evenings with the *Pilot*, usually had twice as many readers, in spite of its Castle connections.

It is tempting to draw the inference from the *Pilot*'s failure that the public despised as spineless an editorial puppet which danced meekly to the party tune, whatever that tune might be. In the early 1830s, particularly, O'Connell's changes of tack were so bewildering that the *Pilot*'s readers could hardly be blamed if they gave up their subscriptions in bewilderment or disgust. Manfully Barrett strove to anticipate possible new departures. For example, when in 1831 O'Connell was suddenly tempted from his out-and-out repeal campaign by the possibility of taking office in the Grey administration, the *Pilot* commented that if O'Connell accepted office, it would be without the compromise of any principle, because he would have attained more power by that means to serve Ireland. 'We will go further', the editorial ran, 'and say that if O'Connell refused office under such circumstances—in dread of the misconstructions of the vile, and the misconceptions of the weak—he would show want of moral courage—be a deserter to his country'. But

O'Connell was denied the office he was angling for, and very soon the *Pilot* was full of invective against the ministers of a kind that suggested they would hardly have made fit colleagues for O'Connell.

In general, O'Connell's relations with the liberal press were unsatisfactory: and if blame is to be apportioned he must accept the largest share. There was some excuse for him in that he had grown up at a time when the newspapers were cowed and malleable, easily persuaded by threats or bribes to take the Castle side. But O'Connell failed to realize the change that came over the Irish press in the 'twenties, largely inspired by Staunton, which put it on a new level. As a result, O'Connell and the liberal newspapers were unable fully to co-operate to the advantage of the causes they shared.

3. RECESSION 1838–41

O'Connell's decision to break with the Melbourne administration and to resume the campaign for repeal brought to an end the period of harmony between the liberal press and the Castle. After Drummond had become under secretary in 1835, prosecutions of newspapers had, for a time, entirely ceased. The *Evening Post* and a provincial newspaper were given notice[1] of an impending action in 1836, for a reflection on the magistracy; but it does not appear to have been pressed. The cases against the newspapers[2] in the following year, although they resulted in the *Freeman*, the *Mayo Telegraph*, and the *Clonmel Advertiser* paying heavy damages, were civil suits. In the summer of 1838, the *Evening Post* was able to assert that since the whigs had come into office, the government had utterly discontinued state prosecutions for libel. But as disillusionment grew, with the failure of the administration to live up to O'Connell's expectations, the press began to reflect his growing discontent. The ascendancy, which since 1835 had been unable to make use of its influence in the courts, again had its opportunity. The crown law officers were still disinclined to initiate prosecutions themselves; but they were willing to take up criminal libel actions started against newspapers by individuals. To the newspaper owners, it mattered little where the prosecutions had their origin: sentence, if passed upon them, would be the same.

The *Evening Post's* comment in 1838 upon the immunity of the press

[1] *D.E. Mail*, 16 Nov. 1836.
[2] *Pilot*, 24 May 1837.

in the immediate past was prompted by the news that that immunity had been challenged, by an action for criminal libel against the *Pilot*, at the suit of the earl of Westmeath. This charge was not pressed; but the following month, another was brought, this time against the *Evening Post* itself. A bigoted Orangeman, notorious then, and destined to be still more notorious later, had been selected as sub-sheriff of Monaghan, to the *Post's* vigorously expressed disgust. The Orangeman, Samuel Gray, collected £250 damages from Conway;[1] the ascendancy's power was still great in the courts. By this time, in any case, the divergences between the Castle and the ascendancy were diminishing, as friendship waned between the Castle and O'Connell. In the same year the attorney general intervened in a civil suit to procure Barrett of the *Pilot* a three months' prison sentence on one libel charge, and a fine on another.[2] Neither libel was particularly offensive, and the Dublin press grew alarmed. The *Freeman* began to express fears that a conspiracy existed against the press; no journalist had been to prison for a libel since Barrett's last incarceration when, as he light-heartedly recalled in his *Pilot*—'Judge Jebb read me a long lecture—a tune which ended in the usual dance— bolts, bars, and vaults for some months in the dog days'. The *Freeman's* fears received confirmation the following winter, when John Jones was awarded damages against Thomas Sheehan of the *Evening Mail*. Jones was another bigot, too Orange even for the *Mail*; yet the jury gave him £300. The *Mail* thought it remarkable that a libeller 'so unreserved and irrespective' as John Jones should have obtained a verdict at all. The *Freeman* and the *Morning Register* joined in condemning the decision. O'Connell, the *Pilot* complained, would never have obtained a verdict for any of the far worse libels heaped upon him.[3]

These prosecutions were too few and too scattered to suggest that they were undertaken with the Castle's connivance; but in order to bring an action for criminal libel, it was necessary to obtain the attorney general's sanction, and to that extent the Castle must have acquiesced. When relations between administration and the press, so cordial in the early months of the Melbourne administration, deteriorated, the ascendancy was able to prove to itself that its hold on the courts was in no way impaired by the accident of whig rule. The duration of the alliance between the whigs and O'Connell had shown that with the help of goodwill and a competent administration much could be done to allay, if not to remedy Irish grievances: and the state of the press had largely

[1] Ibid., 25 June 1838.
[2] *M. Register*, 6, 13 May 1839.
[3] *D.E. Mail*, 4 Dec. 1839: *Pilot*, 11 Dec. 1839.

reflected the prevailing political mood. But the whigs were less concerned for Ireland than for the votes of the O'Connellites in the commons. As this became evident, Catholic newspapers, losing their sobriety, became petulant, and occasionally aggressive. They found that they had not been able to consolidate the gains that had apparently been made since 1835. In that year the *Morning Register* and the *Pilot* had no hesitation in exposing a case of jury-packing to secure the conviction of a Catholic; and a few weeks later he had been released.[1] But as soon as the goodwill of the Castle could no longer be relied upon, the Catholic papers found themselves unable to criticize the courts with impunity. And by this time, as the newspapers had first found in the early 'thirties, the ascendancy was no longer antagonistic only to the Catholic newspapers; it mistrusted the press as a whole. The verdict against the *Evening Mail* was significant. As the *Pilot* sadly commented, juries were at last becoming impartial, as far as the newspapers were concerned; Orange or Green, tory or radical, the damages awarded against the press were 'always excessive'.[2]

Nevertheless, the course of the early years of the Melbourne administration had shown that, given goodwill on the government's side, the Irish press could aspire to act in a fourth estate capacity. Newspapers still suffered severely from the high rate of taxation: but the reduction of the stamp duty and of the advertisement tax in this period, although it was not reflected in any immediate increase in press activity, was a small step towards the acquirement by the newspapers of a wider circle of readers. In other ways, the intervention of the Castle almost ceased. In the late 'thirties there was no Castle newspaper; the proclamation system had gone; and other subsidies, if they existed at all, were negligible.

But these gains could not be consolidated so long as the problem of national independence remained unsettled. Before the whigs left office, the formation of the Precursor Society had brought the period of the O'Connell-whig alliance to an end, and pointed the way to the later campaign for repeal of the Union. When the government chose to resist the demand for repeal, a situation was again created in Ireland where the aim of the leaders of the national movement was not to reform but to overturn the constitution. In such circumstances, as in the 1790s, the Castle, in its concern for self-preservation and the retention of the old constitutional links, was not likely to be influenced by academic arguments in favour of the preservation of the freedom of the press. Yet

[1] 2 Nov., 18 Dec. 1839.
[2] *Pilot*, 4 Dec. 1839.

the effort to obtain that freedom had not been entirely wasted. A few months after the whigs fell from office, a newspaper was to appear in Dublin which, both for its character, and for its influence on the minds of Irishmen, was to gain a reputation unparalleled in the country's history—far exceeding that of the *Freeman*, the *Northern Star*, or the *Press*. It is easy to trace the debt of the *Nation*—founded in 1842—to Staunton, whose *Morning Register* had provided the training ground for Gavan Duffy, Dillon, and Thomas Davis. And it is easy to find in Staunton the central figure in the development of the Irish press after its collapse in the chief secretaryship of Robert Peel. Staunton understood the direction in which the press ought to travel, even if he lacked the flair which would have made his own ventures more successful. That so great a change came over the Irish press in the twenty-odd years following Peel's departure from Ireland, must be credited largely to Staunton's realization that the freedom of the press could be maintained only while the newspaper retains its liberty to criticize the policies, not only of its antagonists, but also of the interests it wishes to support.

Appendix A

THE LAW OF LIBEL

From the year 1694, when the English house of commons had refused to renew the licensing act, the law of libel had been the only outward restraint on the liberty—or the licence—of the press. That law, however, had its roots in the Star Chamber: and it could still be twisted to suit the purposes that had been served by the licensing act. If the judiciary felt that it was their duty to uphold the dignity of the state, they could use their powers to make criticism of the government so dangerous that a state of censorship virtually existed.

This was the position in Ireland in 1784. The judges then, and for many years to come, were bound to the state by close ties of self-interest. The journals of Lord Clonmell[1] and the correspondence of Lord Norbury,[2] chief justices of the king's bench, make it clear that they regarded themselves primarily as servants of the Castle. Their promotion to the bench had been the reward of their services to the Castle: their future promotion through the grades of the peerage was dependent upon their continuing to give the same satisfaction. To them, newspaper condemnation of—say—ministerial corruption was calculated to undermine the authority of the state, and was *ipso facto* seditious. The judges consistently reacted to press criticism of the government as if their own livelihood was endangered—as indeed it was.

The bench traditionally reserved the right in cases of libel to decide whether or not a publication was libellous, leaving to the jury only the decision whether or not defendant had been the author, printer, or publisher. It happened, however, that in 1784, in the case of Rex *v* the dean of St Asaph's, an English jury which had been directed from the bench that the publication in question was a libel, nevertheless insisted upon finding the defendant 'guilty of publishing *only*'. The judge disputed their right to give this verdict, and, on a motion for a retrial, he

[1] Fitzpatrick, *The Sham Squire*, p. 101, ff.
[2] I.S.P.O., Off. Papers.

was sustained by the chief justice, Mansfield, who quoted the jingle:

> *But Sir Philip well knows*
> *That his innuendos*
> *Will serve him no longer*
> *In verse or in prose*
> *For twelve honest men have decided the cause*
> *Who are judges of fact, though not judges of laws.*

But the case against the dean was not resumed; the jury were conceded a moral victory.

Agitation increased to have the right to decide whether matter was libellous transferred from judges to juries. The assumption must be that the class from whom juries were chosen in Ireland knew what was happening in England, because trials in England—such as the dean's—were better reported in the Irish newspapers than trials in Dublin, as it was easier and cheaper to reprint accounts from the English press than to employ reporters to attend the Dublin courts. The Castle could not, therefore, entirely rely upon the courts to do its bidding. A flagrantly unfair charge might provoke a jury to follow the St Asaph's precedent. In 1784–5, notwithstanding the fright given to respectable citizens by the excessive scurrility of the press, the Castle never brought a press case to a jury: and after 1789, when prosecutions were resumed, they found a growing tendency for juries to be recalcitrant. In July 1790 a jury found a Dublin printer, Amyas Griffith, guilty of publishing *only*, in defiance of judicial direction; and when the judge told them that this verdict was unacceptable, they found Griffith not guilty.[1] One of the trials of the owners of the *Northern Star* ended in the same manner.

The executive must have realized that the old system was breaking down, and no serious opposition was offered to the re-enactment, for Ireland, of Fox's Libel Act, which gave juries the right to decide whether matter was libellous.[2]

This act, passed in 1793, ought to have marked the beginning of a new era in the story of the freedom of the press. To have the decision in the hands of a jury is as near as the press can hope to get to trial by public opinion. Had juries been representative of public opinion, the course of libel actions—the arguments of counsel, the judge's charge to the jury, and the verdict—would have become a reflection of the public attitude to the limits of press freedom and, therefore, illustrative of its growth. In point of fact, juries quickly ceased to be representative. After

[1] *M. Post*, 10 July 1790.
[2] *Ir. Statutes*, 1793, xvi. 924.

1793, they were systematically packed. When the Castle and the ascendancy fell out, the newspapers sometimes escaped in the confusion: but normally they stood no chance of acquittal. Libel trials became a reflection not of public opinion, but of Castle policy. The *Dublin Evening Post* in the days of its owner's war with Higgins had coined the definitions:

> *Seditious libel* . . . any publication that contravenes the holy political doctrine of passive obedience and non-resistance. . . .
>
> *Traitorous libel* . . . any publication that asserts the rights of Ireland and its independence. . . .
>
> *False libel* . . . any publication that tells the world that an m.p. always votes, right or wrong, with every administration, because he is a placeman or the hungry hanger-on of a borough-jobbing peer. . . .
>
> *Scandalous libel* . . . any publication of anecdotes relative to the origin and promotion of a beggarly pettifogging scoundrel:

—what the *Evening Post* had described in jest, the government was to enforce in earnest. Libel trials became little more than an executive weapon, for use when bribes and threats had been rejected.

However interesting, then, many of the 1784–1841 libel actions may be—however productive of closely reasoned legal arguments—however illuminated by the forensic genius of such advocates as John Philpot Curran and O'Connell—the legal side of the trials is seldom relevant to the consideration of the freedom of the press. Neither the justice of the newspapers' cause, nor the skill of their advocates affected the results; even where newspapers were acquitted, it was not on the merits of their case, but on account—say—of an ascendancy squabble with the Castle. O'Connell's ideas of a revision of the law of libel,[1] cogent as they were, could have had value only for England. In Ireland, no revision of the law would have appreciably altered the position of the press, so long as the courts remained at the service of the state.

[1] He brought up the subject in the commons almost every year between 1830 and 1838. See index to parliamentary debates in those years.

Appendix B

THE FITZPATRICK CASE (1813)

The prosecution of Hugh FitzPatrick, a bookseller, for libel in 1813 is the only important instance in the period of government action against the press, other than newspapers and periodicals. FitzPatrick published a book on the penal laws written by Denis Scully. Scully's name was not, however, printed, and FitzPatrick allowed himself to be sent to jail rather than betray the author. A full account of the proceedings is given by W. Ridgeway in a pamphlet 'Report of the trial of Hugh FitzPatrick for Libel' (Dublin 1813): accounts of the trial appear also in the Dublin press during the first weeks of February of that year.

Appendix C

NEWSPAPER CIRCULATIONS (1821-41)

The chart has been compiled from the circulation figures given in Parliamentary Papers, 1826–43.

1826	(235)	xxiii. 383.
1829	(164)	xxii. 273.
1830	(119)	xxv. 365.
	(549)	xxv. 349.
1831–2	(242)	xxxiv. 123.
1833	(503)	xxxii. 623.
1834	(510)	xlix. 407.
1836	(146)	xlv. 359.
	(177)	xlv. 361.
1837	(462)	xxxix. 325.
1837–8	(73)	xxxiv. 393.
1840	(266)	xxix. 503.
1843	(174)	xxx. 537.
	(98)	xxx. 513

These returns, which are not quite complete, give the total number of stamps used by individual newspapers over periods of a month, a quarter, or a year. The figures themselves are probably reasonably accurate. Although it was in the newspaper owner's interest to buy as few stamps as possible to save tax, he also wanted to buy as many stamps as possible to impress advertisers with his newspaper's circulation. The object of the chart, however, is to indicate trends, rather than to present exact figures.

The chart's significant features are:

(*a*) The small circulations. Owing to high taxation newspapers were beyond the reach of all but the well-to-do—mainly Protestant or 'Castle Catholic'.

(*b*) The relative popularity of the independent Protestant-Conservative newspapers. Before 1821 the newspapers with the biggest circula-

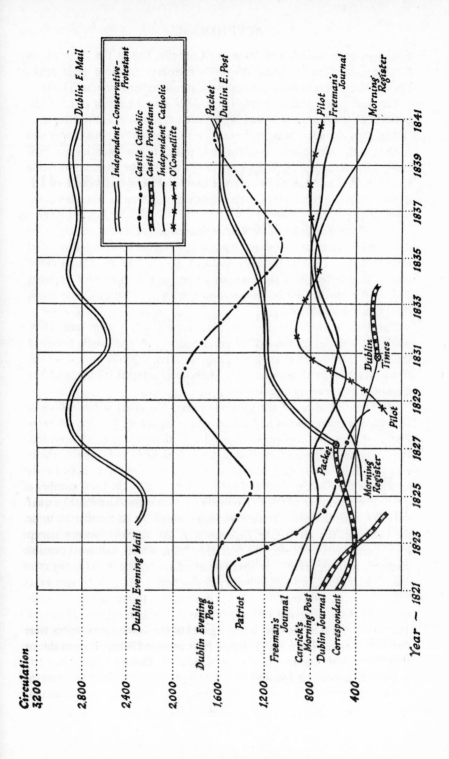

APPENDIX

Circulation

3,200

2,800

2,400

2,000

1,600

1,200

800

400

Year ~ 1821   1823   1825   1827   1829   1831   1833   1835   1837   1839   1841

Independent-Conservative-Protestant
Castle Catholic
Castle Protestant
Independent Catholic
O'Connellite

Dublin E. Mail
Dublin Evening Mail
Packet
Dublin E. Post
Pilot
Freeman's Journal
Morning Register
Dublin Times
Pilot
Morning Register
Packet
Dublin Evening Post
Patriot
Freeman's Journal
Carrick's Morning Post
Dublin Journal
Correspondent

tions had been liberal, and often pro-Catholic. But in the 1820s alarm for the ascendancy's future drove its members to close their ranks against liberalism in order to oppose Catholic emancipation. The temporary fall in the *Mail's* circulation in 1824 was the result of the competition of the *Star*, which was even more aggressively anti-Catholic.

The *Correspondent* was Protestant and Conservative, but it was tied to the Castle, whose middle-of-the-road policy in the 'twenties was mistrusted by the ascendancy. As soon as the newspaper changed its name to the *Packet* and began to take the same independent Protestant line as the *Mail* (the two papers were published on alternate weekday evenings) its popularity grew.

(*c*) The unpopularity of the Castle newspapers. Haydn had improved the *Patriot's* circulation by making it brighter than its competitors, but after he left in 1822 its fortunes declined. By 1829 all the Castle newspapers had failed, and the attempt to revive the moribund *Morning Post* in the 'thirties as the *Dublin Times*, with the help of Castle subsidies, was unsuccessful.

The *Dublin Evening Post* was identified with the Castle until 1824, when it came out on the side of emancipation. A pro-Castle policy in the early 'thirties lost it readers again, but after 1835 the amicable relations which existed between the Melbourne administration and the Catholics restored its circulation.

(*d*) The difficulties of the Catholic press. The chart is misleading in that the *Freeman* always had a Catholic competitor: first the *Morning Post* and then the *Register* were published alongside it every morning. It is reasonable to assume that if there had been only one Catholic morning daily newspaper, its circulation figures might have been nearly as high as the *Evening Post's*.

(*e*) The weakness of the O'Connellite newspapers. The *Pilot* was the only O'Connellite paper to survive long enough for its circulation to be drawable on the chart (the *Freeman* and the *Register* were often at loggerheads with O'Connell). Yet the *Pilot*, which had no Catholic competitor (it appeared on alternate evenings to the *Post*) never succeeded in building up a satisfactory circulation.

Professor R. Dudley Edwards has pointed out to me that the findings of the 1828 Commission of Inquiry into the Dublin Stamp Office (pp. 190–2) suggest that the circulation figures of the newspapers before that date may be even less accurate than I have assumed. There is no evidence that the Dublin Stamp Office ever 'rigged' circulation figures, but the possibility cannot be ignored.

EPILOGUE

'If there be no means left by which public measures can be canvassed, what then will be the consequence? Where the press is free, and discussion unrestrained, the mind, by the collision of intercourse, gets rid of its own asperities; a sort of insensible perspiration takes place in the body politic, by which those acrimonies, which would otherwise fester and inflame, are quietly dissolved and dissipated. But now, if any aggregate assembly shall meet, they are censured; if a printer publishes their resolutions, he is punished. . . . What then remains? The liberty of the press *only*—that sacred palladium which no influence, no power, no minister, no government, which nothing but the depravity, or folly, or corruption of a jury, can ever destroy.'

(John Philpot Curran, Trial of Hamilton Rowan, 1794.)

BIBLIOGRAPHY

SYNOPSIS

A. ORIGINAL SOURCES
(Abbreviations used in references are in square brackets)
I. MS MATERIAL
    1. London
    2. Dublin
II. PRINTED MATERIAL
    1. Correspondence, memoirs etc.
    2. Reports of parliamentary debates, etc.
    3. Newspapers
    4. Magazines
    5. Pamphlets

B. SECONDARY WORKS

★

A. ORIGINAL SOURCES
I. MS MATERIAL

(1) LONDON

British Museum [B.M.]
    Correspondence of
        the hon. Thomas Pelham [Pelham]
        William Eden, 1st Baron Auckland [Auckland]
        Philip Yorke, 3rd earl of Hardwicke [Hardwicke]
        Sir Robert Peel [Peel]
    in the additional manuscripts [B.M. Add. MS]
Public Record Office
    Home Office papers [P.R.O., H.O., . . .]

(2) DUBLIN

National library of Ireland [N.L.I.]
    Richmond MSS
    Lake MSS

Public record office, Ireland, Four courts, Dublin [P.R.O.I.]
    Leveson-Gower letter books
Irish state paper office, Dublin Castle [I.S.P.O.]
    Rebellion papers [Reb. papers]
    Official papers, 2nd series [Off. papers]
    Miscellaneous papers
    Westmoreland correspondence—Fane collection
    Secret service account books
Trinity College, Dublin, library
    MSS of R. R. Madden

The public library, Pearse St, Dublin
    MSS of R. R. Madden (notes for his projected third volume of the
    history of Irish periodical literature) [Madden (I.P.L.) MSS].
    The notes and letters in this collection provide much useful bio-
    graphical and bibliographical material on the press of 1800–1840.

II. PRINTED MATERIAL

1. CORRESPONDENCE, MEMOIRS, ETC.

Historical manuscripts commission [H.M.C. . . .]
    13th report, appendix, vol. viii: MSS and correspondence of James,
    1st earl of Charlemont, vol. ii [*Charlemont* . . .] London 1893
    14th report, appendix, vol. i: MSS of the duke of Rutland, vol. iii.
    [*Rutland* . . .] London 1894.
    13th report, appendix, vol. iii: 14th report appendix v: vols i–iii:
    MSS of J. B. Fortescue preserved at Dropmore [*Fortescue* . . .]
    London 1892, 1894, 1899.

Gilbert, Sir J. T. Documents relating to Ireland 1795–1804. Dublin 1893.
E. Curtis and R. B. McDowell. Irish historical documents. London
    1943.

Barrington, Jonah. Recollections (Every Irishman's Library ed.) Dublin.
    1917.
Beresford, John. Correspondence. *Ed.* Wm. Beresford (2 vols.). London
    1854.
Bowden, C. T. Tour through Ireland. Dublin 1791.
Carey, Matthew. Autobiography. New York 1842.

Castlereagh, Viscount. Memoirs and correspondence. *Ed.* C. Vane. London 1848.

Cloncurry, Lord. Recollections. Dublin 1849.

Cornwallis, earl of. Correspondence. *Ed.* C. Ross. London 1859.

Croker, J. W. Correspondence and diaries. London 1884.

Curran, J. P. Speeches. *Ed.* T. Davis. Dublin 1845.

Drennan, Dr W. Letters. *Ed.* D. A. Chart. Belfast 1931.

George IV. Correspondence. *Ed.* A. Aspinall. Cambridge 1938.

Grattan, Henry. Memoirs. *Ed.* by his son. London 1839.

Gregory, William. Mr Gregory's letter box 1813–30. *Ed.* Lady Gregory. London 1898.

Hall, Rev. J. Tour through Ireland. London 1813.

Hardwicke, Lord. The viceroy's postbag—correspondence of the earl of Hardwicke. *Ed.* Michael MacDonagh. London 1904.

Holt, F. L. The law of libel. London 1812.

MacDougall, H. Sketches of Irish political characters. London 1799.

MacNeven, T. Leading state trials in Ireland, 1794–1803. Dublin 1844. Pieces of Irish history. New York 1807.

Madden, R. R. Memoirs. *Ed.* T. Madden. London 1891.

Melbourne, Viscount. Memoirs. *Ed.* W. M. Torrens. London 1838.

Moore, Thomas. Memoirs, journal and correspondence. *Ed.* Lord John Russell. London 1853.

Morgan, Lady. Memoirs. London 1862.

Mullala, James. A view of Irish affairs. Dublin 1798.

O'Connell, Daniel. Correspondence. *Ed.* W. J. Fitzpatrick (2 vols). London 1888.

Peel, Robert. Private letters. *Ed.* George Peel. London 1920.

Plowden, Francis. Historical review of Ireland. London 1803. History of Ireland, 1801–10. Dublin 1811.

Wellington, duke of. Civil correspondence and memoranda. *Ed.* by his son, the duke of Wellington. London 1860.

Wyse, Thomas. Historical sketch of the late Catholic association of Ireland. London 1829.

2. REPORTS OF PARLIAMENTARY DEBATES, etc.

Journals of the house of commons [Commons jn.] from 1800.

Journals of the house of lords [Lords jn.] from 1800.

Parliamentary debates [Parl. deb.] from 1800.

Parliamentary papers from 1800.

Journals of the Irish house of commons [Commons jn. Ire.] to 1800.

BIBLIOGRAPHY

Journals of the Irish house of lords [Lords jn. Ire.] to 1800.
The Irish parliamentary register [Ir. parl. reg.] to 1800.
English statutes from 1800.
Irish statutes to 1800.

(The *Irish parliamentary register* gives verbatim or quasi-verbatim reports of some of the debates in the Irish house of commons, and a few in the Irish house of lords, for the period 1780–1800. They appear to have been sufficiently accurate not to have provoked parliamentary censure.)

3. NEWSPAPERS

This list of newspapers is not intended to be comprehensive. Others of less importance, or of less relevance to my theme, will be found mentioned in the text: in the bibliography I have included only those which have been studied in some detail.

The brief explanatory notes are designed mainly to help in distinguishing between the newspapers of the period, many of which have similar-sounding names. Such similarity, incidentally, does not necessarily indicate a common outlook; a *Morning Post* and an *Evening Post* running in the same year may have no connection with one another.

Where a newspaper has an unimportant subsidiary title—e.g. the *Public Register, or Freeman's Journal*—only the name which was in general use has been recorded.

End dates are omitted where they fall outside the 1784–1841 period.

DUBLIN

Antidote, 1822–4. Orange, founded to combat Catholic emancipation
Anti-Union, 1798–9. A series of tracts against the projected Union
Chronicle, Dublin, 1815–17. Pro–Catholic, in opposition during Peel's
    chief-secretaryship; Editor, Æneas MacDonnell
Comet, 1831–3. Polemical weekly
Constitution, or Anti-Union Evening Post, 1799–1800. A more virile
    successor to the Anti-Union
Correspondent, 1806–28. Founded as a Castle newspaper by compact
    with the duke of Bedford, lord lieutenant, Managed to ingratiate
    itself with his tory successor, but fell out with Wellesley Pole. Re–
    turned to favour in 1812 and remained a Castle newspaper there-
    after—less violent and less offensive than the others. Regained
    independence under new name of *Packet and Correspondent* in
    1828, and prospered as a Protestant Ascendancy newspaper

BIBLIOGRAPHY

Courier, Morning (see Irish Times)

Empire, 1832–3. Castle evening newspaper

. Faulkner's Dublin Journal, –1825. Independent, non-partisan, conservative, concentrating mainly on advertising until 1788. Then leased by John Giffard with Castle help and run by him as a Castle newspaper until his retirement—except during the liberal viceroyalties of Fitzwilliam and Bedford. Strongly Orange. Merged with *Irish Times* in 1825

Freeman's Journal (throughout period). Liberal until 1784; then undermined by Francis Higgins in his capacity as Castle agent. From 1785 to his death in 1802 a Castle newspaper. Gradually recovered independence under his successor Philip Whitfield Harvey. Backed Catholic emancipation and—under Lavelle—the Repeal of the Union campaign in the '30s

Herald, Evening, 1805–14. Liberal, pro-Catholic. Changed name to *Sentinel*, 1814–5

Herald, Dublin Evening, 1821–3. Pro-Catholic

Hibernian Journal, –1822. Backed Flood in his quarrel with Grattan 1783–4. Liberal under Thomas MacDonnel; flirted with the United Irishmen, but retreated into neutrality when the prosecutions began. Cautious through the rebellion period, but remained liberal until O'Donnel's death in 1809. Became a Castle newspaper with pronounced Orange leanings under the brothers Fitzsimons, until the Castle withdrew support in 1822

Mail, Dublin Evening, 1823–. Protestant ascendancy newspaper, strongly anti-O'Connell and anti-Wellesley in the 1820's; settled down into respectability and prosperity in the '30s, but retained its diehard flavour. Ed. 1823–4 by Timothy Haydn, afterwards by Remi Sheehan, brother of owner Thomas Sheehan

(Rights of Irishman or) National Evening Star, 1791–3. William Paulet Carey's newspaper, brought out to back the United Irishmen

Packet, Evening (see Correspondent)

Patriot, 1810–28. Castle newspaper set up by Wellesley-Pole to replace the moribund *Hibernian Telegraph*. Corbet was retained as owner: Comerford editor. On Comerford's death in 1818 Haydn became editor. Circulation improved: sank again after Haydn left in 1822. Took Castle Catholic course until 1828: changed name to *Statesman and Patriot* but soon afterwards ceased publication

People, 1833. One of the group of artisan, radical newspapers that began appearing after the Reform Bill of 1832

Pilot, 1829–. Edited by Richard Barrett, brought out with the exclusive object of providing O'Connell with a platform. Remained firmly behind him throughout period

Post, Carrick's Morning, 1812–32. An advertising journal, little concerned in politics, until the 1820s when Lonergan brought it in behind the emancipation campaign. Lost ground thereafter until bought up by the Dublin Times in 1832

Post, Morning, 1788–98. Owned and edited by the erratic Peter Cooney. In opposition; but not linked with the United Irishmen. Suspected by both sides. Closed down in 1798, probably as a consequence of the increased taxation of the press

Post, Dublin Evening, (throughout period). Liberal under John Magee, the most influential of the opposition newspapers in the 1780s. Involved in war with Freeman, 1789–90. Favoured United Irishmen until the movement took on revolutionary character: cautious throughout rebellion period. Took up Catholic cause under John Magee jr., leading revival of liberal press, until Peel's prosecutions drove the owners to come to terms with the Castle in 1814. Remained prosperous, becoming the 'Castle Catholics' newspaper, supported Emancipation under F. W. Conway's editorship, but not well-disposed to O'Connell. Backed the whigs throughout the 1830s.

Post, General Evening, 1795–7. Run as a Castle newspaper by William Paulet Carey, until Cooke withdrew support

Press, 1797–8. The newspaper of the Dublin United Irishmen. Founded by Arthur O'Connor and run by him with the help of Lord Edward Fitzgerald, Thomas Emmet, Dr. Drennan, et alios. Nominal owner, Peter Finerty, until he was imprisoned: then Arthur O'Connor took over. Suppressed on Castle orders

Register, Dublin Morning, 1823; 1824–. Founded by Michael Staunton to support Catholic emancipation. The first 'new style' Irish newspaper, concentrating on home events and employing a corps of reporters. In spite of occasional violent disagreements, supported O'Connell in most of his campaigns

Saunders' News-Letter (throughout period). Concentrated almost exclusively on advertising

Star, 1824–5. Founded by Haydn after he had been dismissed from the Mail to carry on his polemics. Anti-Catholic, anti-Castle, scurrilous. Collapsed under weight of libel actions

Telegraph, Hiberbnian, 1795 (approx.) –1810. Run by William Corbet in the Castle interest: obscure, circulation probably negligible. Discontinued in 1810 to make way for Patriot

Times, Dublin, 1832–4. Castle newspaper set up by Whigs to fight O'Connell and Repeal on one flank and the Protestant Ascendancy on the other. Unsuccessful

Irish Times, 1823–5. Protestant. Incorporated *Faulkner's Dublin Journal* in 1825, changing name to *Morning Courier;* soon afterwards ran into labour trouble and ceased publication

True-Born Irishman, 1802–3. An attempt by John Shea to produce Castle propaganda for the masses

Union Star, 1797. Walter Cox's wall-sheet, printed on one side only, for pasting up. Rebel, but not connected with United Irishmen

Volunteer Evening Post, 1783–7. Castle newspaper

Volunteer's Journal or Irish Herald, 1783–6. Run by Matthew Carey until he had to fly the country: then by his brother Thomas. Anti-Castle: its scurrilities provoked the 1784 Press Act. After running itself into constant trouble in 1784, toned down in 1785 and became innocuous

Warder, 1821–. The most successful Orange weekly

BELFAST

Belfast News-Letter (throughout period). Liberal under ownership of Henry Joy until the mid '90s, when it was bought by two Scotsmen, and turned into a Castle newspaper. Regained independence after Union, becoming conservative

Northern Star, 1791–7. The United Irishmen's newspaper. Founded by a syndicate and run by Neilson until his imprisonment in 1796; finally sacked by the military in the following year. The most influential newspaper of its day

CORK

Cork Gazette, 1790–7. Opposition—run by the eccentric Denis Driscol

Harp of Erin, 1798. Intended to be the United Irishmen's Cork newspaper, but suppressed in a few days.

KILKENNY

Finn's Leinster Journal (throughout period). In vigorous opposition until near the close of the century, when it was bought over by the Castle

The British Museum's newspaper repository at Colindale and the National Library of Ireland, between them, have a reasonably complete collection of Irish newspapers, 1780–1842. The British Museum has a printed list of all the newspapers in its collection, in alphabetical order:

a second, chronological list is being compiled. It is not quite true to say that any Dublin newspaper of the period which is not on the British Museum's list will be found in the National Library: but missing files are few. A few minor gaps can be filled from the collections in the Public Library, Pearse Street, Dublin, in the library of Trinity College, Dublin, and in the Linenhall Library, Belfast.

Newspapers during the period were printed off slowly, and they were not published in formal 'editions'—'late', 'special', 'extra'—as they are to-day. The presses might be stopped at any time to add and subtract news items; the final copy of a paper was often markedly different from the first. What is in a newspaper in the files of the N.L.I. may not be in the paper for the same day in the files of the British Museum.

Two serious difficulties are encountered in the use of newspapers as sources of historical material. The first is the physical impossibility of making a comprehensive study of them over a long period of years. The sheer bulk of reading matter is too great—the profitable margin of cultivation too quickly reached. Professor Aspinall has adopted what appears to be the most promising approach to a study of the press, by relying mainly on MS sources, in order to find what was said *about* the newspapers. But MS sources have their limitations, and sooner or later it is necessary to turn to the newspapers themselves.

My method was to go through the files of one Dublin newspaper systematically from 1784 to 1841. It was not always the same newspaper: a choice had to be made of the newspaper appearing most likely to combine independence and reliability. The *Dublin Evening Post* was a standby; but its career, as may be seen, was not consistent, and from time to time others were used in preference. I have normally given only one newspaper in references, but where there might be doubt as to the accuracy of a report, or a suspicion of bias, it has been checked with other newspapers of different points of view at the same date.

It will be noticed that after 1800, little attention is paid to the provincial press. Partly this is due to my reluctance to attempt to cover so extensive a field, but mainly to the fact that with few exceptions, provincial newspapers played little part in the struggle for the freedom of the press between 1800 and 1841. In Belfast, for example, there was no repetition of the struggles of the 1790's. The course of Ulster newspapers in this period is of considerable importance to the history of the Irish press; but not to the story of the *freedom* of the Irish press.

The second difficulty in using newspapers as sources is to assess their value—not in the matter of accuracy, which can usually be checked, but in the matter of emphasis. Newspapers, then as now, were inclined to give relatively more prominence to the abnormal than to the normal. They also gave more prominence to an event which concerned them directly—for example, the trial of an editor for libel—than it warranted. But the whole subject of the value of newspapers as sources for the historian has not received sufficient consideration.

4. MAGAZINES
(in chronological order)

Town and Country Magazine, 1784–6.
Anthologia Hibernica, 1793–4.
Hibernian Magazine (Walker's), –1812.
Dublin Magazine and Irish Monthly Register, 1798–1800.
Irish Magazine (Cox's), 1807–15.
Cyclopedian Magazine, 1807–9.
Monthly Pantheon, 1808–9.
Belfast Magazine, 1808–15.
Dublin Satirist, 1809–10.
Monthly Panorama, 1811.
Hibernian Magazine, 1810
Milesian Magazine, or Irish Monthly Gleaner, 1812–25.
Dublin Political Review, 1813.
Monthly Museum, 1813–14.
Dublin Magazine, 1820
New Irish Magazine, 1822–3.
Gridiron, 1823.
Dublin and London Magazine, 1825.
Dublin Monthly Magazine, 1830.
Dublin Penny Journal, 1832–4.
Irish Monthly Magazine of Politics and Literature, 1832–4.
Dublin University Magazine, 1833–.
Dublin Satirist or Weekly Magazine, 1833–4.
Dublin Review, 1836–.

The Irish magazines of the period were ephemeral, featureless, and dull. Cox's *Irish Magazine* and Dr Brenan's *Milesian Magazine* managed to stir up controversy: Walker's *Hibernian Magazine* survived for over a quarter of a century: and the *Dublin University Magazine* attained a considerable literary reputation. The remainder achieved very little: but occasionally they have references to the problems of the press; they cannot be entirely ignored.

244

5. PAMPHLETS

An inquiry into the doctrines lately propagated concerning libels: a letter to Mr Almon from the father of *Candor*. Dublin 1765.

Dunn, John. Thoughts on newspapers and free trade. Dublin 1780.

Vindex. A treatise on the origins of attachments and informations. Dublin 1785.

Fitzgerrold, G. R. The law of attachments. Dublin 1785.

Towers, Joseph. Observations on the rights and duties of juries in trials for libels. Dublin 1785.

Carey, William Paulet. Both sides of the gutter. Dublin 1789.

The nettle: an Irish bouquet to tickle the nose of an English viceroy. Dublin 1789.

Griffith, Amyas. Miscellaneous tracts. Dublin 1789.

The trial of John Magee for a libel against Richard Daly. Dublin 1790.

Mr Sheridan's arguments in the case of Daly *v.* Magee. Dublin 1790.

Ponsonby, George. On *fiats* (with affidavits upon which said *fiats* were granted against John Magee). Dublin 1790.

Browne, Arthur. Arguments in the court of king's bench and speech in the house of commons on *fiats*. Dublin 1790.

Letters on the subject of the proper liberty of the press, by an Englishman. Dublin 1790.

Mayne, J. A digest of the law concerning libels. Dublin 1792.

Observations on the jurisdiction of the house of commons in matters of privilege. Dublin 1792.

Law, Thomas. Resolutions of the friends to the liberty of the press. London 1793.

The Rights of juries in cases of libel, by a barrister. Dublin 1794.

The trial of the proprietors of the *Northern Star*. May 1794. Belfast 1794.

The Trial of William Drennan for seditious libel. Dublin 1794.

Carey, William Paulet. Appeal to the people of Ireland (2nd ed.). Dublin 1794.

Second trial of the proprietors of the *Northern Star*. Belfast 1795.

Porter, W. Billy Bluff and the squire. Belfast 1796.

Ridgeway, W. Report of the trial of Peter Finerty. Dublin 1798.

Major, Stanley. Proceedings of a general court martial . . . upon Captain John Giffard. Dublin 1799.

Emerson, J. S. A report of the proceedings in the case of the Hon. Mr Justice Johnson. Dublin 1805.

Heron, Isaac (propr. of Waterford newspapers). Memoirs (vol. 1, in-complete). Waterford 1810.

Reports of the trial, F. E. Jones *v.* William Corbet, proprietor of the *Hibernian Telegraph*. Dublin 1810.

A list of the Catholic committee, interspersed with strictures on the calumnies launched upon their views and character by the Castle press. Dublin 1811.

Grace, George (propr. of the *Clonmel Herald*). Letter to the duke of Richmond. Clonmel 1813.

Trial of John Magee, proprietor of the *Dublin Evening Post*, for a libel on the duke of Richmond. Dublin 1813.

Hints to jurors on the liberty of the press. Dublin 1813.

Maley, M. Reports of two trials for libel. Dublin 1813.

Ridgeway, W. A report of the trial of Hugh Fitzpatrick for libel. Dublin 1813.

Barrett, Richard. Prudence true patriotism. Dublin 1815.

Faction unmasked. Dublin 1815.

North's speech in the trial of Magee *v.* O'Gorman. Dublin 1816.

Trial of an action for deceit . . . Magee *v.* O'Gorman. Dublin 1816.

Cox, W. The Mail Reviewed (2 numbers). Dublin 1823.

Bella Horrida Bella. Dublin 1823.

Watty *versus* Dan. Dublin 1825.

The Cuckoo Calendar. Dublin 1833.

Edge, J. S. A report of the trial of John Jones *v.* Thomas Sheehan for libel. Dublin 1839.

Duffy, Charles Gavan. Memoir of, reprinted from the New York *Nation* Dublin 1849.

These pamphlets have been listed chronologically, in the order they are to be found in the Haliday collection in the Royal Irish Academy. Most of them are also in the National Library of Ireland. Irish pamphleteers in this period rarely goaded the Castle to retaliation: few made much impression on the public. They are nevertheless useful. Some of them give trials, etc. in compact form; others discuss problems such as the law of libel, attachments, etc., at greater length than newspaper writers could command.

Pamphlets are distinguished in references by (P).

B. SECONDARY AUTHORITIES

Aspinall, A. 'The use of Irish secret service money in subsidizing the Irish press'. In *E.H.R.*, Oct. 1941.

'The Irish proclamation fund, 1800–46'. In *E.H.R.*, April 1941.

Politics and the press, 1780–1850. London 1949.

Andrews, A. The history of British journalism (2 vols.) London 1859.

Bigger, F. J. The Magees of Belfast and Dublin. Belfast 1916.

Bourne, H. R. F. English newspapers (2 vols). London 1887.

Bradsher, E. L., Matthew Carey, editor, author and publisher. New York 1912.

The Cambridge Modern History.

Chart, D. A., Ireland from the Union to Catholic emancipation. London 1910.

Clarkson, J. D. Labour and Irish nationalism. New York 1925.

Dicey, A. V. The law of the constitution. London 1941.

Duffy, Sir Charles Gavan. A final edition of Young Ireland. London 1896.

My life in two hemispheres. London 1898.

Falkiner, E. Litton. Studies in Irish history. London 1902.

FitzPatrick, W. J. The life, times and contemporaries of Lord Cloncurry. Dublin 1855.

Lady Morgan. Dublin 1860.

Ireland before the Union (2nd ed.). Dublin 1867.

Secret service under Pitt. London 1892.

The Sham Squire (3rd ed.). Dublin 1895.

Ford, D. M. 'The growth of the freedom of the press'. In *E.H.R.*, iv. 1 (1889).

Gilbert, Sir J. T. A history of the city of Dublin (3 vols). Dublin 1854.

Gwynn, Denis. The struggle for Catholic emancipation, 1750–1829. London 1928.

Gwynn, Stephen. Henry Grattan and his times. Dublin 1939.

Hanson, Laurence. Government and the press, 1695–1763. Oxford 1936.

Hunt, F. The fourth estate. London 1850.

Jacob, Rosamund. The rise of the United Irishmen. London 1937.

Landreth, Helen. The pursuit of Robert Emmet. New York 1948.

Lecky, W. E. H. History of Ireland in the 18th century (cabinet ed., 5 vols). London 1916.

Leaders of public opinion in Ireland (2 vols). London 1903.

MacDonagh, Michael. Life of Daniel O'Connell. London 1903.

MacDowell, R. B. 'The Irish government and the provincial press'. In *Hermathena*, liii. Dublin 1939.

'The personnel of the Dublin Society of United Irishmen'. In *I.H.S.*, ii. Dublin 1940.

Irish public opinion, 1750–1800. London 1944.

BIBLIOGRAPHY

'The proceedings of the Dublin Society of United Irishmen'. In *Analecta Hibernica*, no. 17. Dublin 1949.

Public opinion and government policy in Ireland, 1801–46. London 1953

Madden, R. R. The history of Irish periodical literature (2 vols). London 1867.

The United Irishmen (Shamrock ed., 12 vols). New York 1916.

Ó Casaide, S. 'Watty Cox and his publications'. In Bibliographical Society of Ireland, v. 2. Dublin 1935.

Parker, C. S. Sir Robert Peel. London 1891.

Phillips, J. S. R. 'The growth of journalism'. In *Cambridge history of English literature* xiv. 167. Cambridge 1916.

Robertson, C. G. Select statutes, 1660–1832. London 1904.

Rose, J. Holland. 'The unstamped press, 1815–36'. In *E.H.R.* xiii. 711. London 1897.

Simmonds, P. L. 'Statistics of newspapers in various countries'. In *Journals of the Statistical Society*, vol. iv. London 1841.

Smyth, E. L. Ireland, historical and statistical. London 1849.

The history of *The Times* (vol i) 1785–1841. London 1935.

Young, R. M. 'A forgotten Belfast evening paper'. In *Ulster journal of archaeology*, new series, iii. 201. Belfast 1897.

Only two secondary authorities concern themselves closely with the history of the Irish press.

R. R. Madden's *History of Irish Periodical Literature*, vol. ii, provides a considerable quantity of material about Irish newspapers and journalists in the eighteenth century. Madden viewed the subject from a strongly nationalist standpoint, and his verdicts are consequently coloured by patriotic sentiment. He approached the subject mainly from a bibliographical and biographical angle, rather than as a student of the newspapers' place in the community.

Professor Aspinall's *Politics and the Press*, 1780–1850, contains a great quantity of material about the Irish press extracted from MS sources mainly in Britain—for example, from the Peel correspondence in the British Museum. I have commented on his contribution to the history of the Irish press in a review of his book in *Irish Historical Studies*, September 1949.

INDEX

(The words 'Castle', 'Protestant', 'Catholic', 'Orange' etc. have been inserted after the names of newspapers, other than those listed in the bibliography, as a guide to their affinities. Newspapers in the bibliography (*q.v.*) are marked with an asterisk).